Laptop Dancing
Dancing
and the
Nanny Goat
Mambo

Laptop Dancing

and the

Nanny Goat Mambo

A Sportswriter's Year

TOM HUMPHRIES

POCKET BOOKS

TOWNHOUSE

First published in Great Britain and Ireland by Pocket/TownHouse, 2003
An imprint of Simon & Schuster UK Ltd and TownHouse, Dublin

Simon & Schuster UK is a Viacom Company

5 7 9 1 0 8 6 4

Simon & Schuster UK Ltd
Africa House, 64–78 Kingsway, London WC2B 6AH
www.simonsays.co.uk

Simon & Schuster Australia
Sydney

TownHouse, Dublin
THCH Ltd, Trinity House, Charleston Road, Ranelagh, Dublin 6, Ireland

A CIP catalogue record for this book is available from British Library.

Paperback ISBN 1–903650–53–4

Typeset by M Rules
Printed and bound in Great Britain by
Bookmarque Ltd, Croydon, Surrey

To everyone at the back of the plane,
especially Emmet and Paul for all the company and to
Mary, Molly and Caitlín with love as always.

Acknowledgements

Some thanks are in order. So, in no particular order: Thanks to everyone who sustained and entertained during the year. To everyone who talked and some of those who didn't. Thanks to all the people who give us something to write about.

Thanks to Malachy Logan for having faith in me and to Carol Kirwan for keeping us organized. Thanks to everyone in the Sports Department of *The Irish Times*.

Thanks to Treasa and Claire at TownHouse for their support, kindness, patience and expertise. Thanks to my family especially to Mary who has to put up with me when I'm home and put up with listening to me when I'm gone.

I

Beginning

'The best way to be a bum and earn a living is to write sports.'

Jimmy Cannon

Warm Up

My name is Tom Humphries. I am a sportswriter.

Mine is a condition rather than a talent, a disease rather than a trade. We become sportswriters because we can't become anything else. The worst sportswriters are the ones who got into the business because they just love sport. The best are the ones who like deadlines and economy travel and the company of other derelicts.

We sportswriters are a breed in decline. We aren't endangered, there are more of us than ever before – we are just withering. We are further and further from the action and we are shouting louder and louder just to make ourselves heard. It's not very dignified but then if you've seen us as a mob, hustling a nineteen-year-old millionaire for original quotes concerning the choreography of a two-yard, tap-in goal, you know that dignity is low on the list of priorities.

Once we were kings. A long time ago, in the stogie-fumed golden era of what is, essentially, a minor American art form, our predecessors illuminated the big papers in every town from New York to San Francisco. They had elegance. They had dignity. They had an audience.

Ring Lardner, Westbrook Pegler, Damon Runyon, Grantland Rice and so on down through the years and the back pages to the era of Jimmy Cannon, Red Smith and Jim Murray. The old guys had style and influence. They propped up their papers and their papers knew it. Cannon was a $1,000 a week man when that kind of money was unheard of outside of Tinseltown.

They hopped from Toots Shors to Lindys to the 21 Club with punters whispering stories into their ears and ballplayers begging the favour of kind mention. Sportswriters were the medium through which professional sport evangelized, the back page was the spot where a savvy sports star made his pitch for fame. It was there, in neat twelve point that the guys 'godded up' the jocks of the day, turned them into matinée idols and advertizing pitchmen.

We were interesting people once, and sometimes we are still mistaken as such. Richard Ford made his eternally perplexed Frank Bascombe a sportswriter. One half of *The Odd Couple*, the untidy half, was a sportswriter. Ditto, the hero of *Everybody Loves Raymond*. The louche, witless boozers who fill out the casts of movies that are set in newspapers all turn out to be sportswriters taking the inside track with whiskey on their breath and mixed metaphors on their mind.

We gave some of the flavour to certain times and places. A whole generation of Dubliners grew up reading Con Houlihan's columns on the smudgy back pages of the old *Evening Press*. Con's words made a monument that became part of our landscape. It was like that. When the great Texan sportswriter, Blackie Sherrod, moved from the Dallas *Times Herald* to the Dallas *Morning News*, the buses in Dallas carried teaser promotions for weeks: 'The Move'. The hype was justified. Sherrod was a god. God moved newspapers.

Myself, I decided I wanted to be a sportswriter when, during a long period of unemployment, I fished from the bargain bin of a bookstore in Donaghmede a collection by Tom Boswell of the *Washington Post*. I judged the book by the cover, a sportswriter's weakness. The title took me by the ear and led me to a different place: *How Life Imitates the World Series*. I hadn't seen a lot of evidence that sport could be written in these terms. It looked like fun. By and large, it has turned out to be fun.

In the years since, I've always wondered why no comic book superhero has ever tried sportswriting as the day job. All expenses-paid travel, big events in big cities. Continually crossing the paths of other mythical figures: 'Superhack Saves the Superbowl!' The job provides the ideal cover for caped crusaders or alcoholics with frequent-flyer cards.

The vicarious glamour of having one of our number entrusted with cleaning up some gloomy Gotham could breathe a little life back into our moribund trade. It's hard to know what the point of sportswriting is anymore. We have evolved with our environment, we have changed to survive. Our adaptability has subtracted from our beauty and our usefulness though.

In the good old days, we were an actual flesh and blood profession. We had our little tics and our traits. I fancy that there was a time when sportswriters actually called the telephone operator and asked to be put through to the newspaper, whence they then begged to speak to the editor, whereupon somebody would gasp, 'Hold the back page!'

There was a time when a good sportswriter could hold a city, a country even, by the lapels and make them listen while the story was told.

We're smaller than that now. Less relevant. Younger. Today the cursors on our laptops blink implacably and the little numbers in the bottom right-hand corner of the screen, the numbers that tell us the time, they change every sixty seconds and it's always too late. We sit there writing, yet again, an explanation for what happens after a positive B sample in a dope test, after a busted marriage, an arrest, a riot, a nasty case of relegation.

Traditionally, we blame television for shrinking us. Television came and made our trade less relevant. The box sucked the colour right from our cheeks. Words became less important. Punch was what counted. Punch early and punch often. We assume readers to have the attention spans of babies. We assume that they'd rather be watching television. We have adapted to the challenge with the approximate pace of portrait artists struggling through the era of the disposable camera.

Our little business just made itself meaner. Not uniformly. Guys like Murray and Smith on opposite sides of America, writers like Geoffrey Green, Brian Glanville or Hugh McIlvanney or, here in Ireland, Con Houlihan or Paddy Downey, still wrote (as they used to say of Jimmy Cannon) to end all writing. But the papers changed, the business changed. The terrain of sport changed. So many great Alps of money towering over us. We fooster about in the foothills, looking for what falls.

It used to be that sportswriting was a 'wow' sort of business. The sportswriter would point at the athlete and say, 'Wow!' That was fraudulent in its own way. Often the wrong guys got godded up.

Now it's a 'so what' type of game. We are cynical about everything. Especially the old guys who still say, 'Wow!' We've moved on to saying, 'So What!'

We know only what sportswriting shouldn't be. We shouldn't be purveyors of sports entertainment. We shouldn't be the running dogs of prawn-sandwich corporatism. Then again, we shouldn't be sour drunks, heckling all the way through the show. Sport is a form of entertainment. Sportswriting is a form of journalism. In the fog in between the ideals of sport and journalism, we have to make a living, we have to entertain. We have to do it in 900 words or less. And quickly.

When sport became the business of shareholders and agents and chairmen, our role changed more radically than TV changed it. I suppose we could have investigated, could have run stories on sports as one runs stories on virtually every other factor of life – but we didn't and we don't.

We hang on and we cry over spilt milk. It's a common enough lament that every fan feels sport was better and more wholesome when they were a kid. Potatoes tasted better and summers were finer too.

Sport never fooled us. From the moment the first turnstile was invented, money has been the ballast. Journalism fooled itself, at least sportswriting did. As the games went corporate, we kept godding up. Then it was announced that they didn't need us anymore. The shop was closed. No more inside track.

Sportswriters used to come out from the inside and describe to everyone else just what they'd seen. If they could do it with a little grace and style, so much the better. It was old fashioned, but it was artful.

Now we are ring-fenced off. In our surly, sceptical way, we process what is fed to us on a spoon and then we move on. Writing about sport these days can sometimes feel like writing science fiction. It's like trying to explain a world that we can only imagine. We don't know what it's really like inside Sportsworld. We genuinely don't.

And we are tetchy about it. Myself included. We carp and snipe far more than our predecessors did. We enjoy sport far less, but we are more strident about it. We've been rendered less important by the scheme of things, so we puff ourselves out to look bigger. We rail against everything and forget that, for most people, sport is escape and that we are the mere vaudevillians of journalism.

This book was commissioned long, long before the World Cup of 2002 kicked off. I mentioned the idea to a few people and then stopped talking about the project altogether before somebody committed me to a home for the terminally egotistical. Generally those people to whom I spoke asked just one question of the proposed project: 'What makes you conceited enough to reckon that any account of *you* and *your* year would be so interesting?'

'Uhm, nothing.' That was the firm, clear answer. Nothing. It just seemed likely to be a year that had some interesting trips and some interesting people looming. Perhaps interesting things would happen in the proximity of as thoroughly an uninteresting and uncurious person as me. Besides, it would be an experiment to find out how many moments of joy a year covering sport might throw up. And where those moments might arise. And would heavy drinking help.

There were a few great sports events, some chewy scandals and one big controversy that, in this part of the world at any rate, consumed more newsprint and spawned more theories than the Kennedy assassination: Roy Keane left the World Cup.

And 2002 was a long, difficult sporting year to get through. Before memory grows furtive, it seems right to set down an unreliable version of events and to simultaneously trace a finger over the journey that sports journalism has made. From great men riding the rails and covering the grand occasions with a poetical touch to the apologetic shuffling dance we do when a herd of us are admitted to a dressing room to gather the quotes, or the nanny goats, after a game. From poetry to jeering from the sidelines. From waltzes to the nanny-goat mambo.

This was a year when we had influence but not respect, a year when we were cited for several crimes that I think we were innocent of, but got off scot-free for other stuff. It was a year when we fought among ourselves constantly and a time when we realized that, most of the time, most of the thrill is gone.

Sportswriting was never a business suited to sports fans but once, at least, it had its own sort of romance.

More and more, that comfort is hard to find.

Game On: Tooting Trouble

Thursday, 24th January – London

It begins like this. A red light in Tooting. A woman and her son crossing the road in front of me. He tugs her sleeve. Points. Points at me, looming large in a little Clio. I imagine the conversation.

'How did they fit the big man into the little car, Mum?'

She supposes that it must be done in the same way that they get big ships into little bottles. 'They put him in flat, son. And then they just pull a string.'

As they walk away, the boy keeps looking behind him.

His first sports hack.

New year is a slow time for us. The kid has made an unseasonal sighting, the sort that should be recorded in a twee letter to a broadsheet newspaper, 'On Tuesday, while walking in Tooting, I spotted the first sportswriter of the season. Is this a record?'

Technically it's winter but, for our discombobulated species, it is spring. Above ground, the boys of summer are limbering up so, in January, we begin sticking our heads out of our burrows and fiddling around with ideas. We make lists of glorious projects that we'll never complete. January is the month when we take out our homework copies and draw red margins and spaces for the dates and arrange our highlighter pens in a certain order on the desk. In January, every sportswriter is the best sportswriter in the world.

And, in January, we don't answer the phone much. No good can come of it. In fact, very bad things can come of it. You can be asked to cover the World Darts Championships in Purfleet. And there is no clearer indication that you are not, in fact, the greatest sportswriter in the world than a trip to Purfleet.

Apart from the seasonal looking back and peering forward pieces and a few columns, today's journey is my first real work of the year. And, triumphantly, it's not to Purfleet! I am on World Cup business (just about everything for the first half of this year will be World Cup business). The World Cup can be ignored about as easily as an elephant in the drawing room. The tournament, and Ireland's presence in it, looms ominously right in the middle of the year. Till then, it's an all-soccer diet, or near enough.

Speaking of elephants in drawing rooms, I have learned one lesson already: the Renault Clio is a smaller car than the girl at the rental desk said it was. Far smaller. I know because, right now, I am impaled on the handbrake of a Clio.

The lights turn green and I drive on blithely.

I'm lost of course. I'm more lost than a flea on a big dog. I spend a good portion of my working life being lost. If I had been driving the car, the three wise men would never have figured in the Bible except as an obscure footnote regarding four lost men in a car. Being lost is my handicap in life but, I will say this for myself, I am indefatigable and brave. I don't give up. I don't ask for directions. Instead, I try to communicate telepathically with Clinton Morrison.

O Clinton, Clinton! Wherefore art thou Clinton Morrison?

No answer.

This being lost, it's a living but it's not what Red Smith, the greatest of all sportswriters, had in mind when he said that our job beats heavy lifting.

Tooting. Sweet Tooting Jesus.

I've been lost for a good two hours or so now. Not just in Tooting, of course, I have been lost in most parts of 'souff' London and right out into the clear country on the other side. I've been back again. It's not that the scenery isn't spectacularly beautiful around Tooting, or that I'm lacking a sense of adventure, I just don't like to make people anxious.

Clinton Morrison, striker, bon-vivant, wit, boulevardier, interview subject of all interview subjects, you must be anxious by now.

OK. I confess. Twenty minutes ago, beaten like a whipped cur, I let myself down and asked for directions on a garage forecourt. Don't judge me. Only when I'm broken and close to tears do I ask for directions. It's a male chromosome thing. Anyway: 'Awright. It's dahn there innit. You've gawn dahn about a mile and it's left innit. So you've gawn left and it's the third offa the roundabaht innit. You've come off that near the Safeways innit. Arsk some other geezer wot knows the area when you get to Safeways.'

Clinton Morrison, you must be all ajangle by now. I am. Out of your mind with worry. Like me. Be strong. All those anecdotes you have prepared, don't let them curdle, keep stirring them, keep adding stuff.

I know how it is for Clinton. No footballer likes to hear of bad things befalling their friends in the sportswriting business. If I had a mobile number for him, I'd call him and explain. I have a number for the public relations spiv at Crystal Palace, but I'm too proud to use it. Nothing worse than advertizing yourself as a dim bulb to those high-wattage public relations people.

I drive on, imagining Clinton pacing a room at the training ground, concerned for my safety, his nails bitten to the quick, his aides bringing him cups of hot tea. He's wondering who to call if I don't arrive. All week he's been worrying a little as to how the conversation will go once I get there, fretting about what sort of impression he will make. Promising himself that no matter how things go he won't sink to the level of cliché. Cliché? No way, José.

Clinton is the raw material for what will be a 'Big in 2002' type of feature. (Of course I won't be using the word 'big' – already human rights activists are calling for limits on the use of 'big in Japan' headlines. 'Big in Japan' has been declared a cliché of mass destruction and the World Cup is months away.)

Clinton Morrison has just recently been put in touch with his inner Irishman. He and I are going to explore the complex issues of race and identity *vis à vis* the Diaspora. Begob and begorrah, we will to be sure.

We'll do all that and then we'll conclude that Clinton is one to watch.

At least we would if I didn't now believe that no road actually leads to the Crystal Palace training ground, I believe that the training ground is, in fact, a secret garden accessed via a little door hidden behind a hole in a hedge.

Perhaps I was a little cocky. I was born here after all, or first of all. I settled initially in County Kilburn and then in Eltham before opting for suburbia in Ireland. As the joke goes, my parents moved to Ireland when I was five, and when I was seven I found them.

Beckenham! Right now, I am honing in, like a Richard Branson hot-air balloon, on Beckenham. I feel that, if I get to Beckenham, I will be able to flush Clinton Morrison out. That's my new guiding theory of the morning anyway. Beckenham ho!

As Clinton hopes to be disporting himself in parts of Japan and South Korea on behalf of the Irish nation this summer, I'm assuming that he'll see this interview as his chance to meet and greet the Irish soccer public, or that slender part of it which reads *The Irish Times*. Many in the Irish soccer community are still confused by Clinton's ringing declaration some time ago that he had set his heart on playing for Ireland or England. This is Clinton's chance to reject England and all its deeds.

As far as I know this will be the first big interview Clinton has done with an Irish paper. I have high hopes. This will be a gentle stretch and warm-up before the real work of the year begins.

Finally, and entirely by accident, I come across the Crystal Palace training ground. I'm reversing out of a narrow street between two dinky rows of little houses and I notice a little pink-and-blue sign luring visitors down a narrow laneway. Eureka!

Not taking any chances, I swing the car across the road at a fine old speed and hit that laneway hard.

Surprisingly, when used correctly, speed ramps can really launch a Clio into the air.

Fortunately, being jammed tight within the Clio, I become my own airbag and four crushed vertebrae plus a conk on the head is all the damage I sustain – and some internal bleeding from the handbrake.

The Crystal Palace training ground is typical of the genre – hard to find and colder and more windswept than the Russian Steppes. Palace have a nice setup, considering they are a once-fashionable club grown dowdy. In the distance, I can see their first team still training. I have missed the chance to reintroduce myself to Clinton Morrison before he works up a sweat, but I'm here to nab him when he comes off the training ground. My patented, insincere, old-friend greeting act will have to work its charm.

Actually Clinton and I are old friends by sportswriting standards. That is to say we've met once before. I am therefore vocationally obliged to carry on as if that brief encounter changed my life. He must act as if he scarcely remembers it. This is the dance we are condemned to.

Exotically, we met at the airport in Tehran. Our eyes met across an empty notebook. It was the night that Ireland qualified for the 2002 World Cup. Clinton was effervescent, having played the last ten minutes or so of the game and done well. He was sitting in the airport with Mick Byrne, the team physio, and for some reason the two of them were duetting on the theme from the children's television show *The Bear in the Big Blue House*.

Into scenes of genuine happiness, such as this one between Mick and Clinton, we journalists are trained to insinuate ourselves. Given an opening like this, we can insinuate ourselves quicker than rats can shin up a drainpipe. It's not something you'd want your kids doing, but it's a life skill nonetheless.

All over the airport, as the players lounge in happy, little groups, we are scampering with our long, grey tails, hoping that the guys will associate us with this hap-hap-happy time in their lives and not speed dial the exterminator next time they see us.

We move about with our usual toxic levels of insincerity.

Step One: Sidle up to player.

Step Two: Big grin. Cheesy.

Step Three: Hearty handshake, hug if possible. Two hands in contact with the player anyway, as if you are meeting the person who donated a kidney to you.

Step Four: 'Hey! Well done! Jeez! You had us worried there! Ya boy ya!'

Step Five: The Hook. 'Listen, any chance of a few quick words?'

Step Six: Listen to 'few quick words'. Yadda yadda yadda, yeah yeah yeah. Blah blah blah. Yes, indeed, that is football. So true. It *is* a funny, old game.

And at the end of the few quick words you start reeling in.

Step Seven: The Catch. 'Listen,' you say, because you are a sensitive man, 'I'll leave you in peace now. That was great mate, really good stuff. You're very kind. You are the man. You are the oracle. You are the word, etc. Actually,' you appear hesitant now, embarrassed to ask such a thing, 'I'd love to come over sometime before the World Cup and do a proper in-depth feature on you and your extraordinary life. You would? Really? Well, what's the best way of getting in touch with you for that?'

At Step Seven, the older players will invariably tell you that you can call their agent. This is a roundabout way of saying that frankly you can wither and die while on hold listening to *Greensleeves*. Older players are callously indifferent about welfare and health issues in the sportswriting community.

The younger fish are a different story. Approached at just the right time, they are in sufficiently jubilant mood to gobble up the whole 'new best friend' routine. In fact, they are so receptive sometimes that we should be selling them double-glazed windows and life assurance as well. And they cough up their mobile numbers as if we'd done a Heimlich on them. They'd love to meet up. They'd love to peddle you more of these *pensées* that you seem to like so much. And more jokes. They'd never really heard laughter until they cracked a little joke at a press conference. Grown men slapping their thighs in merriment.

And so you emerge triumphant with a number, which you can trade with your sportswriting friends. Phone numbers are currency.

I'll give you a Kevin Kilbane for a Clinton Morrison. Fuck off. A Morrison is worth a Kilbane and a Cunningham.

All fine until such time as the footballer changes his number. Then we begin again.

So it was with Clinton. A mobile phone number scribbled on the back of my plane ticket. Bingo.

'Best number to get me on is this one,' he'd said earnestly before scribbling out the magic digits. 'Best time to get me is this,' he'd said mulling over his routine and advising that, in order to avoid disappointment, I shouldn't ring on match days or the days before match days.

Everybody, in the journalistic end of the team plane, reckons that Clinton's addition to the squad represents a change in our luck. So many of the players on the Irish team are dour and para-noid and just plain hostile these days that we've come to think of them as 'The Glums'. Clinton though is all smiles and irrepress-ible good humour. Surely he must be a raconteur into the bargain.

Everyone wants some one-on-one time with him. Everyone wants to get him to the interview table. He'll be a riot.

Now I have the golden ticket: Clinton's mobile. I am The Man.

I *was* The Man.

Remember Coyote Syndrome? That business of waking up after a blurry night and finding your arm trapped under the carcass of a naked and dozing stranger.

You remember where you are.

You remember, just, who the body belongs to.

You suppress a yelp.

You reintroduce yourself to your God.

You beg forgiveness.

You promise to join a monastery if you can just get out of here without Shrek waking up.

Then, like a coyote in a trap, you gnaw your own arm off rather than wake Shrek up.

I was that Shrek and that's how we made our fun back then.

Not much changes. Clinton has experienced the mobile phone equivalent of Coyote Syndrome. Clinton has woken up the morning after Tehran and realized that he's one step away from media whoredom. So he has done something drastic. He appears to have cut off his own mobile phone. He has performed a mobilectomy on himself. His number has been surgically removed.

For the past few weeks, I might as well have been trying to contact somebody in the late Renaissance period using two bean cans and a piece of string. Clinton's phone is not ringing. I suspect it is entombed in a lump of concrete at the bottom of the Thames.

I have been forced to go through the Crystal Palace public relations staff. This is slumming it. This is an open admission that you are so low on the food chain that you can't even get a player's number. The only thing worse than a PR department is an agent. Journalists, PR people, agents: we are the bottom feeders of modern sport. Each trade sees the other two as being strains of cancer.

Public relations people are my personal phobia. I am a schmoozochondriac. In fairness, PR flaks don't seem to have the personal hygiene problems that make agents and journalists cousins within the animal kingdom. I'm sure you get drunks in PR, but they are probably bright, sunny drunks who are very interested in you.

No, PR departments are the Swiss Guards of professional football. They look cute. They think their bosses are infallible. They flounce. They offer brief audiences, not interviews. They dress funny. They don't understand feature writing.

A decent feature requires at least an hour's worth of interview. The first thirty minutes are just inconsequential faff, all the stuff you know the answers to, but need to ask just to get the wary player warmed up. The second half-hour should be meatier, but not too scary, and by the time that has elapsed, hey presto, you should be having an actual conversation and finding out a little about what the person is really like. You conclude with the hard, scary questions.

All fine in theory, but no PR person will ever tell a player that a journalist needs at least an hour of his time. You may travel to Beckenham on behalf of the *Timbuktu Tribune-Bugle* and a PR serf will do his best to ensure you get no more than five minutes with a player.

So, Clinton comes off the little training pitch (in fact two disused tennis courts that adjoin each other) where the team have been playing a roaring game of one touch. I approach him in the prescribed manner. I'm his long, lost brother.

'Clint-on. Hey!'

Clever reverse syntax there. 'Hey, Clinton' would be much more abrasive.

Clinton looks at me as if I'm a pubic hair he's just found in his coleslaw.

I explain who I am.

'It's me! Tehran!'

I make it sound as though we spent an idyllic summer there picking grapes together.

He frowns. 'Oh yeah,' he says. 'Well how long is it gonna take?'

I say, 'Well you know, as long as you've got.'

He says, 'Quarter of an hour?'

He sounds like a kid trying to imagine what eternity must be like.

'Oh at least that,' I say dreamily as if he's being hard on himself. Eternity plus an hour if you're good.

'Hmmm,' he says and disappears into the dressing room.

I go upstairs to the canteen and wait an hour. Clinton is right. It is a long time.

Finally, he arrives wearing a top with the word 'Duffer' written across the chest. This marks Clinton out as the hippest guy this side of Tooting. I am not equipped for recognizing this, however. Sports journalism is not hippermost among the professions.

Duffer, Damien Duff that is, will be one of Clinton's chief rivals for a spot up front playing for Ireland at the World Cup this summer. I mention this by way of introductory hilarity.

Well, I just point at his chest and say the words, 'Duffer! Heh! Heh!'

Clinton looks at me hard. The music from the shower scene in *Psycho* has just started up in his head.

'Duffer,' I stammer, pointing again at his top. 'It says Duffer on your shirt.'

'Oh yeah,' he says and continues to stare at me wondering how one gets to do journalism as part of an Imbeciles in the Community Programme.

Our interview is one of those nightmares that you often get to share with young professional soccer players. Nothing to say and only a few minutes to say it in. Clinton, a loveable naif, got burned by the tabloids early in life and isn't sure of the protocol for preventing a recurrence. His natural friendliness is doused by the thought that I am about to soak him in petrol and merrily set him ablaze.

His 'bad experience' happened a year ago but this is how it works. A tabloid sins, I do the penance. A silly, jokey one-liner relating to Michael Owen was inflated in the usual manner by the redtops until it began to look like Clinton had threatened to leave a horse's head in the wunderkind's bed. Owen apparently took no notice and Clinton finessed it all through the agent that he and the wunderkind shared, but the 'insult' was uttered after the first leg of a Cup tie. By the time of the second leg back at Anfield, the crowd were on Clinton's case big style. His every touch was a punchline.

That was January 2001 and, after that, his form just evaporated until he was just an opaque presence around the league. The guy who used to be Clinton Morrison. He scored once between January and the end of the season. He went from being mentioned as a future England striker to being told by Mick McCarthy to go away and get his head straight.

So now Clinton comes to the interview table with an actuarial wariness. He doesn't like to take risks in interviews. No opinions. No names. No anecdotes. No one-liners. He knows the precise danger that lurks behind every question.

We talk generally for about twenty minutes. How is the season going? What about this weather? He says some odd, quirky things. For instance, Clinton is keen to prove that he is more than a little bit Irish. He says that, as a kid, he told Ian Evans at Crystal Palace that he'd like to play for Ireland. Ian Evans is the Irish assistant manager. His official biog in the Irish team handbook says that he left Crystal Palace in 1989, which means that Clinton was nine at the time. Considering Evans was an English-born Welsh international with nothing to do with Ireland at the time, it must have been an intriguing encounter with the schoolboy.

I furrow my brow and say, 'Ian Evans? You told Ian Evans?' I can see Clinton is hostile to the idea of being questioned further on this, so I leave it be. I don't mind how Irish he is. I just want to get some sense of him and who he is. And two good anecdotes.

Odd things. Clinton doesn't really want to talk about his family, but his mother and his Irish Granny come in for frequent mention in passing. He owes them lots he reckons. When Clinton talks about his father, he alternates between use of the past and the present tenses, so that eventually I ask apologetically if his Dad is still around. 'Oh yeah,' he says, and leaves it at that until it strikes me to ask if the Morrison name is from his father's side (his Dad is Jamaican). 'No,' says Clinton, 'I changed my name when I was fifteen. I used to be Clinton Chambers, but I changed it to Morrison.'

Clinton's family situation is none of my business really but this is too tantalizing. Maybe he wants to blurt it all out. I ask how his Dad took this. Clinton shrugs. I ask as casually as I can how things are with his Dad. He either wants to tell the story or he doesn't, either way is fine. Clinton just says he's been to Jamaica, hopes to get down there after the World Cup for a holiday, it's lovely down there.

I take it from this switch to Judith Chalmers mode that the subject is closed. No blurting today. He's looking at his watch now, jumpier than ever to be off. We close with a few clarification questions, clearing up the basics from earlier.

He's friendly and polite in a completely distracted way. I try every interviewing trick I know to get him to engage seriously in conversation. Uproarious laughter when he says something vaguely funny. Nothing. Long silences for him to fill in. Nothing. Incredibly detailed questions looking for specifics. Nothing. An awkward question followed immediately by an enthusiastic question, 'You must tell me about . . .' Nothing.

My hero in these matters is my friend Paul Kimmage. Nobody uses the weapon of silence better than Paul does in interview situations. He'll stare at an interview subject balefully as they struggle to come up with some formulation interesting enough to cheer Paul up. And he shocks them too. Once we were jointly interviewing the Irish hurdler Susan Smith in the Olympic Village in Atlanta and she said chirpily how excited she was to be walking in the opening ceremony parade. And Paul said, 'See, I hear that and I think one thing. Loser.' You could see Susan Smith blanching beneath her suntan.

Finally, Clinton hops up to leave. I'm crushed. I've tried silence but he has outsilenced me. I had high hopes for this one. People on the cusp of fame often make good subjects. Of all the various aspects of sportswriting, I like feature writing the best and, of the various aspects of feature writing, the less famous people are, the more I like interviewing them. Today I've had my backside kicked though.

I came here armed with a few Clinton anecdotes, which he dismissed as apocryphal. I have about half a dozen decent quotes but nothing new. Should have been a simple tap in to score, but I've put it wide. Now that he's established that he can leave, Clinton is back to his old self. He makes a joke with the canteen lady who has been on holidays in Jamaica. He's dancing and fidgety.

Desperate that I shouldn't come away almost empty-handed, I raise the subject of his mobile number. 'Just checking this number you gave me in Tehran, I must have scribbled it down wrong and, you know, maybe I'll need to call you to check stuff when I'm writing this piece.'

He glances at the number.

'Nah, that's right. I've just switched it off for the last few weeks. I've got a new one.'

'Uhhm, what's your new one?'

Pause.

'Nah, just keep trying that one,' Clinton says.

Drat. And double drat.

Monday, 11th February

It is said that we sports hacks are hopeless creatures trapped between two real professions, either one of which we would like to be good at: sports or writing. I think of that often, especially when my kids ask me just what it is that I do. I have them with me today. It's one of those occasions they will remember after I'm gone.

He didn't have much of a life, the oul' fella.

'Why are they always late?' asks Caitlín, my eight-year-old.

'Dunno, they just are.'

'And why do we have to stand outside the gate?'

'Dunno, we just do.'

'Why are they not as friendly as the Dublin team?'

'Dunno, they just aren't.'

'Is it going to rain, Daddy?'

'Dunno, probably.'

We are standing outside the gates of Tolka Rovers Football Club on Griffith Avenue Extension on the northside of Dublin. Myself and my two daughters, *Les Miserables*, Molly and Caitlín. We are waiting for the Irish soccer team to arrive.

Les Miserables are on midterm break and, technically, I am on a day off, so they are humouring me by tagging along as I do bits and pieces of work. Our national soccer heroes were due here half an hour ago for a training session. I don't need to see them train again, but I need to see Roy Keane.

We're stuck outside the gates along with half a dozen photographers, a dozen kids and a few other journalists. The sky has turned charcoal black with the threat of rain. The guys with the orange bibs who are guarding the gate are making it clear that they wholly endorse the Irish team's attitude toward the media scum. The orange-bib guys are so surly they could play for Ireland themselves. Mostly, if you ask them a question, they just eyeball you.

It starts to rain, of course. A scene like this needs rain. Great sheets of water chase the traffic up Griffith Avenue. One second we are dry, the next we are goldfish. Caitlín wants to go back and sit in the car now. Molly has a grim determination about getting Mick McCarthy's autograph, even though her little notebook is sodden.

If I have to take the kids somewhere when I'm working, the deal usually is that they sit quietly and don't bother anyone except each other. Later, I buy them treats and beg them not to tell their mother.

Today, though, the team are so late and the gatemen are such bastards and the rain is so damn wet that I don't really care if Molly bothers Mick McCarthy. I don't care if she becomes Mick McCarthy's personal stalker and winds up boiling the McCarthy family bunny (Mark Kennedy apparently) on the McCarthy family stove.

I'm wet and abused and I don't care about these things anymore.

When did dealing with the Irish soccer team become one of the great chores of this job? It used to be fun. It used to be adults talking to each other about football.

Sadly, dealing with the Irish soccer team will be the centrepiece of this year. There was an era, and I just caught the end of it (maybe I caused the end of it, who knows?), when players and journalists stayed in the same hotel together on away trips and often shared social drinks after matches. The hacks and the players would bump into each other around the hotel and there would be some small talk. Generally, life was congenial and civilized. The players were glad of the bit of coverage and there was trust between players and the beasts of the mass-communications field.

Now we are in a state of almost perpetual conflict with the team. They feel as besieged and paranoid as Israel. We feel as abandoned and unloved as Palestinians. Mick McCarthy, for whom I have terrific time on a personal level, is paranoid to the borders of psychosis about the media. He breaks into a rash if he is within thirty yards of an NUJ card. I think this all goes back to his playing days when a sizeable portion of the Irish media lovingly yearned for the return of Dave O'Leary to the national side while pillorying poor old Mick as a 'boil on the backside of Irish soccer' and 'slower than a wet week in Barnsley'. Unwisely, he once accepted a challenge from a journalist to race him over 100 yards. That's not a sign of a man secure in his media relationships. Anyway, since then, he has always had a distorted view of the Irish media. Give Mick a good old *News of the World* stitch-up any day.

So now, on trips abroad, we hacks must take a bath in disinfectant before boarding the team plane. We no longer stay in the team hotel, which isn't a bad thing per se (the old relationships were a little too cosy) except that now we hang around the lobby of the team hotel like groups of strikingly ugly hookers. We behave that way too. We're ready for business with any player who haplessly emerges from the lift.

The players are younger and richer and more callow now. Generally they hate us. Of course, all of them don't hate all of us all the time. Some of them just hate some of us all the time. That's why we keep turning up.

As individuals, if you can separate a player from the herd, there are some fine people among them. There are maybe half a dozen or so whom I am genuinely fond of. A couple of the older guys, in particular, are capable of holding real grown-up conversations. In the main, though, when the players get together, they radiate the surliness of supermodels who have just woken up to find acne all over their faces.

I once asked Steve Carr, the Spurs fullback, if he had a few minutes to spare in order to do a short piece with me. He turned around with almost theatrical slowness, looked me up and down from head to toe and laughed, 'No way pal.' Off he walked, shaking his head. I'd never met him or written about him before, but I came away and bought a bell for around my neck and for weeks thereafter walked through the streets shouting 'unclean, unclean, unclean'.

Three months ago, before the World Cup play-off in Tehran, Robbie Keane, our newest superstar, was scheduled to do one of the daily press conferences through which the team reluctantly drip feeds us some news about itself. It was announced that young Robbie wouldn't turn up if the *Evening Herald* was in attendance. Much consternation and confusion among journalists. An emissary was sent back to Robbie to ask what the problem was. In a rare show of unity, part of the message was that Robbie would have to speak to all of us or speak to none of us. No cherry picking.

Obviously, he would have preferred to speak to none of us, but a footballer lives in a world where tabloidese is the first language. He must suddenly have feared the worst in terms of backlash. He arrived, spoke sullenly and left.

The root cause of Robbie's unhappiness? A few weeks previously, the *Herald* had run a glorious two-page puff piece on

Robbie giving details of a Nike soccer school, which he was involved with, and filling us in on the parts of his interesting life that we don't get to see. His agent wasn't given final approval for this piece. So far as anyone could gather, this is the extent of Robbie's problem with the *Evening Herald*.

So that's how things are between the team and us. Being stuck in the rain on the northside of Dublin stoically waiting for the chaps to arrive goes with the job.

Eventually I break ranks. I announce to the hardmen in the orange bibs that I'm here because I need to see Roy Keane. This is supposed to convey to the orange-bib boys that they will have Roy to answer to if I don't get satisfaction. They are trembling with fear now, but they conceal it well.

'Yeah well,' says the ugliest one, 'we'll see what happens when he gets here, won't we? We'd all like to "see Roy".'

I can tell by their faces that my kids are hugely impressed with me.

The truth is that, though I may need to see him, Roy does not need to see me. The last time Roy saw me, he went through me for a short cut, leaving a neat Keano-shaped hole in my chest.

There are people in this world who you don't want making short cuts through your personage and Roy Keane is one of them. You see him coming at you, menacing as a shark's fin above the water's surface on a crowded beach. He has that vein on his temple that looks as though he's got a worm crawling under his skin, and his eyes, the heat off them could give you third degree burns. He comes at you from far away, like Clint in *High Plains Drifter*, and somehow you know that there's trouble on the way. In this department, he has technique. He gets his face close to yours. He keeps moving. He keeps asking you questions. He doesn't let you answer. If you are a man at all, you'll want to cry.

The worst thing about my presence on the Roy Keane blacklist is that it's all my fault. I have interviewed Roy Keane twice, and each time he has been a perfect pleasure. He turns up and he engages in conversation, which reveals a witty, self-aware side that isn't always on display. Not just that but, unusually for a footballer, he enquires how you got here, was your flight OK, how things are going. On both occasions I have interviewed him, he has gone out of his way to give me lifts afterwards, to make sure I get to the airport on time, and once he even suggested that I come back to his house for the afternoon.

Then I went and gave somebody else his phone number. It was somebody we both knew, the journalist Paul Kimmage. Paul was in Manchester, just leaving Manchester in fact, and he wanted to tell Roy that he'd left him a copy of a book he'd written, at Old Trafford. Paul called me and explained the situation. With a little reluctance, I gave him the number and he left a message on Roy's machine.

Mortal sin. From then on, I was a dead man walking.

The skies darkened and lo there was much thunder and Roy changed his number that afternoon. After that, it was just a matter of waiting for his official retribution.

No complaints. When a Roy Keane interview appears in the paper, the journalist concerned usually gets about a dozen calls in the following days from people whose lives would be made better if only they could make contact with Roy. There are some numbers which journalists will circulate among themselves with the injunction that 'if he asks it didn't come from me'. Others, the rare numbers, the great numbers, numbers like Roy Keane's, are off limits. You chomp down on your cyanide pill before yielding them up. If your dying mother asks you for Roy Keane's number, it is legitimate to lie to her, to fob her off with the number of Michael Kennedy, Roy Keane's agent, or to tell her to call Old Trafford.

Roy gives you his number, it's a matter of trust. It's a matter of life and death.

So I blew it. I don't know why. I made no attempt to appeal the sentence. I cited no mitigating circumstances. In terms of what was coming, the waiting was the worst.

I knew he was coming to get me because he had devoured Paul Kimmage the previous day. Kimmage can take care of himself a whole lot better than I can, but he said he felt two inches tall by the time Roy finished with him. I decided on humour as a defence. Mistake.

We were at the airport in Cyprus when Roy came to ask me why I had done it. I had planned to use a variation on the old Groucho line about not wanting to be a member of any club that would have me as a member. Any number Roy would give me could hardly be a secret number. Yet when Roy came after me, I blurted that I'd thought I was doing him a favour.

'Favour?' he said incredulously. For all Roy knew, of course, I had published his number on a website. You give the number to one person, you can't be trusted not to give it to anyone else. Telling him I thought I was doing him a favour was exactly the wrong thing to say.

'Doing me a favour? You think if I want to talk to Paul Kimmage I can't use a phone book?' His voice is so high at this stage that only myself and dogs can hear it.

'If I wanted to talk to Paul Kimmage, I'd pick up a phone book and find out his number,' repeated Roy, his nose about an inch from mine, his eyes completely black. 'Wouldn't I?'

'Yes.'

Paul is ex-directory, but I could see the general point.

'Can I ask you another question? You think I'm some kind of fool?'

'No, I was just . . .'

'Did I ever ask you for Paul Kimmage's number?'

'No.'

'Did I ever say to you that it was really important that I talk to Paul Kimmage, that I'd love to have him calling my house?'

This all lasted no more than thirty or forty seconds. Then he was gone. I felt like I'd been splashed with battery acid though. When it comes to giving a bollocking, Roy is world class.

People have said to me since, 'Why didn't you stand up to him? I wouldn't have taken that, no way.' I agree. Next time Roy Keane comes towards me at pace with murder in his eyes and asks me if I think he's a fool, I will tell him straight out that yes, I do think he's a fool, that I find him comical and that his physical buffoonery just cracks me up.

Bury me near water.

That was in Cyprus almost a year ago now, and the chances to get to Roy since then have been few and far between. I'm not sure what the lie of the land is, but I need to go bungling on in. It's three months before the World Cup and the paper needs me to interview Keane. Not just the paper, I want to interview him. I think he's the most fascinating and complex sportsperson around and neither of the two interview pieces I have written about him so far in his career have come close to capturing that.

My view of Keane almost automatically identifies me as a member of the Irish media. In England, by and large, they don't see anything in Roy Keane but the cartoon hardman, and they don't like him. The issue of race seldom arises between English and Irish sports hacks, apart from the annual deluge of pieces about punting priests and gallons of the black stuff that the English papers publish to mark the Cheltenham Festival.

On Keane though, we differ. In England, he is portrayed as thick, psychotic and Irish. Irish with all the worst that being Irish can imply. Unpredictable, violent, boozy. Drinkin' 'n' fightin'. In Ireland, most people believe that he walks on water.

Love him or loathe him, it's my job to get people like Roy Keane to speak to me. Professionally speaking, it's not a good thing to have him think of me as something unpleasant that he once had stuck to the bottom of his shoe. I need to make contact today. I need to build bridges, mend fences and generally suck up. Mainly suck up.

There's no point in approaching Roy through Manchester United or through his agent. So I have to come to Tolka Rovers' ground to ask him, face to face, if I'm still on his personal blacklist and, if so, how to get off it. I have the kids with me and, if Roy wants me to, I will sacrifice one of them.

So here we are. Sodden and waiting. Finally the team bus, The Roy Bus, comes into view from the Finglas end of Griffith Avenue. The orange-bib men open the gate in preparation, telling us drowned rats that we won't be admitted now, not until the team have had their official marketing pictures taken.

The coach sweeps past in the usual fashion. Despite ourselves, we look up at the coach windows. Players we have been on trips with for years, whom we have interviewed in press conferences in mixed zones, in one-on-one interviews, stare down at us, frowning, as if our presence here defined Griffith Avenue as a ghetto. By jove! Hobos, crack addicts and journalists. I'm a millionaire, get me out of here.

The bus passes. The gates lock again. It's still raining. We're still outside. Bad words are hissed through the gates at the orange-bib boys. Bad words are shouted back. Not good.

After a while, word comes to us that the photo shoot, which the team had been planning, has been cancelled. None of the orange bibs seems able to think of a reason why we should have to stand out on Griffith Avenue Extension any longer. We are herded in under the corrugated roof of the Tolka Rovers' viewing stand and told to stay there.

The players are already out on the pitch training. This means we have missed them walking out onto the pitch and warming up. In other words, we have missed exactly 50 per cent of the chances we will get to collar one of them for a brief conversation.

The team divides into groups, some of them working with Mick McCarthy, the goalkeepers working with Packie Bonner, the rest working with Ian Evans. Under the corrugated-iron roof, we media are sniffing each other out like dogs, worrying about the competition.

'Who are you here to see?'

'Yeah, is he a talker?'

I announce that I am going for Keane. Instant street cred. I stand and gaze out onto the field with the look that says it all. Down these streets a man must go.

I wander away and lean on the wall near the group that Keane is training with. Even in training, every player defers to him. They each watch Keane for a hint of approval.

Personally, I'm ready for anything. If he peels off early, I'll be ready to follow him. If the ball hits me in the face, I'll be able to throw it back to him with a goofy grin. Who knows? If there is a cold day in hell, he might break away from training and come over and ask me how I'm doing.

I am daydreaming about all the conversational intros I will slay Keane with, when I notice that Mick McCarthy has called a sudden halt to training. The players stand around McCarthy in a circle and I hear him say a few words and then he says that that's enough for today. Suddenly they are picking up orange traffic cones and tucking away footballs and making for the bus. (How did teams train before there were traffic cones by the way?)

I scurry towards the gate through which they will be exiting the pitch. As luck will have it, Clinton Morrison is first off the field.

'All right Clinton,' I say.

Clinton looks at me as if I have suggested that we have rampant gay sex there and then in the rain on Tolka Rovers' pitch in front of a crowd. He is clearly alarmed. He quickens his step and runs on. Possibly, he is going to call the police.

I have no time to be hurt. Roy is approaching. Rather he is looming. On his own as usual. Every time I face him in this situation, I think I hear the music from *Jaws* playing.

The rest of the team walk around in pairs to deflect those who would intrude upon their bubble. They make it a practice never to leave their rooms without a wingman, somebody they can pretend to be having an engrossing conversation with as they pass journalists asking if there is any chance of a quick word. Roy Keane though, Roy doesn't need a wingman. He has his aura – and his glare.

The team bus has pulled right up to the little entrance to the pitch. There'll be no autographs for the kiddies today. The people in Tolka have made tea and sandwiches for the players upstairs. They'll be disappointed too. The players aren't hanging around for snacks. Apart from Roy, who may fancy a piece of me.

I prepare to fearlessly bodycheck the most feared man in football.

Roy is thirty yards away. I'm standing by the entrance to the bus with the team's security man, Tony Hickey. Tony is a good fella, a useful ally on occasions like this.

'Just need a word with Roy,' I tell Tony.

'Yeah, good luck,' says Tony with a little smile. Bastard.

Roy is ten yards away, five yards away. I step forward courageously, almost blocking the entrance to the bus entirely.

'Roy.'

Not a flicker. He is glaring at a spot on the steering wheel behind me. My outstretched hand goes unsqueezed. My gummy smile goes unreciprocated.

'Roy. Sorry Roy, have you got a second. Roy, Roy . . .'

Suddenly, he has swerved and accelerated towards the bus. It's like he's being violently sucked towards the vehicle by forces of the paranormal. He is coming towards the bus now with his head down, and advancing at such velocity that I feel like a drunk out on the streets of Pamplona. Only dumb luck keeps me alive. I dodge out of the way before Roy stampedes right over me. He's determined to make it onto that bus, like it's the mother ship.

'Not your day,' chuckles Tony Hickey through the vapour trail, as Roy steams past and gallops to the back of the bus.

Tony Hickey used to be a good fella.

Mick McCarthy follows. I'm more confident with Mick. He will be my consolation prize.

'Alright Mick,' I say glumly.

Mick ignores me too. Bad weather and journalists are two things that make Mick grumpy. Grumpier. He's grumpy to the nth degree now. By now I'm just hoping that the kids haven't noticed the sad sack way by which their Dad makes his living.

Look away children, I don't want you to see me this way. I'm grotesque.

They haven't been watching. Instead I see Molly step firmly in front of Mick McCarthy, forcing the erstwhile Captain Fantastic to stop dead. She orders him to sign her wet notebook. He obliges.

'I wish it was a sunny day and we could stop to sign them all,' he says to her apologetically.

'Yes,' she says primly, 'the others were very rude.'

I want to run across and get in Mick McCarthy's face. I want to taunt him, to shout ha ha ha, don't you know she's the daughter of a journalist ya big paranoid lump. She got ya. She's fruit of the loins of a hack! But I've lost enough dignity in the last five minutes. Anyway, there are lessons to be learned from Molly's excellent technique.

I bundle the girls back into the car. They both agree that they prefer GAA players.

Good. Me too.

Tuesday, 12th February

Terrible dream. A miniature Roy Keane with a pneumatic drill is hammering away at my head. I keep trying to swat him away, but he seems to enjoy the exchanges and comes back louder and harder each time. That's Roy for ya.

4.05 a.m. Realize Roy's drill is, in fact, the sound of the alarm clock buzzing insistently on the far side of the bed. Have sudden, confused fear that I am in bed with Roy Keane, followed by thought that Roy will hunt me down for having swatted him away while he was drilling or for having impure suspicions about him. I have Roy down as a vendetta-type of guy.

I nudge Mary. Mary nudges the alarm off. I lie on my back for ten minutes, my fingers gently probing my head. Maybe it was Keane rattling away in my brain. Some damage has been done in there.

Finally I raise myself. My head has furniture removers banging about inside it. My throat is sore, like I've swallowed ground glass. And what's this? My chest is tight. I am having a massive heart attack.

I wake Mary and tell her the bad news. I am about to die. Poignantly, in World Cup year. And the paper needs 2,000 words for Saturday. They were going to be the best 2,000 words I would ever write. It's too tragic.

She's heard it all before though. In fact, every time I have to get up early for a trip, she's heard it. I'm dying, I'm dying. Woe is me. Essence of woe is me.

I am dismissed.

Dublin Airport at 5.30 a.m., I meet Ray Treacy. Now Ray Treacy is tanned and smiling and dapper and quite full of chat. There's no jury in the world that would convict me if I killed him on the spot for just being too chirpy. Ray is organizing the team and media travel arrangements for the World Cup later in the year. Right now he's on his way to Japan to make some final arrangements.

'Are you coming on the whole trip?' he says as if it were a cruise.

''Fraid so,' I nod glumly.

'You'll love it,' he beams. 'This island we're going to before the tournament starts, it's seven miles long, four miles wide and nothing to do all day but rest and relaxation. Mick McCarthy says he's not even going to do any media when he's there.'

'Great,' I say. Ten days trapped on an island with the surliest, most paranoid men on earth. No press conferences. Desk howling for copy. I'm a winner in the lottery of life.

Did I mention yet that the paper I work for, *The Irish Times*, had something funny happen to it recently? Not funny exactly. Peculiar. One day we were rich and riding along on massive circulation figures, the next day we were flat broke and management wanted to say goodbye to lots of staff.

Yes. I should tell you that before I go any further. We are sinking. After years of high sales and record advertising revenues, a boo-boo of some sort has been made with our cash reserves. Let's just say that we don't have to worry about our cash reserves any longer.

I am the moaningest minnie in the journalism business at the best of times but, this morning, standing here before the little sunbeam that is Ray Treacy, I'm wondering if the paper will even survive until the summer. I'm feeling especially sorry for myself.

As *The Irish Times* self-combusts, some 113 of us 240 journalists are being asked to look for work elsewhere. In a town with two broadsheet dailies, you might as well be playing the lottery as hoping to get another newspaper job. I figure that with ten years' service, neither too much nor too little, I will survive the eventual pogrom which may have to take place in order to make the numbers work. What sort of paper will we all be working for then? Who knows?

Right now morale is lower than ever. People are bitter and confused. It feels crass and insensitive to be talking about Pacific Islands or to be heading off, as I am this morning, to the Winter Olympics in Salt Lake City and then on to World Matchplay Golf in San Diego.

The paper is disintegrating. Everyone on board is fretting about their future and I'm providing cheery thoughts from abroad. Any wonder they call us the Toy Department?

Not only does this jaunt look like a giant finger flipped at my colleagues, but it will be an award winner when they come to judge the most poorly organized work trip of all time.

My job is a sort of nebulous one. I'm not the official correspondent of any sport. There are no events that I *have* to attend. At the best of times, I piggyback along on other people's big gigs, getting in their way and filching their expertise. At the worst of times, I have to wait and see how healthy Mal's budget is before going looking for my passport. Right now Mal's budget is on life support. So is the entire paper. We have decided at the last minute to go to the Winter Olympics.

That's why we didn't book any media accommodation at the Winter Olympics. That's why we have spent the last couple of weeks tracking down a room for me to sleep in. In fairness, we have found a room. It's somewhere in Canada, but it's a room. By the sound of things, there will be a little ceremony when I check in, just to mark the arrival of the first guest ever to have rented a room for longer than an hour at a time.

My accommodation is to be found in the Golden Pages under the category 'Frills, None.' No food. No bar. No laundry. No media shuttle. Cat swinging not advised within rooms.

I've tried whining to various parties in my life about all this, especially to Malachy. He is the Sports Editor, after all. I remind him of this every time he asks me what I'm telling him my troubles for. I feel his designated responsibilities include listening to all such whines. Mal has a different view. Basically, he feels that no job is worth listening to all my whines. *No* amount of money. No reward.

'Yeah yeah yeah,' he says, 'Winter Olympics and then golf in California. Must be tough to be you. Now go away and stop acting the bleedin' prima donna.'

So I do.

There are other dire inconveniences which have arisen out of the paper's straitened circumstances and which threaten to spoil the enjoyment. I am actually arriving in Salt Lake City on the sixth day of the Winter Games and leaving on the twelfth day. This means there is no point in getting into the real business of daily coverage. I am also going to miss the performances of Tamsin McGarry, the Irish slalom gal because, by the time she slides down the slope, I'll be off to cover golf in California (where, by the way, we have no hotel booked yet and no press centre phone booked. Lawdee! The *annus horribilis* continues).

So what to do? I don't understand any winter sport apart from ice hockey. I don't know any of the big names except Tonya Harding. And then there's the Irish problem. Do you follow the Irish competitors as they pluckily avoid being mowed down by avalanches or by other competitors, or do you cover the people who readers actually see on TV?

One last thing, the capper, the tin hat fastened upon my day. I am travelling to Salt Lake City via London and Chicago, an epic twenty-two-hour day of airplanes and intimate post-9/11 security checks.

Take me now deep vein thrombosis, take me now.

Oh, I lied about that being the last thing, the tin hat on the day stuff. The paper has forgotten to put my advance expenses into my bank account. I have about $40 with me.

If I was twenty, this would be an adventure. I'm not twenty. I'm old and I'm grumpy.

Something else. I'm windy. Scared. Petrified. The more I fly the more I dread it. Today I am on United flight UA929 from Heathrow to Chicago. There's a website you can check called areyougoingdown.com where you input your route, stopovers, plane type, etc., and they tell you the odds on you dying horribly in an air disaster. I tried it out and the computer crashed. I know I am going to die. Statistically, I have worked it out to my satisfaction. The more times I survive a flight, the nearer I am to not surviving one.

Just learning the number of my plane always fills me with dread. I can see the CNN catchline – 'The Horror of Flight 929'. I can see the *Newsweek* cover – 'The Downing of Flight 929'. I can see the sidebar story dealing with my own final minutes – 'The Pathetic Whimpering of Seat 23c'.

It's an epic day and a largely sleepless one too. I have this snoring problem. Or talent – it depends on where you are sitting.

Basically, I can snore louder than a jet engine can roar. In another life, this would be considered a novel accomplishment and I might, for instance, be Snorer By Appointment to the King's Palace or a carnival freak. In this life, I am sorely under-appreciated by passengers and airline staff. There have been ugly incidents in the past, so I do my best to stay awake on long flights.

Today, though, my plan to stay awake is dealt a series of big blows. An early start, a heavy on-board meal and then, cruelly, a Sly Stallone in-flight movie. I find myself drifting in and out of sleep. I keep waking up suddenly when the person behind me kicks my chair violently or the skinny young woman beside me nudges me hard with the granite prosthetic she has where her elbow should be.

My instinct when woken up like this is to turn and apologize profusely, but when I sleep sitting up, I dribble all down my beard and it makes me look droolingly insane. Call me paranoid, but post-9/11, I find it prudent not to appear droolingly insane while on board airplanes. So each time I'm assaulted, I have to make a theatrical little show of pretending to have just woken naturally. I shake my head a little, wipe my face with my hands and, surreptitiously, glance down to see what has just come off my face.

I have twice come close to improvizing a breakthrough cure for the snoring problem. Once on a long haul from Los Angeles, the young woman beside me fell asleep with her head on my shoulder. Soon her head was resting familiarly on the pillowed acreage of my stomach. Her shampoo smelt like apples and the scent of her perfume wafting up caused me to feel at once guard-dog protective of her but also fat-boy fretful about the possibility of my stomach rumbling or betraying me with a sudden passing of wind. So I stayed awake all the way, sitting bolt upright in my seat. Briefly, for comfort, I allowed myself the luxury of draping my right arm over the back of the girl's seat, but it drew dirty looks from the stewardess. She was right too. I was moments from dozing off and risking my arm falling from the headrest and landing on my neighbour's backside. Finally, and smoothly, I feigned a fit of coughing and the woman lifted her head, looked at me accusingly, and went to sleep facing the other way.

Another time, on an early morning flight from New York to San Francisco, knowing that I wouldn't be able to stay awake, I devised a cunning plan. I purchased a twelve-pack of Juicy Fruit, chewed half the packet into a large glutinous wad that I spread out over my bottom row of teeth and then clamped the top row down on them in the hope of clamping my mouth shut.

I awoke in San Francisco, people giving me the usual mix of hostile stares and gape-mouthed looks. I could find no sign of the gum. I assumed I had swallowed the whole wad until the last passenger disembarked and I attempted to leave my seat. I was stuck fast to the seat by means of a powerful epoxy created by six sticks of chewed Juicy Fruit and my entire body weight. When, eventually, I dislodged my backside, it looked as if half the chair was coming away with me. How we all laughed at the good of it, myself and the stewardesses.

Salt Lake City! I've been here before, but arrival always provokes the same memory.

As a kid in the scullery of the little family house in East Wall, there was no hot water and the clothes were washed in a tub and wrung using a mangle. In the scullery, my Aunt Lizzie used to keep a pile of magazines. She'd been to America and was more worldly-wise and fun loving than the rest of the clan. She would keep pictures of the Osmond family for me. I was quite impressed with the musical abilities of the Osmond boys and, among other things, admired their dental care plan, their lifestyle and their sister.

For Lizzie, it was their great manes of shiny hair that did it. When the Osmonds would crop up in her glossies, she would snip the pictures and, passing them over, she would sigh and say with wonder, 'They wash their hair everyday, you know. Isn't that marvellous?' And my granddad would roll his eyes behind her back. He knew that the Osmonds would still grow old and hard-faced and end up hustling their asses in someplace like Branson, Missouri.

Arriving here at the home of the Osmonds, touching down finally at Salt Lake City, we get into line behind the British slalom team at the accreditation desk. They are Generation X Olympians. A nose-ring-and-designer-haircut sort of gang. On the ground, they are met by the traditional Salt Lake City welcome committee.

'Hey, it's the Brits. Welcome! Welcome! Welcome!' booms a man in a tasteful leisure shirt who appears to be genuinely excited.

'What do you all do?'

'Slalom.'

'Well good for you guys. Will you be trying our Salt Water Taffee? Oh we're famous for our Salt Water Taffee. Get yourselves credentialed with Julie over here and then we'll go to the shop and try some.'

'Look mate,' says a slalom geek, 'just tell us where we can get the bus.'

The man is deflated. One fears that, for Salt Lake City, the whole experience will be similar.

Today's trip is a seamless chain of late arrivals, rearranged connections and queues to be searched. It's 4.10 a.m. Irish time when I reach my room somewhere in the gloaming outside of Salt Lake City. In the bedroom, the cockroaches are wearing ski masks with five-ring logos for that authentic Winter Olympics feel. The bed has nylon sheets. As the static crackles around me, I feel more alive than I have in the last twenty-four hours.

Wednesday, 13th February

When you go away on a work trip, there is a pattern to conversations with Mal, The Sports Editor. I point things out. Mal observes that there is a thin line between pointing things out and just plain whining.

'So?' I whine. 'What's your point?'

He says things like, 'It's not that bad is it?'

I say, 'It fucking is you know.'

And he says, 'Oh well. You're always grumpy on the first day. Relax.'

Then he gets down to business. When Mal gets down to business he gives the hit-the-ground-running pep-talk.

'OK. Now. What I need is for you to hit the ground running now that you are there.'

and/or

'I need to hit certain people with your byline out of there from day one. So lets hit the ground running.'

This second injunction concerning 'certain people' feeds into the widely shared theory in the sports department that the rest of the journalists on the paper loathe us. They loathe us and our dim-witted ways. They despise our unstructured jobs here in the paper's Toy Department. They assume that we spend all day, every day, flicking towels at each other's butts and talking about Pamela Anderson. Especially, they abhor our expensive habit of travelling abroad to cover events that are on the TV anyway. When times are hard, their loathing of us increases as an exponential of the paper's diminished revenue and circulation.

Our revenge should just be to live well and screw the be-grudgers, but always we feel we are just one step ahead of the work-study people. We suspect that, out of spite, some pointyhead in the bean-counting department will just axe sports coverage from the paper one day. We know deep down that working in the sports department is really a form of assisted living, that we couldn't survive in the real world. So 'we hit the ground running'. We hit those 'certain people' with our bylines from day one.

Thus we don't get to lie in bed the morning after arriving. It's a stark, gruelling fugitive existence keeping 'certain people' off your case.

Outside it's America, at least it's that briny fold of America to which Brigham Young led the Mormons after Joseph Smith was killed by an angry mob of plain folk in Illinois. Just the sort of plain folk who'll be coming to town this week.

Outside, in fact, it's the Wasatch Mountains and one of the largest sebkhas in the world. Sebkha. How often do you get to admire a sebkha? In the words of Mark Kurlansky, the leading his-torian of salt, this sebkha is 'a flat, thick, 100-mile long layer of salt which became a mainstay of the Mormon economy'.

Any wonder Mormons have a poor reputation when it comes to fun?

Disappointingly, there isn't even a little scab of snow anywhere to be seen outside my motel this morning. The place is either too cheap to get snowed on or I'm in Mexico.

In my dream of the Winter Games, the Wasatch Mountains and their model tenant, Salt Lake City, are spread out over a table of pure white linen. Crisp white and crinkled. From the mountains to the salt flats, everything is pure and everything is white. Purer than

Marie Osmond, whiter than Donny's smile. And all of it, all this goodness, is graciously replenished each night by Mother Nature. Across the road this morning, I can see an In 'n' Out burger joint and an establishment that uses neon to advertise its willingness to cash welfare cheques.

I'm about to investigate the possibility of getting a taxi towards civilization when I spot one of the distinctive lilac-coloured Winter Olympics media shuttles parked outside the relatively salubrious Motel Six just up the road. I'm in business.

Media shuttles can be lifesavers or they can be the express vehicles to hell. Once, at the Atlanta Olympics, myself and some doomed colleagues boarded a bus from the airport. It was driven by a jolly little soul called Venus. She put the foot down and drove us away from Atlanta and towards Augusta. After about fifteen miles, somebody plucked up the courage to point this out to Venus. After about twenty-five miles, she herself became convinced of the truth of it. After about forty miles, we found a spot where Venus felt comfortable turning the bus around.

Today I have Vern instead of Venus. Vern is from Montana and his grandkids are called Virgil, Vern and Vonny. He's a good guy. He gives me orange juice and a banana and promises that he'll swing by the hotel every morning early. He says bananas are good eatin', as if he is the first human to have discovered this.

I love Vern.

My plan for this first day is to gather some colour material on Salt Lake City for a weekend supplement piece that has to hit the computer system back in the office by early tomorrow morning at latest. I'm not expecting much from this piece. Nobody is. It just means that the departments share some of the expense of having me here. In exchange, the magazine will get some polygamy jokes, knowing references to various Mormon scandals in the bidding process for the Games and a quick, largely uninformed survey of life here.

'How things have changed in Salt Lake City. You can party here till 9.30 p.m. some weekend nights, by golly, and teeter home filled to the brim with Grape Knee Highs.' That kind of thing.

On the way into the media centre, I strike feature-writing gold though. Right across the street hangs a multicoloured gay rights flag. A gay bar! Across from the press centre! I'm surprised there isn't a shuffling queue of feature writers right outside the place.

This is too good to be true. What better way to illustrate Salt Lake City's rather self-conscious progress towards diversity than with a few paragraphs on gay life in this buttoned-up Mormon town. This could actually turn out to be a good story. A sign on the door to the bar below says: 'Open 10 a.m.'. It's 11 a.m. now. Still shut. I wait twenty minutes. I bang on the door so that the security men at the press centre across the street stick their heads out to take a look at what's going on. I shrug back. Just hungry for some hot gay action, then I'll be with you boys. I bang some more. Nothing.

Damn their deviant gay hides, they should be ridden out of town on a rail, every last one of them.

I cross from the gay bar to the Salt Palace. The Salt Palace is as big as a medium-sized Irish town, but the average IQ is lower. Security measures will deprive you of a good chunk of your day every time you visit here. Fifteen thousand security personnel surrounding 2,400 athletes. A security budget that, once upon a time, was under $10 million, rose to $310 million. Delays are the least you expect.

I'm not sure why they bother though. I suspect that, if Americans were to nominate a target to sacrifice to Osama, a building full of paunchy hacks would do nicely. If they could squeeze a few lawyers in, they might even paint a big helpful target on the roof.

From the outside, the Salt Palace is a hugely impressive building. To the passing hordes, it must seem as if there are millions of us journalist drones working away inside, extracting the pollen of gossip from reluctant sources and busying ourselves making the sweet honey of media stories. Like most aspects of media operations, how it looks is not how it is. Inside the Salt Palace we live in the sort of listless silence one finds in a library reading room late in the afternoon on the hottest day of summer. By and large, everyone just sits and waits for the bright-eyed and bushy-tailed volunteers to come around with the latest press release. It's a half-life.

I wander aimlessly through the Salt Palace for a while. The place is divided into two halves by a median corridor. One side is reserved for the offices of the big-hitter media organizations, the wire services and those European papers that pay abnormal attention to slipping and sliding. They have shelled out handsomely for the right to have their own small serviced pads. On the other side, the rest of us live together in one big room, teeming and irritable.

I meander down the passageways that delineate the offices of the big media players. All hacks are media groupies and it's always fine and reassuring to see some big-name scribbler walking past you in a hurry. Makes you feel that you're at an event that really matters.

Personally, I like to hang around outside the *Sports Illustrated* office hoping that, at any moment, a harried editor is going to stick his head around the door, look up and down the corridor in exasperation and then turn to me and say, 'Hey kid, looks like this is your lucky day. There's a luge pile-up out on the big mountain and we need three pages. You up to it kid? Can you write luge kid?'

On the other side of the corridor is the big room where the rest of us work. The Garden of the Common Hackery. Cliché Central. At most Olympic celebrations, this is called the General Media Work Area. Here, with some Salt Lake zippiness, it has been made over with a little high-gloss testosterone and designated the Bull Pen. I'm not sure how my female colleagues feel about this, but just ask and I'll throw my weight behind any campaign for a Cow Shed.

Not to butcher the bull metaphor but, as I am about to enter The Pen, I am almost killed by an exiting stampede of journalists. The herd, clearly startled, is making its way towards the escalators. Now I am as spiky an individualist as anyone here (yes, we are all spiky individualists who do the same job), but right now the herd instinct is strong in all of us. When you see a stampede, it's no time to be asking those awkward how or why questions. Wordlessly, I join in.

It could be big news.

Or it could be that the free souvenir bags have arrived.

We stampede upstairs and turn right into Press Conference Room A. I don't know it yet, but this will be my home from home for the next week. Right now I don't even know what I'm doing here.

Presently, a small stocky man with a worried expression comes in and sits at the head table. He has the shifty look of an Italian sports administrator. The old stereotype about Italians and the mafia no longer holds true. These days, the Italians have moved into sports administration. It is their legitimate business. They became lawyers and then they became sports administrators. Good ones too, although this chap looks like he doesn't know where he is or why he's having such a day.

Well, it's Wednesday morning and this is Ottavio Cinquanta, a Milanese business whizz and the don of the International Skating

Union (ISU). He is here to placate us. He is here to bamboozle us. He looks as if he has a very bad taste in his mouth right now. He sits in the chair in this large room for eighty minutes and he sweats a lot. As an act of bamboozlement, it lacks something.

We media, however, we are many and move as one. Apparently there has been a scandal. If not a scandal, something that will be touchlit now and blown into one by tomorrow's editions.

We can sense the story even if most of us can't understand it. You don't have to be a labrador to smell the fear in here. It's coming from Ottavio. Sometimes Ottavio sounds defensive. A lot of the time he sounds surprised. Mostly he's scared. Yup, Ottavio has a real-life breaking news story on his hands.

Here's what went down. On Monday night, during the pairs finals, the Russian team of Elena Berezhnaya and Anton Sikharulidze took to the ice and, if verbal reports are to be taken seriously, they were in a condition of apparent inebriation. Belching and farting as they went they made a string of grotesque errors that weren't just flagrant, they were downright offensive. Women swooned and men reached for their pistols. For a while it was feared that somebody would lose an eye and that would put a stop to the whole thing. All fun and games until somebody loses an eye, isn't it?

They even looked ugly. Ugly and unshaven and very 1980s Eastern European, the pair of them. They looked like they'd pay good money for a pair of Levi 501s. They finished their routine in a giggling, burping heap and left the ice shouting rude and obscene things about the Osmond family.

Not surprisingly, the heart of the audience was subsequently stolen by the unfeasibly good-looking and wholesome Canadians, Jamie Sale and David Pelletier. The Canadians have sheets of white ice where their teeth are supposed to be. Their choppers make Matt Damon's teeth look old and yellowed. As they glide the ice, Jamie and David radiate an aura of simple, uncomplicated goodness. They skated, word has it, like fairies performing a winter dance on a frozen pond. They were *sooo* enchanting. They skated to the theme from *Love Story*.

The conniving huckster judges gave the gold to the Russians, however. Goodness and decency were kicked in the teeth. Everything that Salt Lake folk believe in (while not engaged in Olympic-bidding wars) was repudiated. Salt Lake City has been in a state of revolt ever since. You might as well have contaminated the Salt Water Taffee supply.

We, the media, are in full witch-hunt mode. We shall fight on behalf of goodness and reason here. We shall return serenity to a troubled people. We shall make the world safe for shiny teeth.

Looks like I got here just in time. Local Mormons are so incensed, they've been crushing grapes with bare hands, and there have been two ugly cases of wanton littering. Somebody is to blame for all this and we, the media, will find out who. Meanwhile, we advise the local community to stay calm and to consider Monday night's pairs skating as a mere market testing of the audience. You want a different ending? We the media will go and fix it.

We don't know how we'll fix it, but we will. On occasions like this, we, the media, are both outraged and relieved at the same time. It may be a scandal the finer points of which we know nothing, diddley squat, nada about, but it is a scandal nevertheless. We are all on the same page about that fact. There are perhaps three hacks in this crowded sweaty press-conference room who understood anything about figure skating last week, but now we find ourselves suffused with that feeling of instant expertise. We lean towards each other across the backs of chairs saying things like, 'that Russian double axel was so poorly done it could have killed somebody. Hey, I mean that's Triple Salchow 101 guys.'

Being a sports journalist means never being out of your depth.

I imagine, for a minute, what it must be like to be Ottavio sitting there in the leather-backed chair looking at this great wall of faces and beyond to the stern cliff face of cameras at the back of the room. What must it be like to listen to so many questions pitched with perfect self-righteousness but larded with pure ignorance of the subject? Lawyers never ask a question they don't know the answer to. We hacks, unfortunately, have the opposite affliction.

Luckily for *The Irish Times*, I am an exception. I am a horny-handed veteran of the ice-skating scandal circuit. In 1994, I was dispatched to the Winter Games in Lillehammar. Those Games marked the beginning of the antic tradition of accommodating me in neighbouring territory at Winter Games and are also remembered for the endurance and shining dignity of two of its skating competitors, Tonya Harding and Nancy Kerrigan.

Not only was I there to mine cheap laughs from the spectacle, but it was my good fortune to be one of forty or so journalists whose names came out of a hat in a draw for the right to see the showdown in the flesh.

The other 50 million practising ice-skating experts on hand in Lillehammer had to make do with watching large screens in a tent the size of Denmark. You may think that the large screens would be adequate, but I had the privilege of being among a small group of journalists who were personally asked by Ms Harding to 'get the fuck out of my fucking face' when the competition was over. Treasured moments like that put me in the upper percentile of figure-skating expertise here in Salt Lake City.

We are coursing Ottavio now. I don't know who Ottavio has offended, but I notice just behind me an elderly IOC member feeding tricky questions to nearby journalists who then request the microphone and pass the questions on to Ottavio.

Ottavio has that look on his face, best captioned as 'why me?' He can hardly have imagined that the lucrative dog-and-pony show which is figure skating could have stoked up such passions or intrigue. Or that it could have created so many instant experts among the media. For the second time in a decade! I sympathize. It's only going to get worse for him as we ratchet up the temperature.

Since Monday night, when I went to bed early, right through Tuesday when I did nothing but travel, this scandal has been fermenting. Now this morning, right on cue, the Games have been convulsed. My reaction is typical.

Hurrah!

Instant copy!

Somebody call the Sensations Editor!

Humphries in ground-hit-running shocker!

Bylines from day one!

'Certain People' impressed!

As Ottavio drones on, the room is humming with happy anticipation. We have a witch-hunt and we have a witch. We have, apparently, located a flaky French judge and decided to pile all the blame on her. C'mon down Marie-Reine Le Gougne. To be bleak and wintry about it, we are a pack of howling huskies and Mme Le Gougne is an ailing, but tasty, moose.

Mme Le Gougne has been rumbled. Her deft machinations are no match for our nimble, pitted wits. Mme Le Gougne has been seen crying. She has been observed howling at the moon. Spotted devouring grass outside the Mormon Tabernacle. All very suspicious.

This new French twist suits the American media especially well. If the root of all evil turns out not to be Muslim and fanatic, well then your average American will take short odds on it being French. A French judge diddling the French-Canadian pair? We'll show those hoity-toits in Paris!

And because the victims are Canadian, well, the Americans will feel no need at all to be reticent. Canadians are loveable, library-dwelling creatures who need protection. Because the perpetrators are French and Russian, the American media will feel that they actually have God on their side. Let's free Ottavio. Let the lynching of Marie-Reine Le Gougne begin.

Ottavio finishes up. He doesn't know if Marie-Reine Le Gougne will be available for stockading in the next couple of days. We'll have to ask her.

We drift out. By skilfully deploying that most reliable journalistic technique, talking to other hacks, I am able to piece together the entire background to the scandal and become an expert on the nuances of it all before I go back downstairs.

We have key questions to ask of each other.

'What was all that about?'

'What does it mean?'

'Who was that guy?'

'Spell that?'

'Who'd know about this?'

'Anybody actually at the event?'

We know that ice skating is *big*. There's some statistic that, seemingly, never goes out of date concerning the biggest TV audience for a sporting event being for an ice-skating showdown. Anyhow, in Salt Lake City, it's the only place you can see a man pick a girl up by the crotch and dispatch her like a bowling ball down the ice.

That's got to be worth something.

We're going to have to investigate.

There is an Olympic rule that applies doubly here: when covering a scandal in an Olympic event that you know nothing about, you must *cherchez les journalistes* from *L'Équipe*. If there is a French involvement, you must *cherchez* them twice as hard. At *L'Équipe*, the wonderful French daily sports paper, they have this extraordinary thing called advance planning. A full two years before an Olympic celebration opens, those journalists who will be attending will not only be told that they are attending, they will also be told which sports they will be covering. In the interim period, *L'Équipe* expects those journalists to cover the major events in that sport and get to know the right people.

So the rest of us who never plan anything have two rules of thumb: never go to a big event without a French–English dictionary with which to painstakingly translate *L'Équipe* articles, and gravitate towards the *L'Équipe* person or people when a story breaks. Alternatively, you can gather around some foghorn who has an opinion on everything. You take your pick.

Suddenly, in the middle of lunch, having digested as much second-hand wisdom as I can take, I am visited by a moment of brief and shiny clarity. Hereafter, my own loosely informed view shall be that the Russians are the rightful, hands-down winners.

The argument for the Russian pair, an argument that is scarcely utterable in English-speaking circles here at the moment, is that they were skating a more ambitious programme, they skated with finer and more classical lines. They made a minute error but, for their ambition and classicism, they were awarded a narrow decision over the Canadians who were sweeter and who skated a flawless, but more modest, routine, one that everyone had seen them perform at major events before.

Good enough for me. Good enough, I imagine, for the ISU too.

With these stories, you have to watch and read them. For the next few days, the shutters will be up and very little will be leaking out. We will be picking needles of fact from haystacks of rumour. But we will do it.

Watching Ottavio sweat has made it clear to us all that this is a fine old story that will play big. Right now it's growing. Right now perspective is a dirty word. Everyone has forgotten that, while acknowledging certain elements of grace and courage therein, we generally scoff at figure skating with its absurd theatrics, its camp, pencil-thin men with no backsides, its overwrought kiss-and-cry scenes starring young women with enough make-up on their faces to kill all the fish in the Irish Sea. We have forgotten that this is a sport where nobody wins by two clear goals but everything hinges on the opinion of judges.

As far as we know, right now, figure skating matters more than anything else in the world. The future of mankind depends on triple loops being justly rewarded.

We forget too that, in this matter, the medium is the message. Essentially, television has made this scandal for us. In the aftermath of Monday night, when the Russians were initially awarded the gold, there were scenes of great and squawky hysteria in the NBC television booth, where commentator, and former skater, Scott Hamilton rose to a crescendo of excitement as the Canadians got to the end of their treacly four-and-half-minute *Love Story* routine.

'Throw triple loop, and the gold is theirs!' Hamilton screamed.

They did.

It wasn't.

If Scott hadn't exclaimed so excitedly, if he hadn't so thoroughly lost the run of himself, we'd never have suspected anything. Instead the switchboards lit up.

Soon it became clear that this was the apocalypse of skating, a disaster of biblical proportions which will affect us all for generations. We can feel Canada's pain and anguish. 'Why? Why? Why?' wailed one famous coach, looking as though his crops had failed, a plague of locusts had gobbled his family, the Black Death had taken his neighbours and an unfeasibly large phone bill had just arrived. Why?

Why? Why? Why? Well, Berezhnaya and Sikharulidze received four 5.7s and five 5.8s (out of 6.0) for their technical marks two 5.8s and seven 5.9s and for presentation. Sale and Pelletier got six 5.8s and three 5.9s for technical merit and five 5.8s and four 5.9s for presentation. Even though their total marks were less, the Russians were ranked first by the judges from the US, Canada, Germany and Japan.

'Why? Why? Why?' Because that apparently is the way the sport is. It's judged.

But we're here to change all that. We, the media, are players. Avenging crusaders.

By this afternoon, naturally enough, there are few takers for the argument put forward by the Russian pair's legendary coach, Tamara Moskvina. The coach had asked journalists to note that the Russians made better turns, had more speed, made better steps and used better flow.

'They don't just stay on two feet,' she said. 'The difference is in speed and flow and choreography, it's so easy to see.'

'Yes, my point exactly,' I say to the hacks around me.

'Hmm, sure,' they spluttered. 'But the Canadians didn't exactly fall on their backsides.'

Still. It's Tamara's story and I'm sticking to it. My instinct with these things is always to downplay them. The bigger and more outlandish the story gets, the less likely it is to be true. Somewhere down the road there will be a backlash in this tale and people will start to see reasons why perhaps the Russians did win fairly after all.

And I'll be there to greet the converts.

Already there is a slight change in the mood of some European journalists. Downloading figure-skating trivia by the skipload, one instinctively feels sympathy for the hapless Russians at the centre of all this. What happened on Monday night will always now be the story of Jamie and David, the shiny Canadian victims. The controversy will rob us of the chance to enjoy the story of Elena Berezhnaya and Anton Sikharulidze.

Pity. They are a soap opera on ice. Winner of a silver medal last time out at Nagano, Elena Berezhnaya is best remembered for an incident that occurred with her previous partner, Oleg Shliakov, back in January 1996. The pair were practising in a Moscow ring, both doing simultaneous spins, when Berezhnaya fell, or as the press release says with commendable Russian candour 'became unsynchronized during a side-by-side camel spin', and, well, there's no nice way of saying this, her partner's skate blade 'pierced Berezhnaya's skull'.

Holy guacamole batman! Pierced! Her Skull! The skate blade is not your precision brain surgery instrument.

This woman needs a break. She has suffered brain damage and motor-function impairment and was almost an English football hooligan for a while before making a full and remarkable recovery. And now two slices of white bread from Canada are going to take her gold away?

Not long after becoming 'unsynchronized' during that camel spin and learning the harsh lesson that only a skate blade to the brain can teach, Berezhnaya teamed up with Anton Sikharulidze. This, it turned out, wasn't exactly fate's way of making redress. Elena and Anton have been through the best of times and the worst of times and must still be wondering into which category they might put the present Olympic experience. Suffice to say that Anton is a bit of a lad. He was quoted with some understatement last week as saying, 'Many things have happened to us in the last four years, good and bad. To be here and skate well is just great.'

They won their second world title in Helsinki in 1998 and soon afterwards opted to follow Tamara Moskvina (their coach) to the United States. The move appeared to be a roaring success, especially for Anton.

See, Anton likes to part-ay.

At the European Championships in Vienna the following year, Anton skated with a spectacular cut over his left eye, which he attributed enigmatically to the 'changed environment' he was experiencing living in America. Too many bouncers in that environment perhaps.

Anton's reputation in staid ice-skating circles as a man who likes to shake his funky thing and his unexplained absences from various functions and exhibitions have played their part in the stormy relationship between himself and his partner. Apparently it isn't an uncommon sight to see Elena practising alone before events, when her partner fails to show up. However, given her history with side-by-side camel spins, perhaps that's for the best.

The pair won the European Championships but then, oops, had the title removed from them when Elena tested positive for a banned substance. She claimed then, and continued to claim, that the test was failed as a result of having taken an over-the-counter medicine for a cold.

Now, I never believe drug cheats who claim to have effectively purchased over-the-counter positive tests while suffering from a common cold, but that skate in the brain business has a mitigating effect. I'm a sucker for a gal with a skate in her brain.

The more I learn, the more I'm rooting for the Russians in all this.

And on this fine Wednesday morning, that appeared also to be the position of Ottavio Cinquanta. I suspect, though, that Ottavio's angle is different to mine. I suspect Ottavio is an anything-for-a-quiet-life-type of guy.

Thursday, 14th February

Ottavio's valentine to us is to reveal himself without undue modesty to be a polylingual Ottavio. He speaks many tongues, all of them lovingly and well.

This is part of his problem today. By being willing and able to answer questions in practically any European language, he has reduced this afternoon's press conference to near chaos. The French, right up against deadlines at home, ask him something, and he promptly replies in fluent French. What he should do is buy the time that an official translator could give him. Instead, as soon as he opens his mouth, the Americans are barking, 'Gawd's sake. Whaddee say?' And the French are asking the Americans to hush. Meanwhile Ottavio willingly gives an English version over the din. And the French have to call for him to repeat his answer. And so on.

Ottavio doesn't quite know how controversies work. He loses his temper when he is asked stupid questions again and again. 'Who knew there were so many skating experts in the world?' he asks sarcastically.

He is quite steadfast in his line, however. There has been an accusation. He has secured a denial. Besides, even if you take away the marks of Marie-Reine Le Gougne, well the Russians still win.

Who cares? We know by now, because Ottavio has told us in so almost as many words, that the French judge is a shaking, tearful, flake. What we really want is to get her into a press conference. That would be prime time. Dramatic Scenes! Tearful French Judge! *Sacré Bleu*!

Today, as predicted, there is some sniffy European dissent to the thrust of the American inquisition on Ottavio. Erm, didn't the Russians attempt a more ambitious programme? Isn't there a more classical tradition in Europe? Is it always about being cute? Aren't Americans stupid? As yet, I am too intimidated to ask any questions but I, too, have read the standard text overnight.

We've all been reading books overnight. We've all been reading Christine Brennan's *Inside Edge*.

Count me in on this general wave of Eurocentric thinking. The best sportswriters in the world are American, but this week isn't a good one for them. Of course, I myself am metamorphosing here and now into one of the world's leading ice-skating authorities, and despite advice to the contrary, I have been watching American television coverage of the scandal. Yes, there is more to the story, and if their TV coverage is representative, perhaps Americans are stupid.

I haven't got to the level of full-blown expertise yet. I hold fire at press conferences, but speak scintillatingly over lunches and cups of coffee. It's too easy to make a total fool of yourself at an Olympic ice-skating press conference. I know, I can see colleagues doing it all around me. Anyway, if you have a really good question, it's best to do some sidling and ask one of the more peripheral officials in private. That way, not everybody gets to hear the answer and the official becomes 'a source'.

But I don't have any really good questions.

The press conference drags on and on, conducted in its Babel of languages and steered by some shrewd questions and a steady drizzle of stupid ones that begin with words like, 'Sorry if this is obvious but could you explain how often you have these Olympic competitions.'

It's a law of nature. Somebody asks a question that opens a door in our perception of the event and somebody else follows up with, 'Sorry, could you clarify, would you describe Miss Sale's dress as turquoise or blue? Is that official?'

Stupid questions must follow good ones in the manner of night following day. We are philosophical about this. We adhere to the theory that, if a number of monkeys are placed at typewriters for an infinite amount of time, one of them will write *Hamlet*. If we ask an infinity worth of stupid questions, we might get a salient answer.

Anyway this entire shemozzle is good business. This is all more than any of us could have hoped for. My Olympic debut was the Harding/Wounded Knee Winter Olympics. From there, I went on to cover the Michelle Smith/Incredible Hulk Games in Atlanta and then the C. J. Hunter/Marion Jones Medicine Cabinet Crisis in Sydney.

Given the choice between coming to grips with strange esoteric sports or attending scandal-driven press conferences, I'll take the comfy front row seat just below the podium anytime.

I throw across as much scandal copy as I feel an Irish reader will be able to digest. I explain that if the row isn't resolved peacefully within a week, the world may be at war.

I am too responsible a journalist to christen the entire affair Skategate.

There I draw the line.

People think there must be great variety to the sportswriter's life. It's not coalmining and it's not accountancy, therefore there must be variety. No matter how many times we palm off the same tired clichés to them, they persist in thinking this. They are wrong. It's a treadmill.

Take the Olympics. All sports journalists are familiar with the gruelling phenomenon of the Typical Olympic Day. These are days sent to torment the spirit and crush the soul.

They go like this.

You have spent some hours researching the quirky background of the favoured snowboarder from Ghana who is in action today. You are going to compose a knowing/live report-cum-feature about him and the 'Ghanaian Snowboarder Production Line'.

The Sports Editor calls just as you are leaving your accommodation cell. Instead of going to the snowboarding, he'd like you to go to the women's curling. In the office they've been watching the curling on the television and everyone agrees it would be an amusing and fluffy colour piece.

You sit back down and wade tearfully through the half-ton of paper archives and reference materials you brought with you to the Games. You find just a two-line definition of curling. Curling is the gaping black hole in your expertise. Finally, you pack any book containing references to ice, sweeping brushes or Scotland into your bag, along with your laptop, phone, notebooks, seventeen pens, tape recorder, spare tapes and batteries, electrical adaptors and hotel soaps.

Bent low beneath your burden, you set forth. You get a bus from your remote lodging to the main transportation centre. Then another bus to the distant venue upon which the curlers are curling. By now you are old and grey and you remember that once, in another life, you had a partner, kids and a cat.

Whatever happened to them? The cat must be in college by now.

You sit for an hour at the curling comprehending nothing. Before you know it, the game is over and the only word you have written in your notebook is 'seemingly'. You dash down to the mixed zone with the other hacks. Who won? This we know how? Was this good curling?

The other hacks gather in great numbers around the evident star of the game. You lean in to the scrum with your tape recorder perched on the tip of your outstretched arm. It occurs to you that you know so little about curling that they might as well be speaking a foreign language. You return to your seat and begin transcribing your quotes. The foreign language was actually Norwegian. You curse. You wander around listening in to the opinions of other hacks. What they think will have to be what you think. You start your piece.

'Seemingly . . .'

You grind out maybe 500 of the 800 words required. The phone rings. The Sports Editor.

'You're not at the downhill skiing by any chance are you?'

'No, I'm at the . . .'

'Shit.'

'What?'

'Ah it's just that this Irish young fella impaled himself on a flag in the slalom. Need quotes. Everyone is talking about it. Soo-perb television. Are you near the downhill are you? Can you get there?'

'No. I'm at the curling. It's the other side of the continental land mass.'

'Hmmm. Well listen, as it turns out, the Olympics on TV column for tomorrow is on the curling. Best thing in the paper actually, very funny, very wry, don't want to change it. So keep that curling stuff you are doing to run of play, scores and scorers and some quotes from the Norwegians. Seemingly, their captain slammed the Norwegian Curling Association. Keep it to 200 words and then get over to the downhill skiing.'

You call the skiing venue. Nobody there. Not even a cowbell in the distance. You commence a long series of calls to the Olympic Village. One hour later, a voice, confused but claiming to represent Irish skiing, comes to the phone.

'I'm ringing about the lad who got himself impaled.'

'Ah listen, listen. We don't want to make a big thing of it.'

'Yeah, but it's the Olympic Games. And he impaled himself. He looked like a cocktail sausage on television. It is big.'

'His family were here and everything.'

'Listen is he there? I won't keep him long.'

'No, some of the other lads have brought him out for the evening. He's been through enough in fairness. And enough has been through him. I wish you fellas could just leave him alone.'

'So he won't be speaking to anyone?'

'Well, he spoke to all the press lads who were at the skiing today alright.'

'Shit. Shit. Shit. What did he say?'

'Ah now. Do you want me to do your job for ya?'

On it goes. Day after day of never being in the right place at the right time. Always feeling that the event is so much bigger than you, that it is about to squash you entirely. Always getting back to your room late at night and flicking on the late-night Olympic roundup and seeing no mention of the stuff you were covering.

That's why we have Olympic scandals. It gets all us journalists onto the same page, into the same press conference, talking about the same thing. It keeps us alive. We can drink coffee together. It keeps the morale up. It's better to investigate together than to go off exploring. Exploring is lonely. We'd much rather be Woodward and Bernstein than Scott and Amundsen.

And scandals are democratic in their own way. On the Olympic Media Food Chain, there are several evolutionary steps, from parasite right up to king of the jungle.

People who work for NBC, the television rights holders, are the unchallenged kings of the jungle, they are the jungle VIPs. They can go anywhere, speak to anyone, interrupt anything and, if they so choose, I think they can compete in the events themselves.

Then there are other rights holders who have privileges comparable to NBC's up to, but not including, the right to be carried everywhere upon a sedan.

Next come the common-or-garden broadcasters who have large egos and get better complimentary gift bags than the rest of us. They get a second shot at interviewing competitors when NBC and the rights holders are done with them.

Then the photographers who are impossibly glamorous and oversexed. The snappers dispute this, claiming to be far less exalted than they are, but can offer no satisfactory explanation as to why they also get better complimentary bags.

Then come the print journalists working for the organizations that sponsor the Games.

Then the print journalists working for papers big enough to have their own offices at the Games.

And, finally, at the bottom of the pond, crawling through the ooze in our thousands, are the slimy general-print hacks. We are the lowest convocation of the damned. We are permitted to work in a large hall with nearby toilet facilities. Our accreditation badge points out that, at any time, we may be required to fetch coffee and doughnuts for journalists with higher level credentials.

I am one of these pond creatures.

I work for a small circulation paper that is almost bankrupt. The free bag they have given us here in Salt Lake City doesn't even mention the Olympics. It says Office Depot.

I am bottom of the pile but, when there is a scandal, I still have the right to put my hand up and ask my stupid question. When there is a scandal, we crowd around like rubberneckers at an accident scene. I am free to cough loudly or use expletives near the NBC sound boom.

Today has been a Typical Olympic Day. I still have this feature to write for the front of the paper's weekend supplement and I am already a couple of hours behind deadline. At least there's a nice warm scandal to look forward to.

In the short term, though, before I go back to the leather lodgings, I must scoot around Salt Lake City looking for little bits of colour and froth to cram in. The subject of the required piece is the Mormon Games or the MorLympics as we call them. Really it is the sort of piece that should have been written for last Saturday as a warmer-upper for the Games but, hey, we're broke and I just got here.

The problem is that no matter how much colour and froth and quotes from yokels who have no locals I squeeze into the piece, the skating story will be bigger. I can't write about the skating story because there will be 'developments' between now and Saturday morning and these 'developments', which may in fact transpire to be 'revelations' or 'sensations', may make our story redundant.

So I run around Salt Lake City gathering bits of colour and vox-popping cleancut people. I hate interviewing strangers. First, I have no personality as such, and hence am very poor at reaching out to people I don't know.

Second, I am six-foot three-inches tall and almost as broad. I have very short hair and usually dress like a vagrant. Strangers are scared of me.

Third, no matter how many people I vox-pop, the hacks in other papers always seem to happen across the real 'characters' in town. I encounter folk who have lived most of their lives in sensory deprivation chambers but would prefer not to talk about it.

Still. Down these clean streets a man must go.

Today I'm in the market for a little bible-thumping, a little moral castigation. I want to get it on with some holy rollers.

To be fair, the city has put religion aside for this month. We heathens can have no complaints. I have heard no tedious boasts to the effect that you'll never beat the Mormons. When the weather delayed the start of the women's downhill, the crowds didn't break into a chorus of 'We don't care if it rains or freezes, coz we all got a little plastic Jesus, sitting on the dash of our S.U.V.' Indeed the 4,000 or so missionaries who make this city their base (trivia nugget: there are 60,000 Mormon missionaries worldwide) have effectively been stood down for the month. No buttonholing, no knocking on visitors' doors. No soliciting. No conversions. Strictly no miracles.

I hover for a while at the food court in a downtown shopping mall. In retrospect, this is probably a mistake insofar as it looks as if I am about to mug people for their burgers, nevertheless I will hover until I pluck up my courage.

The plan is simple: When I see some people, who I deem to be square-looking enough to be out and out, heavy-metal Mormons, I shall move in on them and get them to burble their brief potted biographies and then I'll rile them a bit until they cough up some pretty darn controversial views on the Games being in their town. Hopefully, they'll be polygamists into the bargain.

It's promising. Everybody looks real square. This is Wholesome City. I am the only person here who has definitely committed sin. Even their dinky, little meals suggest that they avoid the sin of gluttony at all costs.

The crowd is so bland, white and generic that I'm beginning to think that maybe I've miscalculated. Maybe I should be doorstepping the gays, looking out for Utah's gay scourge. Real paydirt at this point would be to meet one of the mythical Straight Edgers. Seldom seen but often heard about, the Straight Edgers are a down-home security headache for Salt Lake City. The Straight Edgers are a vigilante gang of do-gooders. Mormons with attitude.

Which isn't to say that they forcibly enter your house and then tidy it for you. Nope. Utah's Straight Edgers are a clean-living gang of youths who look and dress punky, but who use violence to get their message across. Their message is basically what your parents used to tell you. No drinking, smoking, drugs or pre-marital sex. At least not in this house. At least not when visitors are coming. Several Straight Edgers are in prison after a 1998 incident that began with fists, progressed to knives and ended up with gunshots.

Like travelling from Cork to Limerick to Belfast in the space of a few moments.

The Straight Edgers have been known to linger outside rock concerts waylaying hapless smokers on the way out. Drunks are also a regular prey. In the main media centre, Straight Edgers are the al-Qaeda of our imaginations. Every form of depravity exists within the media centre. Suppose the Straight Edgers just begin attacking us at random? Maybe the gay bar across the road is just bait to lure us.

I change tack. Go for some deadbeats instead. I pin my slender hopes on a middle-aged couple sitting in the corner with what looks like a wantonly sinful pair of milkshakes. They might be distant relatives of Straight Edgers. Gentle Curvers. He looks like an accountant who maybe siphons off a few dollars here and there, she's an attractive well-built woman who, if I'm lucky, will turn out to be just one of his six wives.

I sidle over, squat down on my hunkers and announce myself in my usual prolix way.

'Hi I'm a journalist from Dublin, Ireland, and what I'm doing is this, I'm writing a colour piece on the Winter Olympic Games and, right now, I'm hoping to speak to people such as yourselves about the whole experience of the Games and what impact the Games have had on your lives, not just right now but all the scandals leading up to the Games; all the construction, the hopes, the arguments and now the reality. It'll only take a few minutes of your time.'

There is silence as they chew the cud ruminatively. Finally, he says, 'So, shoot.'

'Thank you,' I say and, while still on my hunkers and moving now like an obese cossack dancer, I fish out my faithful recording machine, set it up and place it on the table in a clearing between the limp fries and ketchup lakes.

'Well. First of all I'm Tom. I'd better get your names for the record.'

Another silence. They look at each other.

'Rather not say if it's all the same to you, Sir.'

'Sure,' I say.

What else am I going to say? Names are mandatory?

I continue. 'Are you guys married, how should I describe you? A Salt Lake couple?'

'We're sister and brother,' says the woman.

'OK,' I say. And then, for some reason, I announce that, 'There's nothing wrong with that at all.'

I spin into a long-winded question of many clauses. 'Tell me about the history of Salt Lake City and the Games, tell me about when you first heard of the idea of bringing the Games to Salt Lake, what was your initial reaction, and now that you see the whole thing laid out before you, has it changed the way you feel about Salt Lake City or about the whole idea?'

Another silence. Exchanged glances.

'We're from Montana,' he says, 'big sky country.'

I stop short of enquiring if they know Vern the media-shuttle driver. *The Irish Times* will be getting froth and colour. No good local quotes.

I file. Late. I go to another ice-skating scandal press conference. Ottavio is sticking to his guns. He will look into the matter at his own pace and the results of his investigations will be announced when they are ready. Sometime between the start of the baseball World Series and the end of the soccer World Cup is my bet.

It's Thursday night. Still haven't seen an actual sporting event.

Friday, 15th February

Well, the fuss worked its way through the system like a rabbit through the belly of a snake.

We have a little digested pile of doo-dah presented to us just now. Understand this first: when it comes to the Winter Olympics, it's the figure skating and the kiss-and-cry business that draws the punters to the sofas.

If figure skating ever gets to be as discredited as, say, athletics well the jig is up. Most spectators can accommodate a form of doublethink when it comes to athletics. They know that virtually everything they see is dirty and drug-tainted, but a good race is a good race. Figure skating though? If it's bent, well then, it's just Disney on ice. If kiss and cry is all fake, well then who's interested?

Mr Jacques Rogge, the IOC President, knows this. When it comes to figure skating, well he couldn't just let things slide.

Rogge, looking shaken and suddenly old, leads Ottavio Cinquanta by the ear into a press conference and tells us that Ottavio has something to say to us. Haven't you Ottavio?

Poor Mr Cinquanta. He stood up for his sport as he had a right to and explained again and again that skating comes down to subjectivity. You like. You don't like. You vote.

We, the media, didn't like. Mr Rogge didn't like. NBC didn't like.

Ice skating's problem is akin to that which besets art. We don't know much about ice skating, but we know what we like. We like happy endings. Good-looking couples. The lottery numbers tension as the scores come up.

So, quite improperly, Rogge has put extreme pressure on the ISU to come up with something, anything, by way of an exit plan. Rogge's weakness is that he can't stand to look bad. He's in the kitchen and he doesn't like the heat. In that regard, his predecessor, Juan Antonio Samaranch, was made of asbestos.

The ISU executive had been due to meet next Monday evening but, seeing as how all sirens were flashing, the panjandrums brought forward their meeting to Wednesday night. There was no confession from Marie-Reine Le Gougne, but apparently, evidence seeped out that she 'had been subjected to a certain pressure'. Nobody acknowledges where the pressure came from. Mme Le Gougne is suspended indefinitely. Nobody else is. Rogge is grinning like a game-show host who has given away the big prize.

You can tell that the man beside him, Ottavio Cinquanta, doesn't like it. Just yesterday afternoon, Mr Cinquanta had been adamant that the ISU would be looking into the matter at its own pace. In this regard, Mr Cinquanta is old school. He is an Italian, of course, and all the most cunning sports politicians are Italians. Yesterday, he realized that all he had to do was make the investigation last longer than the actual Winter Olympics and then everybody would go home and forget about it all until the TV movie featuring the Canadian couple came out.

Today, Mr Cinquanta must announce that a second gold medal shall be minted and handed to the Canadians. There had been unspecified impropriety on the part of the French judge, Marie-Reine Le Gougne, but Ottavio, all shot through with bullets earlier in the week, had realized that the story was almost over. Stay quiet was his counsel. The media abhors a vacuum. He has obviously failed to persuade either his ISU colleagues or Jacques Rogge of the wisdom here.

'Is the investigation finished?' we ask.

'Well no,' he says, glancing at Rogge in a way that suggests that he feels that Rogge should be taking more of the shrapnel right now. 'No. But last night the ISU made a decision and a deliberation. The decision was to suspend Mme Le Gougne. The deliberation [although outside the ISU's actual remit] was to award a second gold medal. This was passed on to the IOC executive, wherein seven of nine members voted in favour.'

Wait a minute though. This scandal broke on the night of 11th February. It concerned rules and propriety. Ever since then, the ISU has had quite a bit of difficulty sticking to its rules. Awarding a second gold isn't even within its remit. It's a bit of choreography. In fact, this is all a fast-shoe shuffle. Just now the ISU have thrown out all nine judges' votes, not just Mme Le Gougne's. If the other eight votes count, the gold still goes to the Russians.

And the Canadian judge's deviation from the average in favour of his compatriots is even greater than the bias of which Mme Le Gougne is accused. Benoit Lavoie of Canada awarded 5.9 for technical and 5.9 again for presentation to his compatriots.

Sissy Crick of Germany did the same but gave the Russians two 5.8s. Lavoie managed to give only a 5.7 to the Russians for technical merit, the only judge to see 0.2 of a difference between the respective technical merits of the performances.

We mutter among ourselves that the whole thing stinks.

That's what this has been all about though. Plonking a potpourri of sickly fragrances over the whole stinking pile. However imperfect the behaviour of Mme Le Gougne, however great the pressure applied to her from her own Federation, or from the ISU during their inquisition on the morning of the 12th, this has been about a media earthquake. This has been a sport creaking under the weight of so many media bigfoots until it has collapsed.

In the big room where we have all spent so many happy hours baiting Ottavio, we are all a little deflated. The frenzy is over and the business is complete in a curiously unsatisfactory way. We know this outcome to be wrong, but we know that the story won't handle another twist. There is Skategate fatigue out there. Rogge has just stuck a Hollywood ending onto the story and washed his hands of it.

The investigation is incomplete, and 99 per cent of us here know that, when it is completed, we won't be making any phone calls about it or getting frothy at the mouth. We'll be carrying a couple of paragraphs' worth of wire copy at best. If we think about this week at all, it will be to try to figure out why we got so worked up or how we let them resolve the matter in this way.

Rogge and Co. are getting up to leave now. In the corner of the room, there are a battery of TV cameras and they mingle among them explaining the new happy ending to their movie, how they changed things after test marketing.

Cue violins. Cue weeping. Cue continued career for Cinquanta.

The rest of us tramp out quietly. We devoured this story like wolves tugging at a lamb chop. This is a result for our ferocity, but it's also frightening.

The Salt Palace has been buzzing with rumours all week: bribes, pressure, coercion, deals, conspiracies. You ran with your theory of choice, except the possibility that the Russians were perhaps technically better, but televisually challenged. This week we would have believed anything except the possibility that we were involved with what was a pretty dumb sport to begin with.

The story of Mme Le Gougne's instant notoriety is the most interesting part of the media explosion that occurred here this week. By Tuesday, an American referee had come forward to say that he'd heard that Le Gougne was pressured to 'act in a certain way'. By Wednesday, there were unnamed sources retailing any rumour you cared to run with. By Thursday, she was featuring as the lead in monologues on the American late-night talk shows. 'Hey. Lonely on Valentine's Night?' said Dave Letterman. 'Well why don't you give that French judge a call? With a little pressure she'll screw anybody.' A few days ago, Mme Le Gougne was nobody. Now, she's public enemy number one, the perpetrator of a hazy crime in an obscure sport few of us understand.

And we ran with anything. Anything. At one minute Marie-Reine Le Gougne was alleged to have fled back to France, the next she was living the high life and cackling like Cruella de Ville in the suite of a top Salt Lake City hotel. We went with 'unnamed sources' and 'unsubstantiated reports' and 'observers' and 'rumours circulating' and 'informed speculation'.

And that was just in print. The television folk just went wild altogether.

NBC, whose money pays for most of the gig, led the charge. We have to assume, because they have the most journalists here, that they had the best access and the best sources. Whatever. We assumed it anyway.

Most of us rushed out and quickly purchased some expertise in the form of one of Christine Brennan's fine books on the world of figure skating. Christine Brennan herself was involved in a little media sideshow when a column she had written early in the controversy alleged that Mme Le Gougne had promised to deliver her vote to the Russians and that her motivation for doing so was that she, herself, was looking for Russian votes in order to secure a place on the technical committee of the ISU.

This column appeared briefly on the *USA Today* website before it was removed, never to appear again. Nobody from *USA Today* would say what happened, but one assumes that Christine Brennan, as a serious student of the sport, has impeccable sources and that, somewhere among the sources, was somebody who would speak but was wavering about backing it up. So, to the credit of the journalist and/or media organization, the column came down.

But, by then, the story had grown legs. These Olympic stories always do. In the heated frenzy, it's kosher to publish anything that's 'out there'. A TV newsreporter will conclude a report with some outlandish rumour that he introduces with the words 'and now people here in Salt Lake City are even wondering if . . .' and by tomorrow morning newspapers will be using the rumour as headline fodder.

Now Rogge and Cinquanta are announcing that the fun and games are over. There will be no Mme Le Gougne press conference spectacular. There will be another medal ceremony. We are disappointed. In truth, we wanted Le Gougne. Her tears and her shakes and her fragility would be better stuff than some rehashed medal ceremony.

Survey the hundreds of journalists who have been trooping in and out of Press Conference Room A all week to find out which they would prefer, gold medals all round or a Mme Le Gougne press conference – and Le Gougne would win by a landslide.

We have been cheated. We go back to our desks sullenly to file. I get ready to file a short piece on how all those people who have been deprived of medals by drug cheats over the years must feel. Their results have been declared immutable by the Olympic move-ment. If only they'd thought to go on the *Jay Leno Show* or to play air guitar with The Barenaked Ladies downtown or schmoozed with Larry King. Who knew?

Memo to self. Time to go see some sport.

Saturday, 16th February

Here's an odd way to screw up. And I should know; I've tried them all. Down behind the Delta Centre in Salt Lake City, there is a large, and not unpleasant, shopping mall. On the other side of the mall is a park in which various local tribes of Native Americans have mounted cultural exhibitions to make up, I suppose, for having been slaughtered and dispossessed.

I wander through here for a while rubbing my chin in my polit-ically correct way. Then I slip away to the large Barnes and Noble bookstore that sits at one end of the shopping mall. I'd like to get my hands on another skating book if possible.

The aisle where the sports books are is blocked, however, by two teenage Native American girls who are sitting on blankets having their lunch. No problem. I'll outwait them. I busy myself looking at the mountaineering books, which are in the section next to sports. I'm sort of half reading a chapter when the two girls leap to their feet and are suddenly all a-fluster. I'm eyeing them furtively, getting ready to move in on the sports books, when they suddenly march right up to me and hand me a couple of cameras and ask if I will take their photograph. Of course, I will.

I look for somewhere to leave down one camera while using the other and then work out which button to push. When I look up and get ready to stick my eye to the viewfinder, the girls are standing with a couple, the four of them with their arms linked around each other. I take a shot of the four of them and reach for other camera. Do the same again.

I hand back the cameras and all of us bow at each other. Then they all disappear. I'm thinking that I've seen the guy somewhere before, when a flushed Barnes and Noble assistant comes around the corner with a camera in his hand.

'Jeez. They gone?'

'Yeah.'

'Darn. How's about that, huh?'

'Sorry?'

'Berezhnaya and Sikharulidze! In here!'

'Yes. Yes.'

Berezhnaya and Sikharulidze. Knew I'd seen them some place before. There goes the greatest interview I never got.

The Winter Olympics was my first real gig as a sports journalist.

I'd got some short skites to grey Eastern European cities with the Irish football team but, in terms of going off to a big event on my own just like a real grown-up journalist might, well, the Olympics in Lillehammer was where I surrendered my virginity.

That was 1994, before the Irish economy boomed. The paper was pretty broke back then too. Being sent to Lillehammer was a *big* deal. Still, the planning was typically chaotic. Something in the title of the event should have tipped us off that it would be cold at the Winter Olympics. Still, we neglected to book a hotel.

It took hours of negotiating at the press centre with jolly Norwegians before I secured a place in out of the snow. I'm not saying where they eventually put me was out of the way, but the first person to come by and complain about my snoring was Santa Claus.

We had to get a bus every night back to the lodge, myself and a merry brass band, who lived together in a valley somewhere beyond the mountaintop I was staying on. We'd all have to pile off the bus in the early hours of the morning to push the wheezy old bus up ice-caked inclines. I loved it.

The first night I got there was in the early hours, having spent an eternity of trying to finagle somewhere to stay. I flopped onto the bed that, being made of rotting wooden slats, immediately collapsed. I slept on the floor for the next two weeks.

First morning at the Winter Games and I woke up to find myself on the top of a mountain with nothing but six feet of snow and some trees outside. And, in the distance, a bus stop and a telephone booth.

It was the Games of Tonya Harding versus Nancy Kerrigan. It had been arranged that I be on the *Pat Kenny Radio Show* that very morning talking about this. I trudged across the fields to the telephone booth, called home and found out what the teletext was saying about Tonya and Nancy. I called the *Pat Kenny Show* reverse charges and, from the top of my mountain, told the nation what the teletext said about the Winter Olympics. When I finished, a bus came over the brow of the hill and the driver introduced all the passengers to me, and me to them, before we drove on to Lillehammer. Perfect day.

Well Salt Lake City is nothing like that. I've been here since Tuesday and I've seen nothing but press conferences and possible incest cases from Montana. So I figure, if it's Saturday night, it must be short-track speed-skating night. Am I right or am I right?

Short-track speed-skating – don't know much about it, but I love the energy without understanding anything beyond that. It's the donkey derby on ice. It's Uncle Lars with too much drink on him sliding home on a snowy night. It's men going around in circles very, very quickly. Short-track speed-skating is what the nose-ring-and-green-hair crowd do for leisure activities in North Dakotan towns like Fargo and Grand Rapids. It's one of those sports that draws a blank from everybody you mention it to.

'I'm off to the short-track speed-skating.'

'Hmm. Well that shouldn't take long. Should it?'

If you announced that the field was restricted to red-nosed reindeer, people would have no trouble believing you.

The Brits are still doing well in the curling, but curling and Mormons spell trouble in anybody's language. I'm not up to that sort of action this Saturday night and I know that those lame 'clean sweep', 'end-to-end contest' jokes are going to sneak into my copy if I go.

So here I am. Short-track speed-skating, I'm yours to be wooed.

Short-track speed-skating makes good TV, apparently, but, from the press box in the Delta Centre, it just looks like people with abdominal pains skating around in circles until they are dizzy. Most of the time they are bent over so far, they can almost smell the butt of the contestant in front. They skate in this way for several laps until, in the last lap, when almost everyone is dizzy enough, some of the competitors fall down, careening off the padded walls in all sorts of artistically valid ways. While we watch this and are truly entertained by it, the race is awarded to some timeserver who has stayed standing.

This happens again and again. Don't these guys ever practise? In the press box, we ask each other is this normal? Are they drunk? Those who know circulate a two-word answer that serves for every occasion in this sport, 'That's speed-skating.'

In a panic, I look around for a representative from *L'Équipe*.

I may not know what I like about short-track speed-skating, but I know what I don't like. The poster boy for this activity is Apolo Ohno. I'm sure he speaks highly of me, but I have taken against him. Apolo has alienated me with his little smig, which looks like he stole it off a lap-dancer's genitals, and his big hair (elsewhere on his head). I also have a lifelong rule of not taking kindly to anyone called Apolo.

NBC, who are contractually obliged to provide a heart-rending tale to be broadcast before any American competes in any event, have already explained several times this week just how Apolo was raised single-handedly by his father. Harrowingly, Apolo stayed out past bedtime once but has since learned his lesson. Through speed-skating he has achieved redemption. Or has he? Tonight he skates for redemption. Tonight he is due to win the first of his four gold medals and it is felt that, next week, he will move on to the more lucrative part of his redemption.

Apolo Ohno is the sort of person I don't expect to like and, even before I settle down in my seat, I have wished him ill. Too much dude in him. Not enough dude in me. Besides, he's better looking than anyone with talent has a right to be. And every American in the press box is referring to him by his near-celestial first name as if they were lifelong friends.

I hoover up some other little facts with which to stoke up my anti-Apolo animus.

Afraid to travel anywhere after 9/11 when, of course, we all feared nothing more than that something awful might happen to short-track speed-skaters. Totally cracked under pressure at the US Olympic trials four years ago. Accused, wrongly it turned out, last December, of being involved in a race-fixing scam. Plus, he's a rallying point for the raucous American media who beat the drum all the way to Salt Lake City talking up Apolo's drive for four golds.

No thanks. Mine's a regular.

So, on this Saturday night in downtown Salt Lake, in the same arena where Michael Jordan finished the second portion of his pro career with that buzzer beating final shot to win his sixth NBA title, I watch the men's 1,000-metre short-track heats and final in a state of sublime ignorance.

I have come to mock Apolo, not to praise him.

And lo two great miracles occur here within the barn that is the Delta Centre – Apolo loses and I am forced to change my mind.

I'd say that the circumstances of Apolo losing the final were so dramatic and unusual that the race will be popping up on the 'What Happened Next?' segment of sports-quiz programmes for decades to come (except for the fact that the same thing happens in every race).

By the time the heats were done and the five-man field had come around the last bend in the final with Apolo in front, the crowd was apoplectic. A week ago, nobody had heard of short-track speed-skating. Now it seems that a gold medal in the sport would heal America's national pain. Apolo Ohno is holding off Li Jiajun of China, with Mathieu Turcotte of Canada and Hyun-Soo Ahn of Korea in pursuit. Steve Bradbury of Australia was dead last, skating in a different race apparently. He's been doing this all night.

Then the Korean takes a tumble, just hits the deck without warning. And the front four fall like dominoes. Swoosh! Scrape! Slide! The crowd is in sudden uproar. Crikey! Goodness gracious! With a big, sheepish grin on his face, Steve Bradbury slides unmolested over the finish line and wins Australia's first ever Winter Olympics gold medal. Goodonya! Apolo Ohno bounces back up off the ice to claim second place. I haven't been this excited or amused since I saw Argentina beat England in the 1998 World Cup.

In the press area, the Americans are convinced that they have witnessed another scandal. The rest of us mill about asking each other the usual pertinent questions.

'So, erm who won?'

'You know this, how?'

'Was this good speed-skating or bad speed-skating?'

'Is this a scandal?'

The Americans are tentative.

Nobody from *L'Équipe* tells us Europeans what to do. So we are tentative too.

'Let's wait to hear what Apolo says,' advise the Americans. It's as if the Sermon on the Mount is about to have a sequel.

Finally a ripple in the pressroom. Apolo will be here in two minutes! Well here goes I think, as we go about setting our tape machines to long play for the beginning of the sort of double-album whine that Mary Decker Slaney produced when Zola Budd tripped her up back in 1984.

Come and hit us with your moaniest shot, pretty boy.

As we waited to hear what Apolo would tell us, we gathered in clusters and gazed at the slow-motion tapes of the race that NBC were showing over and over again. The crowd in the Ice Centre, watching the same thing on the big screen, booed solidly, encouraged, perhaps, by the new Olympic tendency, which we had helped create, whereby gold medals can be handed out to crowd favourites.

Looking at the replays, you had to admit that Apolo had done pretty well to bounce off the wall with a six-inch gash in his leg and stick his skate out for a silver medal, but the sight of him being tended to and pampered by half the American Olympic community afterwards rubbed even that generous thought out for me.

A rumour runs around the pressroom to the effect that Apolo is in a wheelchair. Give us a break we say. He may be able to manage courageously with crutches, they say. Oh, boo hoo, we say, just get him in here.

And dammit the kid comes in and he speaks and he conquers our hearts reminding a few of us just what the Olympics are supposed to be all about.

'Is this a scandal or is it just the sport?' he is asked.

'Hey, it's just the sport,' he says.

And the rest of his words are an outburst of generosity and decency that we thought had no place in modern Olympism. Turns out that Steve Bradbury, the bleach-haired Aussie who found the gold dropping into his lap, makes Apolo's skates. The pair of them had been e-mailing each other best wishes on the night before the race.

'Yeah, it's a wonderful opportunity for Steve and I congratulate him. He's the guy that makes my skates. Last night he sent me an e-mail saying, "Apolo if you win tomorrow be sure to give a shout out."'

And on he goes, happy as a lark as we pick, pick, pick away for a little piece of bitterness. 'Who's fault was it?'

'I have no idea. I still have got to look at the tape. This is short-track. It was out of my control.'

'What about those four gold medals?'

'My quest, my journey, is not about winning four golds, it's about coming to the Olympics and experiencing it and enjoying it and performing my best regardless of the medal outcome.'

If that wasn't enough . . .

'I thought it was one of the best efforts of my life. I was definitely happy with the performance. Regardless of what medal I have.'

And Bradbury, the lucky Aussie, is a good fellow too. Can you be a journeyman speed-skater? If so he is one. He has a CV stuffed with lower ranking finishes and, this evening, he was just thrilled to have made it to the final. In fact, come to think of it, he was thrilled to be alive. He is the Mr Magoo of skating. In 1994, after an accident on ice, he lost four litres of blood. Four litres! I picture it in terms of large, plastic fizzy drinks bottles.

Two years ago, in another accident, he flew into a perimeter wall and broke his neck. Surely this guy should be appearing in *Jackass* on MTV? His accidents are the second and third most unusual anecdotes Steve will be telling his grandchildren. He got through the quarterfinal stage at the Olympics when two of the skaters in front of him went down. In the semi-finals, you won't believe this kids, same story. In the finals? Ditto!

'Obviously,' he says with a grin, 'I'm not the fastest skater, but those were my tactics. Luck was on my side. I won't take the medal for the minute-and-a-half of a race that I won. I'll take it and think of it as something for the last decade of hard slog. I was the weakest guy in that field. Everyone went down and I'm the winner. That's just unbelievable to have everybody go down like that. But I'll take it. It's good, but it doesn't feel right, you know. I wasn't as strong as the other guys. I consider myself the luckiest man. God smiles on you some days and this is my day.'

And off they all went. Apolo Ohno, wheeled out, vowing he'd be all right for the next three medal attempts; Steve Turcotte, the third placed Canadian with a cut on his backside, grinning and saying he'd be back too; and Bradbury, the man who won the lottery.

We sit around wondering if this mad, little sport can survive itself, if the television people and the sponsors and the men in suits won't pick it up and corporatize it and queer it with grudge matches and nationalism and money. Hope not, because, right now, here this evening, short-track speed-skating has done what great sport should do, it has made us long to be kids again and just get out there and try it.

I wander out into the bracing Utah night, reborn in Apolo.

Sunday, 17th February

Day of rest, my backside.

I have my regular Monday-morning column to fill and, with the time-difference deadline, time for this comes about quicker than usual. My technique for columns is simple. I stay mindful of the old columnists who say that every column you write is better than your next, so I don't aim high. I don't think about the thing till an hour before it's due in. At that stage, any idea will look good.

Also, it takes eight or nine years to establish yourself: you have the freelance struggle, the casting couch for the staff jobs, the rat race therein. By year ten of your career, you are burned out with nothing original left to say. One shouldn't be too self-critical about columns.

Anyway, try thinking of a column idea, one that you might lovingly graft and shape and research, and you are guaranteed to find that:

a) The idea has major holes in it, your opinion won't stand up to the refutation of a five year old.

Or

b) Somebody else has just written the same column in a Sunday paper.

So, wait till the last minute to write your column. You will find that the flaws in your position actually diminish in importance until they become part of the essential charm of the piece. For want of something to say, you'll fill the lines out with dumb jokes. What might be construed as a lightweight rehash of a Sunday-paper column can become, in my mind, the definitive but humorous last word on any subject. A series of these disasters can become your 'distinctive style'.

So I am up at 7 a.m. pacing the floor, trying to think of a flaw-less, definitive, humorous, last-word piece. There are party people in the motel corridor outside, still giddy from last night's fun. Then it strikes me! C'mon down Shirley Babashoff.

Surely Jacques Rogge has made this *your* time Shirley. Surely, Shirley. Again.

Even if Jacques Rogge is not sparing a thought for Shirley, I am. She is one of the great standbys for the column. Her name springs to mind any time the topic of sporting injustice comes up and, if I'd been more than half awake on Friday, I would have put up my hand and asked Jacques about Shirley Babashoff, the most-cheated woman in Olympic history.

Instead, we all sat there and listened as Rogge put himself across like a father giving in to the clamour from the back seat on a

Sunday drive. Jacques pulled up outside the ice-cream parlour and shook his head indulgently. OK kids! Gold medals for everybody, now how does that sound?

Babashoff's story is the parable that needs to be read to all those who don't understand why drugs in sport matter, it's the refutation of the glib denial and the dumb 'everyone is doing it so why shouldn't we?' argument which we Irish comforted ourselves with through our own Olympic drug scandal. It's the cure for doublethink.

Shirley Babashoff's story is a poignant morality tale about the brutality of cheating. She is the reason why, even if there is only one clean swimmer left in the world, her rights are worth fighting for.

Shirley Babashoff retired from swimming at nineteen with two Olympic gold and six silver medals in her drawer. She slammed the door shut and never opened it again. That she walked away branded a bad loser was sadness enough, but inside in her soul she felt she was a loser too and closed the door on what had been the joy of her life.

As a fifteen-year-old, she had gone to Munich in 1972. It was a time when the world hadn't yet begun to wonder how East Germany produced female swim teams that looked and sounded like Welsh male choirs, but Babashoff, the golden Californian, won gold and two silvers. Four years later, they said, and you'll be unbeatable Shirley.

By 1973, she was already beginning to doubt that. The East Germans showed up at World Championships in Belgrade looking like a different species. They won ten out of the fourteen golds on offer. Won them easily.

At Montreal, Babashoff swam four individual freestyle events: 100 metres, 200 metres, 400 metres and 800 metres.

Since Belgrade she had brought her training levels up and up in stubborn defiance of the laws of chemistry. She thought she could beat the little blue pills that the East Germans took for breakfast.

Wrong.

Kornelia Ender beat her in the 200 metres. Worse was the fact that Petra Thumer beat her in the 400 metres and 800 metres. Thumer was a late replacement for the established star Barbara Krause. She was just plucked from the system, wound up and placed in the pool. Remarkably, Babashoff beat the old world records in both events, but still finished second in each. After the 400 metres, she sealed her fate in PR terms by refusing to shake Thumer's hand. The world demanded sporting behaviour in the face of cheating.

If there was consolation, and for Babashoff there wasn't really, it came in the 400-metre freestyle relay, the final swimming event of the Montreal Olympics. When people talk fondly of great sporting upsets, and this week America's 1980 ice-hockey victory over the Russians has been fondly reheated, they overlook possibly the greatest upset, the most heart-warming win of all time. The Americans qualified third for the final. You would have said they were lying in the long grass waiting for the East Germans except that the world knew everyone else was competing for silver. Instead Babashoff anchored the team and led them to a remarkable victory, an achievement that deserves to be remembered as a shining moment in Olympic history.

Instead, it is brushed under the carpet with the sweepings of the times. Shirley Babashoff now delivers the mail for a living. Jacques Rogge talks a good game when it comes to drugs in sport. Imagine, though, if Shirley had been Irish and all of us on this little island knew the story of what her parents had sacrificed to give her a swimming career. Imagine if she'd been our big Olympic hope, if we'd hung the bunting out getting ready for a Welcome Home Shirley party. That's the flipside of every cheat story. The lonely, desolate loser who wonders what it was all about, who wonders what happened to all the high-minded editorializing about the glory of sport when the hard questions had to be answered.

Last week, Rogge inadvertently opened up the door to renewed requests to clean up the muddied record of the Olympic Games. I don't think he has the guts to do it. Everytime I think of Shirley Babashoff and the doughty, determined kid she must have been, it makes me want to cry for sport and its lost innocence, it makes me want to shake all those journalistic beaten dockets who sat and defended Michelle Smith to the point where they were more of a disgrace to their profession than she was to hers.

Those years of the Smith controversy were a defining time in Irish sport. They drew a line between the segment of the population who want nothing but inane, meaningless parties built around sporting success and those who'd rather salute an honest loser than cheer a counterfeit winner.

Every time there is a drugs cheat in a race somewhere, we make another Shirley Babashoff. We let it rain on all the kids who go out and get a kick from busting their guts on sports fields.

I don't really believe that sports columnists should be in the business of picking fights. We just shouldn't be in the business of avoiding them either. There are not many worthwhile stands to be taken in sport, but drugs is one of them and if I ever want to draw a line that divides this job into the people I respect and those I don't, then the stance that any writer has taken on drugs does just fine.

I tell the Shirley Babashoff story once again and go out to see some people built just like Kornelia Ender.

I go to an ice-hockey game.

Monday, 18th February

It goes something like this. I awake in the spartan lodging house somewhere on the Utah-Nevada border at about 5 a.m. I can smell the weekend's refuse still stinking up the corridor. For some reason, the hotel insists on keeping its rubbish in the ground-floor corridor. I would have chosen to regard this as a conciliatory gesture to the rodent world (no reason why a rat should have to freeze just to earn a crust), except the hotel doesn't seem worried about whether or not I freeze. My thin nylon eiderdown has slipped to the floor, leaving me blue-mottled cold and naked as a Lucien Freud painting. I grab the sheet and curl up under it, dreaming, for some reason, that I am the last prisoner on Alcatraz. I know the bright lights of San Francisco aren't far away but . . .

I have decisions to make. Being an experienced Olympian, I know I must make these decisions without consulting the office. I sit on the edge of the bed and weigh up the possibilities for the day.

OPTION A: I can go to the skeleton event at Utah Olympic Park. I don't know what skeleton is, but there's an Irish guy competing. He won't win. He may die. There are no odds posted.

OPTION B: I can write up all the stuff I had done for the weekend and then hope that the skating scandal will take another twist. That would be two pieces.

Not only do two pieces present a grander illusion of hard work being performed by the paper's willing field hand, but Option A has very little going for it. Sure, there is an Irish competitor sliding in the skeleton for sure, but he'll be sliding for less than a minute. He'll start off lying down so he can't fall over. He'll just slide by on a credit card and then I'll have to approach him, introduce myself and ask him if that was a good slide he just had. I wouldn't know what to ask him. It would be embarrassing being there at the finish line never having spoken to the geezer in the first place. Anyway I don't know his name.

One competitor noted the other day that luge is the champagne of the sliding sports and skeleton is the moonshine. That may be so, and it would certainly explain the Irish presence, but skeleton just ain't a great spectator sport. It's the visual equivalent of standing at a railway station and watching the express go past. Paddy Irishman will go blurring by into last place.

I won't be around for the finals anyway. No point in luring readers into the odd world of skeleton. Besides (and this is a biggie), it would take three hours to get into town and back out to the skeleton venue.

I opt for Option B.

Option B is simple and spacious and reasonably priced. It is a starter plan. Modest, affordable and with a simple style of its own. The beauty of Option B is that it comes with its own built-in bonus as standard: extra sleep. I turn the light back off and graciously accept my four hours of that fine slumber.

Experience Doc. Experience.

The day comes out sweet as a nut. I write up my considered thoughts on Sunday's ice hockey, a cracker of a game between Sweden and the Czech Republic as it turned out. Then I wander along to a highly entertaining press conference on the skating business at which several French journalists go theatrically insane.

L'Équipe, bless it, has published an interview with Marie-Reigne Le Gougne herself. In the interview, she states, in effect, that everyone is bent except her. She states that she was placed on a rack and held over a furnace. She states that she is Joan of Arc.

The French media and the American media are no great fans of each other by now and the *L'Équipe* interview is further evidence to French journalists that the loudmouth Americans have been disrespecting them. That makes the French a little tense, but there is also the fact that the press conference begins at 3 p.m. Salt Lake time, which means newspapers all over France are holding the presses waiting for comment from Ottavio Cinquanta.

Sadly for the French, Ottavio has grown into his role as circus wrangler. He has come to love these little press-conference performances and he is hamming it up for all he is worth. The French, bang up against their deadlines, point out that there are earphones through which English speakers may listen to spontaneous translations concerning the Mme Le Gougne scandal. They point out that, at Olympic press conferences, this is what they, the French, politely do all the time. We English speakers are unmoved. 'This is America,' says somebody. 'What about NBC?' says somebody else. NBC can't be showing a press conference with people yakking away in some foreign language. If there's not going to be yakking, let there be fighting then. That would be a story.

It transpires that it is just more fun to let the linguistically dexterous Ottavio translate his own answers. The comedy proceeds. 'The question is,' says Ottavio, 'was Mme Le Gougne upset when I questioned her? Of course she was upset. My friends, I was not, at that time, the champion of sweetness.'

Hugely entertained by all this, and knowing that there will be a pleasant and amusing colour piece to be wrung out of it, I dander back to the main press area only to meet Ian Chadband of the London *Evening Standard*. Ian is in a state of high excitement, like Flipper when he swims to shore with news of pirates out at sea.

'You've got to tell me all about this Irish skeleton guy.'

'Why? Whatisit, Chad?'

'He came fourth in the heats!'

'Fourth, Chad! Tell me more.'

'Yeah, he's a lord and he owns a vineyard or something. What a story!'

'Oh, so it's bad news then, Chad.' Bad for me. Shit.

'Whatshisname? Lord Clifton Lancelot de Vere Chinless Wrottesley or something?'

'Oh Jesus.'

'Yeah, he's a lord and he owns a vineyard and he has servants or something. Absolute cracker of a story, Tom.'

I hit Chad firmly on the head with a piece of lead piping and go back to my desk.

It's almost midnight at home now. I know nothing of his slippery lordship. The Olympic computer system is vague on his actual lordliness but, apparently, he carries a bona fide title. I fill out many paragraphs with a dry-as-dust description of the nature and history of skeleton. Basically competitors lie on a little rectangle of plastic and slide off at breakneck speed. This is the third time skeleton has been part of the Olympics. Once in the 1920s, once in the 1940s and now. It may be another few decades before they can find people willing to compete again.

I find an old *LA Times* story on the web and lift a quote from Lord Wrottesley about the run at Cresta in St Moritz. '"She's a cruel mistress," he said recently.' The piece makes him sound as though he were dead. Who cares? It doesn't make the editions anyway, but when the post mortems are held back in the office, it will give the impression that I tried.

I tried. Like the Champion of Sweetness, I tried.

Wednesday, 20th February

Golf! Sport of Sports Editors. Ticket to air-mile heaven.

The golf course at La Costa is the usual setup. Deep-pile money with eighteen nicely trimmed greens in between. You can smell the cash in the air like the sweet cicadas. Everyone moves around with a bespoke elegance and the tanned confidence that comes from years of country-club living.

I'm not really a golf journalist but, over the years, I've wound up covering lots of tournaments, and I always come away wondering how the regular golf-beat guys can stand going to a different part of the world each week and sitting in the same tent, all day every day, with only each other for company. Occasionally, one or other of them must disappear away into the big world outside saying bravely as they leave, 'I'm going out. I may be some time.'

Those that remain behind aren't journalists so much as survivors. On the one hand, covering golf is the easiest gig in sportswriting, everything is spoon-fed and you have the day to mint your words and build your piece from the bottom up. Yet it is the most dispiriting job – the job that requires you to travel the most to see the least, the job where the depressing sameness of the environment must gnaw at your soul.

Even the good access to players has its downside. Most of them are friendly and appreciate that media is part of the gig. The friendliness, in most cases, has a cloying and pragmatic feel to it, though, and doesn't survive a polite approach after a round in the high seventies.

Journalists aren't well paid. We're not badly paid, but this is the only sport in which a disparity of wealth exists, not just between the participants and those who cover them, but also between the journalists and the rest of the audience. Everyone here is wealthy except the beery chaps in the press tent. I remember a golf correspondent telling me once that, after some gentle ribbing about where his next trip was going to be, and some of the traditional comments ('Well it's all right for some, but when are you going to get a real job, or could you afford to get a real job?'), he asked the company to guess how much he earned. The lowest guess hazarded was about three times his actual wage.

Then there is that matter of actually seeing some of the sport you cover. Most of the guys never leave the press tent from morning until dusk. There are two reasons for this. Firstly, all sports editors are golf fanatics and the life-support machine from which they must not be removed is the golf correspondent. They ring every two minutes looking for information on who played which stroke and used what club. It keeps them happy if there is somebody answering the phone all the time. And when they go to the afternoon editorial conference with 'certain people', there will always be questions asked about the golf.

Secondly, at the typical golf tournament, going out and actually watching golf is a mug's game. You can only watch one golf-playing group at a time, whereas sitting at your desk you have not just the TV coverage, but the scores of all the players on the huge board in front of you. You also have a legion of volunteers dropping pages with flash quotes from players on your desk and you know that any unusual shot which is made will not just be shown on TV, but a piece of paper will quickly appear on your desk telling you which club was used, what distance was involved, how many times this shot has been made before, along with the precise genealogy of the grey squirrel who lived in the hole by the tree at the back of the green upon which the unusual pin position was set. Plus a quote from the squirrel.

Here at La Costa, well it's no different to being at Birkdale on a rainy day. *The Irish Times* has a seat near the front of the press rows. The *Irish Independent* is next door to the left. The *Irish Examiner* in the next seat. The various Irish Sunday papers have seats to the right. In the row behind, the English boys sit bantering. Further back again, the 'foreign-language media'. Across the aisle, the Americans.

I am at a little bit of a disadvantage today. Due to the parlous state of the paper's finances, we haven't booked a telephone for the event. Back in Dublin, we worked all this out. I was central to the hatching of the money-saving masterplan that involved a rare excursion for the paper's one and only tri-band mobile phone.

We were all excited about the plan and behaved as if it would rescue the paper. Filing via mobile from America would be a fresh and exhilarating new experience that would also allow me to accept regular calls throughout the day from my incredibly large circle of acquaintances. So I booked my laptop in for elective surgery so that it might have local American free-phone numbers on it. My laptop having come through its little op, I went to collect the tri-band mobile.

'It's wonderful,' said Doris, the guardian of *The Irish Times* mobile phones, as she handed the sacred instrument over on the day before my departure. 'Remember, it can't be used with a laptop. Never. Or else you'll turn into a pumpkin. Aha.'

I've been carrying the useless thing around with me for over a week now. Not once has it rung. Not once have I been able to work out how to make a call on it.

I know the fault is mine and not that of my incredibly large circle of acquaintances who are missing me with a sense of grief so clean and pure that it precludes involvement with tone-dialling apparatus. There appears to be some minor adjustment that my Luddite fingers must make to the setup of the phone in order for the thing to spring into life. I spent half of last night fiddling with the thing, at one stage calling a number that flashed up on the screen only to get through to the message service of Maeve Donovan, the paper's new managing director, at 5.30 a.m.

When I arrive in the press tent, I note bitterly that, right beside me, is the desk of Karl McGinty of the *Irish Independent*. Of course Karl's desk is equipped with a splendid phone. I will have no choice but to beg him for use of the phone while my useless mobile sits on the desk like a paperweight.

Seeing Karl's phone reminds me of one of my favourite journalism memories.

The World Cup of 1998, and Argentina are to play Holland on a slow bake of a Saturday afternoon in the Velodrome at Marseille. I arrive at my desk and, to my immense surprise, this being a Saturday game and no copy being required of me after the game, there is a telephone all connected and lovely sitting waiting for me. The great John Brennan of the *Sunday World* is sitting two seats down, completely bereft of any communications technology. I wave my phone at him, teasingly, at which point he stands up and barks at the French volunteer in the aisle behind me, 'Hey!

How come the Protestant *Herald* has an oul' Wolfe Tone? On a Saturday?'

Harrington and Clarke are already out on the course by the time I get settled in. No sign of Karl. I look at his phone and hope, small-mindedly, that some non-fatal accident has befallen him. I badly want some breakfast, but decide I had better wander out and show my face. Outside the sun is up. It was a mistake to bring only Winter Olympic clothing to a southern Californian golf competition.

This is the Accenture World Matchplay Championship. So it says on my nice complimentary computer bag. I rail and rant against all manner of freebies taken by journalists, but I am a sucker for computer bags. We are at the Accenture World Matchplay Championship for two reasons: one, they give good free bags and, two, Darren Clarke won the thing two years ago, beating Tiger Woods in the final. We were the only Irish paper on site. Lightning may strike twice. If it does, may it strike Karl first. I want that phone.

Harrington and Clarke are the Irish hopes. An Irish golf-writer's life is spent writing about and extracting quotes from Harrington and Clarke. Clarke and Harrington. They are the Mason and Dixon of our Irish golf explorations, charting new territory for us all.

I interviewed Clarke once in Baltray, Co. Louth but, in the intervening years, I have frequently been able to assure myself that he doesn't remember it. When he's coming off a course, I'll stand in his way and say 'Hi Darren', and he'll give me a diabolical look and swerve past me with astonishing agility for a big man. Boy is he going to be so embarrassed when, eventually, he finds out that it's me he's been snubbing, me the guy who did the favourable little Baltray piece back in 1992.

So I wander towards Padraig Harrington's match. There are several reasons for this. He is a hero of mine, a hard thing for any golfer to be. The way he works, the values he brings to the game and, perhaps most impressively of all, the fact that he always talks to me. That's the fibre of true heroism.

Then there is the matter of his amiable and lovely wife, Caroline, who is always in the gallery following him. If you've just missed the first nine holes of his game, Caroline will happily fill you in with all the necessary stroke-by-stroke details and some useful colour as to what movie they saw last night and who else is over. Long may they thrive as a couple.

Harrington and his opponent Steve Flesch are just coming off the ninth when I join the group. No sign of Caroline in the small gallery, I notice. Damn her fickle ways. Flesch disappears into the toilets at the ninth while Harrington limbers up on the tenth tee. He is one behind. As we are near the clubhouse, a good crowd has gathered to throw its eye over the eleventh-ranked player in the world.

Suddenly, the silent communion between gallery and player is interrupted by the loud shrilling of a mobile phone.

This is a cardinal sin on a championship golf course, but a little gift to a colour writer. I, of course, am delighted. How will the players react? Some yuppie in a Pringle jumper is going to get the death penalty from the stewards and the hard stare from Harrington.

The phone keeps ringing, loud and insistent, its owner apparently willing to brazen it out. I see Harrington and his caddy Dave McNeilly cease their planning for the tenth hole. They stand scanning the crowd like a couple of secret-service men. The stewards turn around and do likewise. The phone tweets on. My eyes meet Harrington's and I nod towards him, rolling my eyes in sympathy.

Just then, the man beside me pokes his finger into my side. 'Switch off your phone dammit,' he says. I turn to him to shrug my shoulders theatrically. I'm as baffled as he evidently is. In our collective confusion, I am willing to forgive him for carrying on like a vigilante. As I shrug, I naturally slip my hands into the pouch of my hoodie. And there it is, the shrilling *Irish Times* Motorola tri-band cellphone, almost jumping with impatience, having broken its fortnight-old silence.

I fish the damn thing out, showering it in a spray of expletives. It's an unfamiliar phone and I've never been faced with the problem of having to answer or switch it off before. I begin pressing every button frantically, fingers and thumb moving all over the face of the thing.

It's like one of those movies when Sean Connery has five seconds – no four, no three – to decide which wire to pull before the bomb blows everyone to smithereens. Finally, one button stops the ringing. I take my finger off the button, and a second later it starts again.

Finally, the caller gives up.

The ringing dies.

I look up. I have attracted the biggest gallery of the morning. Harrington is beaming across. 'Made my day,' he says loudly.

I can tell by his face that he's joking but if there is a person here in southern California who has not turned to stare, well they swivel their head now taking in the inappropriately dressed fat man standing in the morning sun with a treacherous cellphone in his hand. I fall back on the position of the National Rifle Association – mobile phones don't bother golfers, people do.

And that, the first, as it later transpires, of a thousand calls from Mal, is about the highlight of the day for everyone. The gamble we have taken in spending the money on coming to La Costa backfires spectacularly. Clarke is beaten by a guy called Matt Gogel. Bad enough. Just time to ask Clarke to glower into the tape machine before Flesch knocks Padraig Harrington out. Then Tiger Woods gets beaten by somebody called Peter O'Malley. And David Duval goes belly up. Phil Mickelson flops. It's Wednesday and all the stories are used up.

I meet Karl. Bless him, he knows nothing of the phone on his desk, only that it's no use to him because he has some new wonder gizmo for filing. Wonder gizmo is the phrase that the technical support staff of newspapers use instead of 'heartbreaker'.

I tell Karl that there is nothing for it but for him to immerse himself fully in the new technology. Embrace, don't resist. And I do Karl the favour of taking the phone away from him lest he backslide. Then we wander out towards the scene of Harrington's exit.

Karl is all a-fluster this morning. Not bad enough that the stage here is scattered with more bodies than the last act of a Shakespeare play, but Karl is staying down the road in San Diego and, to get up here to Carlssbad, he hired a rental yesterday. This morning he woke up and couldn't find the keys and had to take a taxi up. Karl is an obsessive genius when it comes to saving money on trips, but the cab ride up and the one he faces back to San Diego will wipe out all his money saving devices for the trip. Still at least he's in the city.

Padraig Harrington's exit shouldn't have come as a surprise to us really. This is the third year in a row he has bounced out at the first-round stage of this competition. Every January, his game is a work in progress. He meets us and grins ruefully.

'Same old, same old,' he says. 'Maybe I shouldn't have started the year with matchplay. On the other hand, I wouldn't have made a cut this week either. I hate to say it, but I could do with the four days' practice now. I'm not distraught. I had low expectations.'

And that's it. All we need. Expressed frankly and openly. We all walk back towards the clubhouse together. When Padraig leaves us, Karl and myself turn to each other and say virtually the same thing, 'Wish they were all like that.'

I am the only journalist staying in the hotel. To celebrate this, the manager has asked if he can see me. He is a man from Belfast as it turns out or, as he pointedly tells me thirty-seven times, he is from the UK. We inspect each other, talk small talk for about half an hour, and decide that we'll never be friends and had best avoid eye contact on all future trips through the lobby.

Indeed, after a while, I take to leaving the hotel by the back entrance lest we excruciate each other anymore.

My status as the only journalist incarcerated in this UK-run hotel has distinct drawbacks. I discovered the biggest of these just this morning after fifty minutes of waiting for the media shuttle, which is supposed to arrive every forty minutes. Naturally, thirty-nine minutes into my wait, I'd begun to grow a little excited about the bus, wondering from where it would suddenly pop, seeing as how it was nowhere on the horizon. After forty-five minutes, I went back into the hotel and made a timid call to the media centre and, a few minutes later, a surprised shuttle bus driver pulled his gaily decorated vehicle up outside my primitive lodging house.

It is agreed between us that he shall be my personal shuttle for the week and for future trips he shall come only when summoned. He thinks this is a splendid arrangement and laughs loudly at the good of it. I laugh along, but my tightwad, journalist heart is telling me that on Sunday night, a generous tip will be in order. It is unlikely that a receipt will be provided for this tip.

Maybe he'd just prefer a big hug.

I call home when I get back to the hotel. Get the headlines.

'Lord Wrottesley fourth in the Skeleton Final!'

'Nation agog!'

'Wrottesley real charmer!'

Certain People Wondering Why Humphries is Not In Salt Lake City Still.

Thursday, 21st February

All our eggs are now in one basket. The basket is called Paul McGinley and he has one big eyebrow running right across his forehead. Graucho style.

Paul survived yesterday's bloodbath, beating Joe Durrant easily in the last match of the day, which finished much too late for our first editions. We have decided that Paul will be the story. On the front nine yesterday, he made five birdies and looked confident and unbeatable. With so many of the big names gone, maybe he can mill through the field and win the thing. He's playing with a new putter too. He just woke up yesterday and decided he needed a new, heavier putter, went out and got one – and hey presto!

Seems like a small thing but, in a bad week at the golf, we can turn that into seven or eight paragraphs of anecdotal backup.

Today Paul is playing Kevin Sutherland. Tee-off is twenty-four minutes before midday, which makes it hard to make the editions back home. On the bright side, who is Kevin Sutherland?

It all unfolds like this. McGinley plays wonderfully. Birdies five of the last ten holes and he is three under at seventeen when the game finishes. Does everything right. Problem is, Kevin Sutherland just does it better.

McGinley stops and gives Karl and myself a few quotes. He's thoughtful and reflective. A big, silver courtesy car comes purring across the grass to take him back to the clubhouse. He declines the offer and walks off up the gentle slope alone. Unlike his old friend Padraig Harrington, a few days' practice isn't what he wants right now.

For Karl and myself there is a silver lining, of course. This is a nothing tournament now. It's only Thursday. It's southern California. You wouldn't fill a postage stamp with the amount of copy our papers will be needing between now and next Monday morning.

We head off for lunch with Karl telling me merrily how he almost door-stepped Sergio Garcia and Martina Hingis last night.

Friday, 22nd February

Grim scenes. By this evening, the fairways at La Costa were littered with the bodies of TV executives who had taken their own lives. The tournament goes live on the box tomorrow and the only name left playing in it is José Maria Olazabal. Sergio Garcia left town today saying thanks, he had fun.

Colin Montgomerie left, saying he wouldn't be back. Ever.

I leave early. The paper is too dispirited to want anything extra for the late edition. I'm waiting for the shuttle and there's a guy outside the clubhouse taking down a big canvas banner with the tournament's logo written on it. 'The World is Watching,' it says.

Saturday, 23rd February

You don't want to know.

Sunday, 24th February

Well Doctor, its Sunday in California and I've been feeling odd for about a week now.

The motel says that I'm welcome to free continental breakfast. This means free coffee and the choice of red or green apples.

On what continent or planet does this count as breakfast, Doctor?

Outside the window, the shuttle bus to the final of the Accenture World Matchplay Golf is waiting, and it waits for me alone.

Me and Bill, the shuttle bus driver, get along fine, but there is a crunch coming in our relationship this evening. A watershed moment. Last Wednesday, when we discovered that we were to be a couple, we could both see this coming, I think – but, just in case, Bill took the precaution of providing me with visual reminders. By Thursday morning, there were several stickers adhered to parts of his bus telling me that 'Gratuities Are Graciously Accepted'.

Well, Bill Stickers, I thought to myself. How very ungracious of you.

Anyway, this evening will be the last time that Bill will drop me back to the motel. We are both glad, I think. We have reached the limits of our small-talk reserves. He's not interested in golf. I said to him on Thursday that this was the first time I'd ever been involved in a golf tournament longer than Tiger Woods and Bill just said, 'Yeah, I guess', as if he'd been thinking the very same thing but didn't think it worth saying.

For my part, I have discovered that, in southern California, commenting that the weather is lovely today gets to be redundant quite quickly. Every morning I say, 'Hey Bill, that's a beautiful day', and Bill says, 'Yeah, you bet', and starts up his bus. In the evenings, when he drops me back to the Coffee 'n' Apple Motel, he says, 'There you go buddy, home sweet home.'

I wish that Bill and I had become a little closer. Then this evening I could give him a big hug and just say thanks big guy. Instead, I've got to fumble in my pocket and fish out a big tip. No way will Bill provide me with a receipt for the office. He may be gracious, but he's not thoughtful. Not in that way.

Even apart from that pending awkwardness, it seems a little strange to be heading off to the final day of this particular golf tournament. There's just two guys left, Scott McCarron and Kevin Sutherland and, if they were sitting across the tiny lobby from me right now tucking into red apples and black coffee, I wouldn't know them.

Yet one of them is going to win a million bucks in a few hours' time. In fact, if it's McCarron, he'll win a whole lot more because he'll be crowned King of the West Swing or something like that. Whatever it is, Scott doesn't have to worry about not getting a receipt from the shuttle-bus driver.

The fact that there are only two guys left in the golf tournament makes it unique, but it's been a weird week anyway. On Tuesday, as planned, I left Salt Lake City after a week or so of covering the Winter Olympics. Leaving was a gamble, and with gambling, Doc, I've found that you win some and you lose some.

And that's how the week has gone. Off to California last Tuesday. Writing obits for Clarke and Harrington by lunchtime Wednesday. Call home. The lord came fourth again. He's been on the radio and everything. What a story! Write obit for Paul McGinley on Thursday.

So, Doc, it's this persistent chronic feeling of being in the wrong place at the wrong time all week long. Today there's this historic ice-hockey match between Canada and the US back in Salt Lake City but, for me, there's this awkward parting with Bill still to come. I can see him out at the shuttle now, his fishing hat pushed down over his eyes. He's dozing softly, waiting for me and me alone. Bless his heart folks, he's a good man, but lemme tell you, it's no consolation.

Oh, and Kevin Sutherland took that million-dollar cheque.

March: The Ides (or thereabouts) of Irish sport: a Quick Sampler

The Bertie Bowl!

There aren't many areas in which I stand up and demand to be counted. In ten years of sportswriting, I've done little more than my duty in keeping the clichés circulating. I aspire to be nothing more than the fat man jeering from the sidelines. On one issue alone am I firm as opposed to jiggly – the Bertie Bowl.

Not so much the controversy regarding whether or not it should be built. No, it's the actual phrase 'Bertie Bowl' I'm concerned with. I made it up, see. Coined it. Minted it. Launched it. I have seen it credited to Mr Pat Rabbitte of the Labour Party but am sure, as one with a fine canon of memorable phrases already to his credit, he repudiates it. He is no thieving magpie, no plagiarist. I doubt he can sleep nights with the inference that he is a shameless larcenist hanging over him.

Myself, I sleep the sleep of the just. I know that it was me, thirty seconds or so before the rest of the Irish population, who first thought of and launched the phrase Bertie Bowl. I was the first to reach for the easy alliteration.

Let that be my epitaph. A big man, but in many ways also a small man.

I debuted the Bertie Bowl and Stade Saint Bernard on the same day in a dazzling showcase of my writerly talent. Two brand-new phrases to be worn threadbare and entered into the lexicon of sporting cliché. The Bertie Bowl, being the national stadium dreamed of by An Taoiseach, Bertie Ahern, and Stade Saint Bernard being the salubrious coliseum craved by his rival, Bernard O'Byrne of the Football Association of Ireland.

Stade Saint Bernard never really caught on but, years later, the Bertie Bowl is still with us. Bertie can't leave it alone.

This week though, the dream died. It's possible that we won't have the Bertie Bowl to kick around any longer.

The cancer has spread. The Aquatic Centre attached to the Bowl, as part of the great Sports Campus Ireland vision, has itself become tainted with scandal. Our national birdbath was intended to be one small damp corner of the immense leisure gardens conceived by the Taoiseach himself and modelled, as we were proudly told at a press conference eighteen months ago, on that great Australian loss maker at Homebush Bay, Sydney.

Now we know that critical information about the company, Waterworld UK, that runs the centre has been withheld from the government. When they say critical information, they mean critical information like the fact that the man selling the *Big Issue* on O'Connell Bridge has more financial backing than the company who actually won the bidding process to build the Aquatic Centre. In fact, they should never have been allowed to bid at all.

The State is now in a trickier position than a swimmer with yellow clouds seeping from his Speedos.

For the newspaper, this is a news story as much as it is a sports story. There is an odd territorial arrangement in newspapers wherein it is deemed that everyone is an expert on sport, but that sportswriters only know about sport. In other words, a political correspondent may sit down and write a column on a sports issue and, even though the column is filled with laughable errors of fact and judgement, nobody will say anything. A sports columnist, however, is not expected, under any circumstances, to devote a column to his or her views on, say, foreign borrowing policy. During the Michelle Smith controversy, some of the most offensive and laughable pieces I read were by people who fancy themselves as heavyweights of the news pages.

With the Aquatic story there's enough to go around, however. Will an unsuccessful bidding consortium now sue? Will the European Union take action over a perceived breach of the rules regarding public procurement? Should the State sit tight and hope it all blows over? Should it move against Waterworld UK and thus openly concede that the entire process was dodgy?

I have enjoyed the time of the Bertie Bowl, viewing it as the government's little gift to columnists, a bountiful provider of good column material. Now I'll have to look elsewhere for six columns a year.

That's another sports column rule you need to know before you get started: once is never enough. If a thing is worth saying, it's worth saying a dozen times. You need to write about a subject and then write about it again and again and again before people will begin to appreciate you have anything to say about it.

Not many sports topics have that sort of durability, but the Bertie Bowl has played and played. I love it. It has given me a sheaf of columns so thick that you could brain a donkey with them.

Thank you An Taoiseach.

For his part, the Taoiseach is showing signs of mental instability on the issue. Little wonder. These are the Taoiseach's personal plans for a stately pleasure dome (with velodromes measureless to man) to be built out in Xanadu West, where every road is clogged like a fat man's arteries. The project towers above all other current examples of ludicrous ego-driven pomposity. Those who oppose the plan, on the basis that it is the wrong stadium in the wrong place at the wrong time, have been dismissed as 'nitwits'. Ouch!

Ah, the Bertie Bowl.

Start anywhere. For instance, the Aquatic Centre should be the baby of the Irish swimming authorities. Instead, the justification for building it is the Special Olympics, which Ireland will host in the summer of 2003. Irish swimming is still reeling from a drug scandal, child sexual abuse revelations and a double murder. Nobody really wants to come right out and say that Irish swimming deserves a big Aquatic Centre right now.

Throw in the machinations of the various other sports bodies, whose support for the project is being bought and sold on an almost weekly basis, and you have a fine overview of the current state of Irish sports administration.

The Bowl itself and its gaudy trimmings have survived the accusations of sweetheart deals in the matter of the consultants appointed to nurse it. It has survived widespread ridicule as regards its size and inconvenient location. It has survived the 'High Point Rendel Report' of just a few weeks ago, an independent inquiry that produced a judgement so damning of the whole business that it should have brought forth a bundle of resignation letters. Nobody resigns anymore though.

Instead we got the grim pathos of Paddy Teahon (Director presiding over all matters Bowlish but now damaged, perhaps terminally, by the Aquatic Centre scandal) fulminating that we had his personal guarantee that he'd get the Bertie Bowl built for the original price.

Speaking rationally, and with only the slightest hint of a twitch, the Taoiseach has continued to let it be known that plans for the place will be scrapped only over his cold cadaver.

And yet the game is up! The only true measure of cunning and deviousness in Irish politics comes when you mix it up in the fight club that is Irish sports politics. In that shady world, poor Bertie has been biffed about like a bantamweight.

The pantomime that begat the shambles began back in 1998 when, in the midst of the solemn deliberations of a governmental committee to examine the feasibility of a national stadium, the Football Association of Ireland began to feel strange and excused itself. The condition the FAI was suffering from was initiative. They weren't going to wait around for things to happen. By golly no. From this day forth, they would be movers and they would be shakers.

The FAI stages an unbelievable amount of action every year, perhaps six home fixtures in a busy year (or just one competitive home fixture in 2002, for example) and, therefore, they came to a decision. A national stadium wasn't good enough. The FAI needed its own place to bring people back to after the pub and to hold the odd decent soccer match in.

The FAI announced that it wouldn't have another decent night's sleep until it had a gleaming stadium of it's own. They would build it and they would call it Eircom Park. That was the plan.

And there was much worried lowing among the beasts of the field.

The Taoiseach, wounded and worried by these developments, did the only sensible thing he could. He proposed that yet another stadium be built, that the populace of Dublin never be out of sight of a great, big white elephant to remind themselves of how much money there was in the good times.

The FAI boys got their foolish Eircom Park proposal up and running before Bertie could flesh out the dimensions of his Bowl, but it was all quite macho for a while. Tragically, the FAI's numbers refused to match up and there were looming difficulties with planning permission as well as the usual infighting.

With nobody willing to put the final bullet into its chest, the ailing Eircom Park/Stade Saint Bernard business had eventually to be bought out of its own folly with a huge wedge of government money.

Having paid one sports organization not to build its own stadium, the Taoiseach was hooked on the idea. He became a serial briber. There began a brief era of wanton money-waving, during which Bertie kept his eyes on the prize and went around town shoving bundles of notes into the breast pockets of sports organizations, 'There's more where that came from if you stay away from builders.'

The Taoiseach's dream survived. Viva el Bertie Bowl. On a clear day, Our Leader could stand in a field in Abbotstown and almost feel the glory of his erection. Manchester United perhaps winning a European Cup Final in the bright and shiny amphitheatre. The Taoiseach shaking Roy Keane's hand, joining the boys for a lap of honour, the populace cheering lustily, 'Keane-o! Bert-ie! Keane-o!'

With Eircom Park gone, another threat loomed. Perhaps the GAA would come over all happy-clappy ecumenical and permit soccer into Croke Park, their newly redeveloped super stadium. Or perhaps the GAA would prefer IE£60 million in the breast pocket? On the eve of the GAA Congress 2001, some IE£60 million more of government money fell, like manna, on the shoulders of the delegates. The whisper went down the lines, '£60 million. Just to say no to soccer in Croke Park. Just to say let there be a Bertie Bowl instead!'

The GAA is a proud and independent-minded organization. It trousered the money quickly and took the big PR hit on Monday. It has suffered worse flak before and, privately indeed, there were the sort of smiles that follow the receipt of money in exchange for old rope. The vote to allow soccer in actually succeeded by one vote, having needed a two-thirds majority. Thirty-two delegates left the room while the vote was being taken.

Of course now, just a year later, the government has come back with a big omelette's worth of egg on its face. One shambles begets another. Always.

Just as the Bertie Bowl looked as if it would sink into the bog of bad management and scandal it was founded on, the FAI had an idea. No ideas for a century and then two in a couple of years. Must be trouble ahead. The FAI wanted to play a part in hosting the 2008 European Soccer Championships.

The opportunity to do so came about through almost stereotypical parsimony on the part of Scotland. Our braveheart Celtic cousins, being that little bit too mean and cowardly to spend the crucial extra £10 million or so on their own bid to host the championships, came knocking on our door instead. We're loud-mouthed and beery, but we have our uses.

The Scots see themselves as canny folk (even though canny folk shouldn't get so much amusement out of asking strangers to guess what's under their kilt, we know already – a prat) and they must have had forebodings. We Irish aren't trustworthy.

We are a hubris-ridden race who, in the extraordinarily unlikely event of the joint bid succeeding, would immediately claim the entire venture as our own great big party. Nevertheless, the Scots came knocking. Typically, we Irish threw the door open and gave ourselves a clean bill of health for the campaign ahead. No problemo!

Later, on a tiny point of clarification, we conceded that we had one problemo: no stadiums and no real reason to build any but, listen, we're a good laugh when we've drink taken.

For lots of sportswriters, the wish fathered one thought at this stage. We were going to host the European Championships! We would bathe in what we call the 'Feelgood Factor'. Never mind that we are an ungovernable country run by halfwits.

Suddenly, in some sports columns, it was justifiable to spend oodles of money to host three football games, to put football fans in hotel rooms that, at that time of the year, are already filled by paying customers.

And by tickling journalists on the feet with this feather, the Taoiseach bought a little more time for the Bowl.

Now though, it's time up. Settlement day. The Aquatic Centre has as much prestige left as a cracked birdbath. The Bertie Bowl is dead. The Euro 2008 bid needs the GAA to come around and do what it was paid not to do – open its doors. When the inspectors come this summer, the bid team really needs to at least be able to show poor, ramshackle, old Lansdowne Road and Croke Park to their visitors.

There's an election coming. At present no other party, except Bertie's loyal retainers, favour the construction of a national stadium.

There's a GAA Congress on the way. The Taoiseach would like Croke Park opened up now *and* the Bertie Bowl to be rubber-stamped.

Rocks. Hard places.

The FAI is convulsed with embarrassment. They are making whimpering noises about the Abbotstown/Bertie Bowl development being their preferred choice of venue in terms of their own future and the Euro 2008 bid.

The fate of the Euro 2008 could lie entirely in the hands of the GAA. For the Football Association of Ireland, nothing could be more humiliating. Soccer people who dislike GAA, hate the GAA with a Balkan passion. They despise, loathe and abhor GAA people. They wish them ill at every step. Given the choice, they would prefer that their neighbour's horse died than to get an extra horse for themselves – that's something that's not going to improve.

As media stories go, it's all wonderful. It gets space on the news pages and the sports pages. Nobody gets shot at. It pulls in the political corrs, the environment corrs, the finance people. It's also very boring for readers.

I get a couple of easy columns out of it all. Making hay while the sun is still shining.

So kids, these are the things you get to write about when your dream of being a sportswriter comes true.

Tuesday, 19th March

The dizzy day when I got my first byline in a national newspaper (above two overwritten paragraphs on club rugby on the inside back page of *The Sunday Tribune*) was the day before I signed off the dole.

The day after I signed off the dole was the day I began the long wait. Deep down, every journalist suffers the long wait. Somewhere in the pit of your stomach every morning is the feeling that this is the day when the rug is pulled from under your feet. This is the day that the world decides it doesn't need another chancer.

The wait is over.

I am being sued.

Specifically, I am being sued by Jim Bolger, the racing trainer. I have only met Jim Bolger once and I have never written a word about him. Nevertheless, here I am in a roomful of lawyers and the sun is waning outside. There are enough lawyers here to make the seriousness of the business unavoidably obvious.

It's like seeing a priest at the side of your sickbed.

It's getting on for tea time and I've told my friend Tommy Clancy that I'll be late for the training session of the under-11 camogie team I help him run. By that I meant perhaps ten minutes late. Myself and Mal arrived here assuming this was a house-keeping meeting.

Bear in mind that this is 2002.

In early September 1994, I was in Riga, Latvia, on a trip to cover the Irish international soccer team. I had a long and pleasant dinner with David Walsh and the late Peter Ball. I can remember that the meal took place in a baroque, high-ceilinged dining hall and that we discussed motor racing, as I had recently been forced to cover the Hungarian Grand Prix and was keen to share my dim view of motor racing.

I mentioned that one of the many things I disliked about motor racing was the artificiality of the contest when two cars from one team are first and second in a race. We also talked about how it's virtually impossible to cover the sport decently and honestly as the corporate hospitality is almost everywhere and the cost of getting around from race to race is prohibitive. Many of the reports are literally from fans with typewriters.

Out of that discussion, there arose a subsidiary discussion about horse racing. Again I remember only fragments. Peter was in fine form and told a story about a former colleague famous for milking the expenses system. Once he handed in a bunch of receipts that included a claim for a Big Mac Meal and two Happy Meals. The accountant, who had long been hoping to catch our friend in what we might call a whopper, summoned the hack to his office.

'A Big Mac and two Happy Meals?'

'Yes,' said the hack indignantly, 'I had lunch with Lester Piggot and Scobie Breesley.'

Peter and David chatted away about horse racing, a subject I know next to nothing about. David, a lifelong race-goer, mentioned that, at the Galway Races, one well-known trainer had often been accused by punters of not running horses on their merits. There was a broader discussion about racing and how the French had rules about trainers with more than one horse in a race or trainers backing their own horses. All news to me.

We discussed the old weakness of racing journalism and many other specialist branches of the game – the problem of being too close to the travelling circus. There had been a couple of one/two finishes in the weeks previously, and the frequency of such occurrences and the unlikelihood of racing journalists investigating such outcomes was discussed in terms of racing being a very closed, cliqueish type of business and it being very easy to find oneself with access cut off.

I don't remember any specific references to Jim Bolger, but it seems likely that we would have spoken about him. David Walsh was, and is, an admirer of Bolger's and he has written about him frequently. What little I knew of him was as a good Wexford hurling man and an implacable foe of the old West British element who made racing seem so alien and elitist to lots of ordinary people.

And that's the limit of my recollection of the relevant conversation, as it is David Walsh's. It was seven-and-a-half years ago after all. I would scarcely remember it at all if it weren't for subsequent events.

Not long after the trip to Latvia, I found myself presented with a column to write. I was to cough up a weekly piece for the Weekend Review section of *The Irish Times*. This would be a light look at sport for people who weren't hardcore sports people. The column would be called 'Locker Room'. I would be given a few bob extra for writing it, thereby swelling both ego and pocket.

About the third week into this new part of my career, I wrote a column that dealt in a light, slightly humorous way with the conflict sports journalists are faced with in dealing with sport – access versus independence. By way of criticizing my own profession, I drew down a compounded version of my conversation with David, citing an instance where two horses run by a prominent trainer fought out a race: one pulled up and the other won and the trainer pocketed a few quid from the bookies. It happens, I said, it happened recently.

The intent was to illustrate that newspapers usually acquiesce in these cases where there is rumoured to have been some fixing of the outcome. Meanwhile, punters must come away wondering if we aren't all in league against them. With the various cases we had recently discussed in mind, I was trying to draw down a notional compound to make the point. The relevant paragraph wasn't at the core of the argument I was making. It was merely a tool.

Just a day or two later, it transpired that I'd bumbled into a minefield. We received a solicitor's letter indicating that Mr Bolger had decided that the paragraph referred to him and the case of Pozzoli and Tirolean. Specifically, this was a race that had taken place in Naas that summer. Pozzoli the 11–10 favourite has beaten Tirolean a 12–1 outsider by a head. The Turf Club had decided for some reason that Tirolean hadn't tried hard enough. His jockey explained that he had been gurgling as he came down the straight.

I didn't think, when I saw the solicitor's letter, and I don't think now, that the case fits the notional one I wrote about. Tirolean was 12–1 and only lost by a head. It seems to me that a bent trainer would have engineered things the other way around with Pozzoli winning.

It transpired at the time that Mr Bolger had lost an appeal to the Turf Club, having been fined IE£1,000 for not running a horse on its merits in the race.

He would later take High Court action against the Turf Club and win. Rightly so, and fair dues to him for fighting the good fight. Reading now through the documents relating to his case, it appeared that not only was he emphatically in the right but that he helped racing rid itself of a rather stupid rule whereby the trainer was forced to take responsibility for anything which happened out on the course.

Today, though, it seems that I am to be a casualty of this war. I am to expect receipt of a ricochet bullet that has been whizzing about for over seven years.

1994. It was a summer during which I had been at the World Cup and had written a quickie book on Jack Charlton. I knew nothing, absolutely nothing, about Jim Bolger or his troubles.

The Pozzoli case was actually an example of action being taken in the sort of instance I was writing about. The circumstances didn't at all fit into the argument I was making all those years ago. Although, as I've said, he was eventually vindicated, Mr Bolger, at the time when the column was written, had some weeks previously lost his appeal to the Turf Club against the fine imposed upon him. I, meanwhile, was making a general point about cases where there was no Turf Club investigation or appeal, merely strong and widespread rumours that journalists dare not look into or report. I was asking if the ordinary reader/race-goer was well served by racing journalists in those cases?

The great frustration now is that I didn't know enough and I should have. By knowing nothing about Jim Bolger and his troubles, I'd left myself exposed to this. Had I known of his case, I could have pointed out the extraordinarily careful, neutral language used by all racing journalists in reporting a case that went right to the heart of the ethics of racing (and the seriousness with which Jim Bolger reacted to the charge bears this out).

I have just been handed a great sheaf of such reports. It's hard to think of any other sport or sphere where an apparent breach of the rules would have been written about so delicately. There wasn't silent acquiescence in that there was plenty of reporting and coverage of the case, but neither were there condemnatory editorials. Journalists were hanging back. Waiting and seeing.

I didn't want to refer to Jim Bolger, however. I didn't know about his case. If I had known, in all likelihood, I would have used it in some way. You never let a little nugget of a storyline get away from you like that.

The fact was, and always will be, that I wasn't writing about him. A few weeks into a new column, only a fool would go picking a fight like that on a subject he knows nothing about.

A couple of other things happened that week in 1994. The paper offered to clarify that it was *not* Jim Bolger who was being referred to in the previous week's column. I was invited to write a letter as part of our legal team's reply. I had completely forgotten about this letter until it was read out to me in the solicitor's office. Regrettably, it seems that I continued the equine theme of the exchange by getting on my high horse. The letter is angry and not a little pompous, but very firm on the point – I didn't know what Jim Bolger was talking about.

I wrote the letter in 1994 and handed it over. That, until yesterday, was the last I ever heard of the case. It went from being a cause of alarm to being an anecdote I told whenever the subject of libel law and libel cases came up amongst journalists. I got seven good years out of it.

Journalists often discuss libel cases. The libel laws in Ireland are so outdated and so palpably unfair that we like to joke that these cases are the Oscars of our profession. Still, the prospect of being sued chills us. English tabloids are occasionally rumoured to build the cost of a legal case into a story that will bring big circulation numbers. Irish papers operate at the other end of the spectrum, we are scared rigid of the courts. I know why. I'd never come close to being sued before and it doesn't feel pleasant right now.

Right now, I'm just bewildered. We have been in this room for an hour. We are talking about things that I haven't even thought about for years. Everybody else has a pile of briefing documents with them – I have my hands in my pockets.

I am astonished. Nervous. Reeling.

The column, with its offending paragraph underlined in dayglo green, is shoved across the big, shiny desk in my direction.

See! I think to myself. See.

The language and words right in front of me don't seem to me, in any way, to make Jim Bolger identifiable on any reasonable reading of the piece. Why would they? I say in the column that one horse pulls up. This did not happen in the race Jim Bolger refers to. I state that the trainer has had a bet on the horse that won, etc. I don't know Jim Bolger's betting habits but, in the race at Naas, the favourite won at 11–10 by a short head over a horse being ridden by an apprentice. That scarcely seems like the stuff of a betting coup or scam and has since been proven in the High Court not to have been.

Thus I am certain that the race in Naas would not have been identifiable from any reading of my column.

I make my argument. It's one I can swear to. In a box. On a Bible. On my kids' lives. Just let me.

The lawyers all say nice sympathetic things about my argument. 'Very good,' they say. 'We understand,' they say. Then they clear my argument away. They demolish it. That's why they get paid so well for doing what they do. Speaking softly about hard things. 'Now, here's how it works,' they say . . .

All Jim Bolger has to do is produce a line of people who will disclose that they were shocked when they read *The Irish Times* that Saturday, people who could not believe that the great man was being attacked in such an underhand way.

Then it's just down to whomever the jury likes the look of. Will they choose me, sitting there recounting a boozy meal in Latvia that led to a smartass column? Or will they like the better-known, much-respected horse trainer who describes his long battle to clear his name against this genuine injustice visited upon him by the Turf Club? Will they be moved as he details every increment of the additional hurt that this column of mine caused?

Nobody needs to say any more. I'm not beauty-contest material.

It doesn't really matter if myself or David Walsh can recall a name to whom the offending paragraph in the column might have more specifically applied. That will look twice as bad to any jury. It will appear as if we are hanging another man so that my neck can go unwrung.

There are three hopes:

a) That, at this late stage, it will go away.
b) That a judge will find the whole thing to be arrant nonsense and make us all go away.
c) That I will die peacefully before it all happens.

Right now I'm filled with dread and anger and confusion. I want to fight the damn thing to the death. It's the sort of case that will make for entertaining reading in the papers and I want someone to ask Jim Bolger how all that publicity will stack up against a column that never mentioned him and never meant to refer to him.

I want to ask him about the case he took against the Turf Club. The judge overturned his suspension and fine, but declined to award him damages. Afterwards, Jim Bolger was quoted as saying, 'I was never concerned about damages and this is the reason why I chose to give no evidence.'

I want to ask him why he would have no concern about damages when suing the people who wrongly made a case against him and why he is suing us for damages when we never mentioned his name or intended to write about him and indeed offered to clarify that.

On the other hand, I know that defending litigation is a high-stakes game you play with other people's money. Once we go through the door into the High Court, the legal bills quickly ascend to that place where the air is thin and hard to breathe. I probably won't get to hear Jim Bolger answer those questions.

And there's no great journalistic principle here. No source being protected. No great truth being defended. Just a stray paragraph written seven-and-a-half years ago from which somebody has taken the wrong meaning.

By the way, the lawyers tell me, as a parting shot, that it's set for 17th April and that Jim Bolger has none other than Mr Garreth Cooney acting for him. Mr Cooney is well known as a man who eats journalists between meals. I can imagine his pearly white incisors snacking through my flesh.

The meeting ends.

Mal and I wander out into the evening sun.

'Fucking hell, Mal,' I say.

'Yeah. Fuck,' he says.

'Can't believe this, Mal. I cannot fucking believe this.'

'Ah. Might never happen,' he says. But he looks as pale as I feel.

If there's a bad time in the history of the paper to get sued, this is it. The rug is being tugged sharply from beneath me.

I wish I'd known more back in 1994.

I wish I'd been more smart, less smartass.

Fuck.

Friday, 22nd March

Today, the Artists Formerly Known As BLÉ hosted a couple of press conferences at Leopardstown Racecourse. Straight up it has to be said that the guys and gals seem to be doing a reasonable job on hosting the World Cross Country Championships. Their difficulties in coming to grips with the task of running Irish athletics have been well documented down through the years but, today, I even felt a little bit sorry for them.

The backdrop to the press conference, the wall with the logos of all the sponsors on it, just fell down. Sonia O'Sullivan, the star of a second press conference, was late, lost somewhere on the road to Wexford because the championships weren't signposted along the N11. There were some embarrassing questions as to why people with black faces had such trouble getting visas to compete here. The ghost of Breda Dennehy Wills – a casualty of an impossibly complicated selection debacle – hung over everything. And, of course, through nobody's fault, the championships are here a year later than they should have been.

Just another day on the Irish sporting stage but, hey, we've seen worse.

Finally Sonia arrives. She's carrying her three-month-old baby, Sophie, in her arms. She's also chasing her older daughter Ciara around the place. It's tiring just to look at the three of them.

It's a curious thing about Sonia. Besides having immense time for her personally, I reckon she has to be the greatest athlete this windswept, little, septic isle has ever produced. She's had great dramas in her career, but nobody has competed at her level for so long over so many distances. No Irish athlete has ever been so clearly the best in the world like Sonia was in 1994 and 1995. And nobody has ever looked so good and so exciting when winning a race. Seeing Sonia O'Sullivan pull away down a home straight is one of the great sights in sport.

And yet, and yet, despite the dramas, the illnesses, the tragedy and all the great moments, despite the fact that here is patently an honest athlete who gives it all every time, lots of people seem to hate her.

She has been denounced from a church pulpit as a slut. She still gets criticized by tin-pot patriots for not carrying the Irish flag all the way around an arena in Gothenburg seven years ago. She is perceived sometimes (to borrow a soccer phrase) as a Bertie Big Potatoes. She is aloof. She is ego driven. She is tough. You hear more backbiting about her in athletics circles than you'd get in a year's worth of gossipy coffee mornings.

Every time I write about Sonia, I get letters. Two kinds. One asks, seeing as how I was so quick to identify Michelle Smith as a drug cheat, why don't I do the same to Sonia. The other asks why we give so much space to a woman who has let us down so often.

On the drugs, I can only say the following. Sonia likes people to come and see her train. She takes pride in it. There's no secrecy. There's no secret about where she trains or her schedules. Usually it's in public parks. She often mentions the precise times in a diary she occasionally writes for *The Irish Times*. She has been a world-class athlete since her mid-teenage years, when she became the World Student Games champion in 1991. Nobody she trains with or associates with has ever been done for drugs. No coach of hers has had a runner done for drugs. She came back to running from both her pregnancies and ran remarkable races while she was still breast-feeding. Her two lovely daughters show no signs of having ingested anything dodgy. She has given many blood tests over the last few years, several while participating in a study about female athletes.

Besides, I have asked her, and asked her till she is blue in the face answering, and never once have I found an inconsistency or a chink in the armour. I have heard her talk privately about her suspicions about other athletes. I have heard her be angry about these things and then put the anger away as a waste of energy. I asked her once why she didn't wear the red ribbon that her friend and rival Paula Radcliffe wears as a declaration that she'd like blood testing introduced. She said that she didn't want it to be the case that everyone started wearing them. It would get to the point that people, who she just knew were cheats, would be turning up with red ribbons. It's the great triumph of the cheating community that the rest of us have to go around inspecting and suspecting genuine heroes.

And as to her having let us down? It's scarcely worth replying to. She is one of a handful of people in top sport who gives it all, every time. Losing breaks her heart. Losing just crumples her. She has lost, she has made mistakes, but she's always busted her gut for us and for herself. And she's a woman. World-class Irish sportswomen are rare creatures. She's an inspiration and a joy to most Irish people but women, especially, identify with her.

And this afternoon in Leopardstown, she is here doing everyone a favour. It sours them slightly that they need her to be here, but they accept their need.

This weekend she's running because the event is in Dublin and the event needs her.

It needed her to run in the qualifiers a few weeks ago. So she did.

It needed her to crop up on the *Late Late Show* and push it. So she did.

The event needs the media interest, she always stirs because, otherwise, it would have turned into a private function and the IE£2.1 million budget would largely have slipped into the red and the efforts of over 750 volunteers would have been wasted.

But, of course, the rabid backbiting continues. During her press conference, I can hear two tracksuits behind me muttering about 'madam' and 'Who the fuck does she think she is, bringing her kids here?' Naturally, the pictures of Sonia and her daughters will be what makes the front page tomorrow. Nobody realizes that it was Sonia and her daughters or nothing. She's doing them a favour here.

Afterwards, outside in the sunshine, Sonia does a couple of TV and radio interviews. I'm waiting to talk to her about a diary piece. The same two middle-aged tracksuit wearers are lurking in the background. One says to the other, 'Tell you one thing, since she had those kids she's got a grand pair of tits on her.'

Sunday, 24th March

These Cross Country Championships could have been a genuine disaster.

Except Sonia O'Sullivan turned up, rallied the troops, did the PR and ran well. All bow. Sonia's presence today drew a crowd twice the size of the one that was here yesterday. That is her almost single-handed achievement. And we all went home happy.

If she'd stayed at home? Even as the great little sporting nation that we imagine ourselves to be, we would still have needed an impossible amount of prodding and a massive advertising budget to get us off the couch and out to see one of the last great and true sporting icons, Paula Radcliffe. We'd have watched the majestic Kenyans on the telly. Unless there's a party and some flag waving, we'd just as soon stick to the chair, thanks very much.

But it was worth being here today. As a sports hack, I wasn't really looking forward to it. Too cold. Too crowded. Too much going on that you can't really see properly. And the people who run Irish athletics, those Artists Formerly Known As BLÉ, sure know a thing or two about chaos and catastrophe. Today was good though. Wet and muddy and raw. Great excitement and a sporting occasion filled with nice old-fashioned romance.

We have little enough going for us on this wintry island, little enough apart from the character of a few remarkable people, a handful of determined heroic souls like John Treacy and Sonia O'Sullivan. People who escaped our sodden little cabbage patch and went out to light up the world.

When I was a kid, I watched Treacy win the World Cross Country in Limerick. When he finished, he had half the mud in Limerick stuck to him. Today is just as good.

Paula Radcliffe, a hero of mine and loved by an Irish crowd today like no British sportsperson has been in my memory, won the big prize but she won't have the headlines in the morning. The Irish women's team run their considerable guts out to claim a bronze medal. It mightn't be a big deal to the rest of the world, but today in south Dublin it was all that mattered.

The aftermath of the race, the mixed-zone interviews, etc., all take place in the shadow under the stand at the old racecourse. On the way in, I meet Kay Guy. On a day for heroes, Kay and her husband Al are in a league of their own. They were the husband and wife couple who performed the drug test that finally exposed Michelle Smith. For that they almost had their lives ruined. I know a little of what they went through, because I took many calls from people slandering them both in the most outrageous terms.

For what they went through in the space of those months, they would be forgiven for thinking that they had done their bit for sport and could now move on. But Kay is here delicately directing those who have been randomly picked for tests to the doping-control area. It's quiet, thankless work, resented by most athletes, but it's heroic work, the only thing that keeps me believing that athletics might one day be redeemable.

And here, amidst a welter of people, like a boxer making her way to the ring, is Sonia. The tape recorders are stretched towards her. We begin calling her name, 'Sonia, Sonia, over here Sonia.' She has come seventh, and on other days when she has come seventh, there have been tears and harsh questions. This afternoon, though, she stands on one side of the barrier and beams at us. We, the media faces she's been looking at for most of her career, make a disorderly, cheery crush on the other side. Recorders outstretched, cameramen jostling, radio guys making space for themselves. An old familiar scene. You need sharp elbows to get Sonia quotes on the good days.

You'd wonder by now if she isn't jaded with it.

Suddenly though, while we are talking, Christy Wall, a famous BLÉ artist, steps up behind Sonia and whispers something softly into her ear. The computations of the team event are in.

'Whoa!' she squeals and jumps clean off the ground and her face explodes into a mile-wide grin. Jesus Christy, we think.

'We were third!' she shouts. 'The team was third.'

And it's infectious. She's as happy as we've ever seen her! And we're all smiling too! That's fantastic!

'We've done the job now,' she gasps. 'If we'd lost by one point I wouldn't be happy, that Ethiopian in front of me was too close. While we were waiting there, waiting to hear where we finished, that was in my mind the whole time, one more person, I could have passed one more person. It's great!'

And I look at her and wish I could bring all those people who write catty letters about her to this place right now, to let them see how proud and deliriously happy she is with this team bronze she's won running for Ireland. This is a woman who has won individual golds in both cross-country distances on the same day. You've never seen her look this happy though. Not even when she put her career back together and came back and won silver in the Sydney Games.

'Ah, this is extraordinary,' she says when she recovers herself. 'We were third in Turin, but third in Dublin is ten times better. The job here was to be part of the team, people were shouting at me going around, "Come on Sonia, every place counts."'

It did count. And a funny thing is happening here. Sonia's happiness is becoming the story of the day. Five minutes ago, we were all going to write leads about Paula Radcliffe. We were all wondering if she would come to the mixed zone or if she would have her own press conference. We were expecting Sonia to be disappointed but brave faced. She's ecstatic though, and the happier she gets, the bigger the story gets.

'The girls were fantastic,' she says. 'They deserve it. Anne and Rosemary have been running the cross-country races here all season. While I was in Melbourne out walking, I was reading about them in *Athletics Weekly* and I was thinking that I'd have some catching up to do to make sure we went well as a team. I probably won't win another bronze like this, this and the other team one [from Turin when she wasn't happy at all] are about the only bronzes I have.'

She leaves us to hug her team-mates. We look at each other. 'That went well,' we say. There have been so many tough mixed-zone scenes with Sonia over the years that we half dread them. I once travelled to Milan to interview her at the end of a tough, tough season. When I got there, she had changed her mind, and I got the first flight home the next day with an empty tape recorder.

But this was a happy day. For a woman who has won so much and seen so much, this was an extraordinary afternoon when the emotion of the occasion connected cleanly with her personal needs. I don't imagine there'll be a better sporting highlight all year.

So we write the story. The cross-country weekend is a triumph. The key figure, cast in epic light against the cloudy sky, is Sonia O'Sullivan. We draw her gritted and muddied, clawing out seventh place in a World Championship event just three months after giving birth to her second child, doing it in the context of the other great Irish performances behind her and with ghosts scenting the afternoon. It's only months since her former ABC (as she used say, agent, boyfriend, coach) Kim McDonald died. Kim would have loved this. This was something special, a medal with so much good and a moving back story attached.

Three months training is not enough really to get a person a medal in this event. Not in the real world. But this girl is tough. It was tough at the start with the Kenyans going pell-mell as usual, but it got worse. She could feel pains in areas she had forgotten that she could have pains, but the best thing about Sonia O' Sullivan is watching her when the passion fills her blood and she runs fast enough to punch a hole in the wind. People jump to their feet and roar. She has an elegance and a toughness wrapped into the one package and when you see her loping strides you understand why so many people are in a constant state of fury with her. She is one of those athletes whom people invest in emotionally. They take her defeats harder than they take setbacks in the real world.

This is what it's all about, this mud, this bruised, spring sky, this mad cheering. An afternoon speckled with a few heroes you can actually believe in. A joy that's not jaded. You can still watch cross country in a way you can't watch sprint events, you can feel that possibly, just possibly you've seen a clean, cheat-free race.

After the month we've had, it's a tonic. If we want a sports policy for the next fifteen or twenty years, it shouldn't involve the self-aggrandizing cack we have been wading through recently about stadiums and domes. It should just be the sowing of seeds. Plant something democratic and ethical, grow it with our health and education plans, and produce a happy, healthy, sporting generation. That's all.

Here endeth the day. Here endeth the lesson.

Three Interviews

Monday, 25th March

Dublin Airport hotel. Irish team in town again. No Roy Keane again.

This is starting to hurt. Over the weekend, somebody told me a wonderful Roy Keane story. Well, maybe not wonderful but feature-writing gold, the sort of thing that gets to the heart of the guy. It seems that, after the famous victory over the Netherlands last year, Roy let his hair down a little and found himself in Lillies Bordello with a few of his fellow players. The night was long and lively. Finally, Keane stood up and sang a song that, if you were to rifle through all the songs in the world and choose one for him, couldn't be more apposite, 'Positively 4th Street', the Bob Dylan classic. It so bristles with Royness, it should be his signature tune:

> 'You got a lotta nerve
> To say you are my friend
> When I was down
> You just stood there grinning

> You gotta lotta nerve
> To say you gotta helping hand to lend
> You just want to be on
> The side that's winning'

The story enthuses me once again, so I put in another call to Michael Kennedy, Keane's agent. Michael tells me that I am in a queue. He won't say how long the queue is, but I get the impression that, from where I am standing, I can't see the front of it.

So I switch tack. I have a series of player interviews to do before the World Cup. I start with a favourite, an easy mark – Jason McAteer.

Interviews are the staple of how I make my living. I get more letters about columns I write and probably get more of a short-term buzz from covering live events, but what I enjoy most and consider to be my only really saleable asset is the interview/feature gig.

I've been interviewing Jason since he was a bright, young thing at Bolton Wanderers and Bolton were just a dowdy club with a pie shop across the road. Since then he's been through the media roller coaster. Up, down, around again and spat out the other side. Still he's game. He'll always step on for more. I think media fascinates him.

Jason's not in the country of middle age yet, but he's close enough to its border to be able to look back on his antic youth with affection and perspective. It's not a bad time to add another interview to the canon.

Nowadays, he divides his days into that time before and after the baby goes to bed. It's been a fast eight years since that hopeful springtime when Jason and his amigos Phil Babb and Gary Kelly came down the catwalk and straight into the Irish squad.

Three cheeky chappies with big hunger. Take That with a Sinatra soundtrack.

We hacks lapped it up. It was the first time there had ever been anything sexy about Irish soccer.

They hit the big time. Up and away like a carnival ride they went. Swoosh. Gravity was for losers. They hit the big time and it hit them back and put them on their arses. I got a good view of it all.

Back then, Phil Babb did a ghosted column for *The Irish Times*, for free. Just because he was interested in journalism. We'd be working on his columns and Jason would provide most of the fodder for the comic diversion and Gary would provide whatever interruptions he could to prise Phil away from the work at hand. Jason's trick was ever the same. He'd pretend that he was dumber than he is (not very dumb at all) and people would fall for it and underrate him everywhere he went.

Within a few years, Jason and Phil were among the dreaded Spice Boys set in an under-performing, overdressed Liverpool team and, one day, when asked if he wouldn't mind doing an *Irish Times* interview, Phil replied that no, he couldn't be arsed.

Life dropped them like pieces of battered cod into hot oil. Jason ended up training with the kids at Blackburn. Liverpool sent Phil so far into anonymity that the medical for his eventual transfer to Sporting Lisbon involved checking whether he still had a pulse.

So football has enough gravity to go around. For the lads, football hasn't been one, long-running, cartoon-strip adventure after all.

This month they are both back on the upswing. Jason is at Sunderland, adoring it and being adored. Phil is playing every week for a successful Sporting Lisbon side.

I plan to do Jason and then revive the paper's relationship with Phil Babb.

'Football,' Jason says. 'Loved it, loved it, loved it. Hated it. Love it again.'

Usable.

All the time when you are interviewing people, you wish you had a little remote control on hand for your tape recorder. You need it because, as you listen to answers, your mind filters what you hear into two categories. Usable and dross.

Most stuff you hear isn't worth recording. Footballers never get this, but feature writers like anecdotes and detail rather than opinion. Yet, footballers are conditioned. You ask a footballer what his favourite colour is and he says that it's hard to write off any of the colours – primary is good, pastel is good, the whole lot to be fair. And in your head you have grabbed the remote and switched your tape recorder off.

With Jason though, 90 per cent or more of what he says is usable. His speech pattern is a rhythm of vivid stories and self-deprecating yarns. You keep glancing at the recorder, making sure that it's on, that it's getting all this stuff.

In Lansdowne Road a few months ago, Jason scored the goal against Holland that just about sealed World Cup qualification for us. Then he went back to Blackburn and Graeme Souness didn't throw a word his way for a week. So sullen and complete was the silence that Jason began to wonder had Lansdowne happened at all.

He says all this and he articulates it perfectly. No need to prod him or push him for detail.

The good thing about Jason is that, if he trusts you, he'll assume you won't make a complete fool of him in print, so he'll tell you things. And he's frank.

Aer Lingus, bless them, have this habit, which nobody much likes, whereby they place that day's newspapers on the players' seats when the team and media are picked up the day after a big away match. So players who have done well sit beside players who have done badly and, awkwardly, they both read the reports written by the scribbling bastards in the cheap seats at the back of the plane. They read the reports, what Mick McCarthy said, what each other said, the marks out of ten that some papers give. Last spring against Cyprus, Jason had a stinker. The island had to be fumigated after his performance. What most of us remember about that evening is listening to Roy Keane shouting at Jason. All night long.

Jason played poorly and paid more attention than usual to what was coming from Keane's mouth. He admires Keane hugely and, in Cyprus, every arrow of Keane's was finding purchase in McAteer's hide. Jason came off and talked himself down further to the media. Next day, he got on the plane for the hop from Cyprus to Barcelona for the game against Andorra and there was a little pile of papers sitting in his seat.

'Time's up with Ireland.'

'McAteer should retire.'

'Move over, say goodbye to the cheeky scouser.'

Each headline was as bad as the next.

So he got up and looked for Mick Byrne. Found him. Asked Tony Hickey to move over and sat there in tears.

'I just said, Mick, I come here, I always turn up, I've always loved it and I battle my bollox off, but I'm fighting a brick wall. I love going away on these trips, love playing in these games, but reading all this after last night, I told him I was finished. I was retiring. And I was.'

But he got talked around. And I'm glad.

For a start, he's here telling his story, frank as ever. The media is forgiven again.

He's always been brighter than he lets on has Jason, and he knows that putting his personality across in an interview will serve him better than pouting and sulking.

And he's a far better player than people give him credit for. He's one of those players that a team needs. One of those guys who is up, virtually all the time, who takes the jokes and makes the jokes. He seems essential to the character of this Irish team.

He tells me what he likes about playing in the green jersey. During the week of the last friendly, the team were in the bus going to training and Jason was sitting beside Gary Kelly. Mick McCarthy turned around and handed the boys a catalogue and a task. They had to go through the glossy pages and pick the Irish team's World Cup outfits before they got to the training ground. Five minutes to do it. Jason loved that.

'Mick says if you take that away, we'd be just another team. Another day, I was having a cup of tea with Mick and he takes a call and, next thing, he's screaming blue murder there's no portable goalposts at the training ground. And he puts the phone down and he's laughing. National team! You fellas write about people turning into big-time Charlies. Spend a week with us. We stay at the Holiday Inn with airplanes taking off every two minutes. That's the glamour of it! When that goes though, when we lose that, that's the end of the good times. I don't want us to be like everyone else.'

'I'm a raw to the bone footballer,' he says when we're finishing up. 'I believe in old-school methods of taking training and man management. The French brought in a lot of stuff on the back of their success, but it will swing back. You are going to need coaching badges and myself and Kevin Kilbane have looked into it. We'll try and grab a week in the summer, do a crash course, get it started. One ball, eleven players, get it in their net. It has to be simple!'

I love interviewing Jason. He insists that Phil Babb could be a journalist or a TV presenter, but Jason, well Jason is a student of people. As always, today, we end up talking about *him*. Roy Keane.

Last week at Sunderland, where Jason now plays, they had a World Cup press conference, parading all their players for the media. The media traipsed around from player to player asking the same things.

Mostly they asked Jason, 'So what's Roy Keane really like?'

'Same old, same old,' Jason said with a laugh, 'treading on egg-shells there.'

Saturday, 6th April

Next to Phil Babb, the ghost of World Cup past. He was the first amigo. He was on board for that bitter sectarian night in Windsor Park nine years ago when a draw with Northern Ireland proved enough to get Jack Charlton's old team to another World Cup final.

We shared a few things back then. Phil did his column for the paper, a good one too, throughout the World Cup. I visited him for an interview in Coventry and he showed me around Highfield Road. He was extraordinarily decent and friendly. He flew to Dublin one day for a photo shoot for the paper's 'World Cup team' promotion and, again, he never looked for a penny. I can't imagine that happening this time around with anyone.

I was his ghost. It was the first big tournament for him and ditto for me. We squeezed good fun out of the experience. Two things stick in my mind. In the aftermath of the Ireland and Italy game in Giants Stadium, for my money the greatest day in Irish soccer history, I sat with Phil and Paul McGrath for an hour as they waited to be drug tested. They'd just played what for both of them would prove to be the game of their lives and they stayed there in the shade under the stand sipping from cans and chatting as if they'd just knocked off after a day at the office.

And I remember the last day in Orlando, when Ireland got knocked out against Holland. A tame, limp performance by a team who thought somewhere inside that they'd done enough and had enough. The players were refusing to come out and speak to the media. We, in turn, were under immense deadline pressure. And Phil came out into a dark corridor and stood speaking the column into a tape recorder. When it was finished, I said cheers and shook his hand and went to get back to the press working room. And he said, 'Nah, hang about for a while, I don't want to go back in there', and he nodded at the tomb that was the Irish dressing room.

We learned a thing or two about the media together also. We did a column not long after Eric Cantona performed his Kung Fu kick on that loudmouth Crystal Palace supporter. Phil was beginning to know what stick was like at the time, and could understand Cantona's point of view. In the piece, we dealt with the issue jokily and re-ran one or two of the gags that were circulating in the Liverpool dressing room. The next day, an Irish stringer for *The People* picked up on a line from the piece and the paper ran it as a 'Babb Slams Eric' front-page sensation. Our wonder didn't cease until envelopes started arriving addressed to Phil Babb, c/o Anfield; envelopes with razor blades glued into the lining where you run your finger along to open them.

Other things in life changed Phil Babb of course. He came into our orbit as captain of Coventry, a serious young man engaged to be married. His people came from Carlow. We expected he'd captain Ireland someday. And he left the Irish setup (or more correctly it left him) in controversy. He was a Spice Boy with, it seemed, a great future behind him. I knew things were changing for him when I drove up to Monaghan one day in the year after the World Cup. There was a match looming and I found Phil uncommonly tired. He'd been up all night with some journalists from *Loaded* magazine. 'Shhh!' he said, giggling. I felt like a scolding aunt armed with my prim questions.

Yet somehow Phil has put himself back together again. Footballer. Party boy. Footballer again. He deserves a shot at the World Cup squad and he hasn't got one.

And he knew that, a long time ago. Maybe he didn't know it at the very moment when he and Mark Kennedy slid across a car bonnet in Harcourt Street in the early hours of a September morning before Ireland began their World Cup qualifying campaign back in 2000, but he realized soon after. Real soon.

He realized when the story hit the papers. Front pages.

Looking back, he's right when he says that it wasn't *that* big of a deal. Still. Early morning in Dublin. Huge match against Holland looming. Two international players arrested for clowning on somebody's car boot. The car's owner, as it transpired, was a police officer. It wasn't a big deal, but it wasn't going to be stuck in at the end of the court reports either.

He and Mark Kennedy were jettisoned from the squad that flew to Amsterdam that weekend, but Kennedy was forgiven and rehabilitated. Babb never has been. I'd like him to talk about that, but suspect he won't want to. He's always played this image as if he's outside the code but, in reality, he adheres to football's rules.

This has been a good year for him, the best in some time perhaps. He's just helped Sporting secure the Portuguese league title and he's playing in the cup final soon. This season he played in front of 85,000 in the Benfica derby. He played UEFA Cup football in the San Siro against AC Milan. Got Maldini's jersey in the away leg, Inzaghi's in the home leg. They sought him out both times. Last week, he picked up a trophy as best foreign centre half in the Portuguese league. Sixty per cent of the popular vote too.

Mick McCarthy hasn't been to see him play, however.

Do I expect Phil will have some traces of bitterness? That he might want to stir the pot?

Not really. I get what I expect. The same old shrug. A quiet loyalty that he isn't always given credit for.

'It's Mick's decision. If you're asking do I think that I've been unfairly treated by Mick, it's his decision. He's picked a squad that have done well for him. He can feel that he doesn't need me, I can see that. He's got young players, who'll do a job. The flip side is that I'm enjoying playing well, I'm enjoying football. There's been ample opportunity to, well, forgive and forget. If I'm disappointed, it's not over that though, it's that the door seems to be closed on my international career when I'm playing as well as I have ever done. Better. I know, though, if I've made my bed I have to lie in it.'

I ask him, a bit mischievously, if we lined up all the Irish centre halves going to Japan and invited them for a sprint race, would he beat all of them.

He pauses. And laughs. 'I'd like to think so. Jesus, I'd hope so, yeah.'

But he's quick to dig himself out. For all that he gives the impression that he doesn't care, he's not going to rock the boat. He lists all the Irish centre halves and their individual virtues. Makes a case against himself.

He has changed with his environment. Sporting Lisbon train twice a day. Hard fitness work in the morning, tactics and ball work in the afternoon. The players take the odd glass of wine, nothing more. If a Sporting fan saw Phil Babb in a place he shouldn't be, he has no doubt the fan wouldn't call the club. He'd run him out of the pub or club personally.

He has a daughter now. Mia is four and a half years old, and life in Lisbon is good for her. Recently, Phil's even been speaking to his club directors about integrating some family-oriented facilities into the new stadium that Sporting are about to build. They've taken the ideas on board. And he's wondering about retirement and what will come afterwards. Something to do with golf is his feeling. 'Golf,' I say, feeling betrayed. Yup, he's changed.

I like the interview we do. There's a little edge to it. He's loyal to the players, many of whom he is still close to, but he's disappointed too. Most people would have put him down in the 'won't play, doesn't care' category.

'You know,' he says when we finish, 'I've always had this shrug-the-shoulders image, but you have to have an inner drive in football. I have that. It's never waned. It's people's perceptions of me and the shrugged shoulders. I suppose I never bothered to change it.'

Regrets?

'Life's too short for regrets,' he says. 'You just look forward to the next day. Regrets? Nah, sod it.'

The piece runs on Saturday and, that weekend, Phil's life in Lisbon changes. He has flown his old friend Jason over to see him play in the cup final. A couple of hours before kick off, though, he is told that he's not playing. An Argentinian reserve is being given the chance to impress his national manager instead. Nothing personal.

Thursday, 11th to Tuesday, 16th April

Duffer.

This will sound odd, but I believe it to be true: everyone who meets Damien Duff falls a little bit in love with him.

Everyone who knows him, worships him. You cannot meet a person who will say a bad word about him. He is just a few goals away from becoming the national pet.

I thought I was inoculated against all this Duffermania. A couple of years ago, having failed to get Duffer to come to the phone, I drove up to Blackburn's training ground and presented myself for a surprise interview. Not only could the shy and retiring in-house genius not be persuaded to do the interview, he couldn't be persuaded to come and tell me this himself.

At the time, I thought this was a little prima donna-ish and that no good would come of the boy. I know now that Damien Duff genuinely feels that the less said about him the better his world will be. Fuss gives him the bends. If he could play football in a Balaclava under the name A N Other, well then, he would. In fact, for one who likes anonymity so much, it's surprising he's not playing in the League of Ireland.

Duff is genuinely, blushingly shy, constantly bemused at the attention showered upon him and frequently in agonies as to how to dodge it.

Which is a pity, because he is a good character. He's funny and personable. The only player who can walk into a press conference and say, 'How's it going lads?', and be greeted by a charmed chorus of 'Howya Duffer'.

He told us once, with a worried look on his face, that they'd given him the player of the season award at Blackburn the previous summer, 'even though I was just a fat old yoke'.

As far as anyone can make out, when he isn't playing football, he does nothing but sleep. He puts himself into a sort of cryogenic suspension and comes out again when the next game looms. He lives, as he puts it, 'up a mountain outside Blackburn' in a three-bedroom house his mother picked out for him.

He lives in this half-lit dreamworld, drifting happily through his stardom. Whenever I see him, I wonder what it must be like to be Duffer. The answer of course is the one that Einstein gave when he was asked what it was like to be a genius, 'What does a fish know about the water in which it swims every day?'

To his discomfort, Duffer is forever being 'linked' and 'associated' with clubs far more glamorous than Blackburn Rovers, but I think that he belongs in that old-fashioned, quartered strip of Blackburn's. He's a tousle-haired, shimmying winger, clipped right out of a 1950s comic book and born to entertain this grimy northern town. He's not a bright-lights, big-city guy. You can't see him in a zippy red Ferrari nipping around Rome or Barcelona.

I've interviewed him once since that failed attempt to entice him into conversation at Blackburn. I cornered him in the team hotel one afternoon and he sat down for a while and explained, in earnest detail, how he felt there was nothing interesting about him. He made unfootballer-like statements that could have got him drummed out of the profession. He said that he loves his Ma and Da to bits and just wants a quiet life. That all his friends are 'loved up' and going out with people but he wasn't bothered. Then he shook hands and said, 'Thanks very much'.

Shocking stuff really.

So now it's barely a year later, but I fancy doing a big piece on him for our World Cup magazine. That last interview we did had to be padded out with stories and anecdotes from independent witnesses. This time, I'm hoping Damien will be comfortable enough to show me a bit of his life. I fancy he'll become a big, big star over the course of the summer, during which time, owners of the glossy *Irish Times* World Cup magazine will be able to refer to the definitive Duffer piece and find out everything from what watch he wears to what makes him tick.

I call him in Blackburn. He doesn't know how to act the big shot. He just wants to know how things are in Dublin. 'Any news?' he says.

I suspect I've woken him. I hit him with the big plan: me coming to Blackburn, spending a day or two or more hanging around; him getting on with life, showing me some sights that will spark reminiscences for him.

I'm saying 'interview'.

He's hearing 'root canal treatment, with no anaesthetic'.

He's charming about it though.

'Yeah,' he says, 'give me your number, I'll let you know what's a good day. When we have some time off.'

This is an unprecedented step. Footballer looks for journalist's phone number!

I blurt it out girlishly and, when I've hung up, it dawns on me that, not only have I no firm arrangement, but I have lost the momentum in the entire arrangement-making process.

Then to my surprise, two days later at 10 a.m., the phone rings.

'Tom?'

'Yeah?'

'It's Duffer.'

He calls himself Duffer. I wonder if his Ma and Da do this too. It's a footballing curiosity this. I know somebody who once had to call Graham Rix's house and his wife referred to him as Rixie. Do Roy's kids call him Keano? Does Big Niall answer to Quinny when he's at home?

'I've a better idea about the interview,' Duffer says. 'I'm in Dublin at the weekend, why don't we do it there?'

Better idea? The man is a genius. What could be finer? Old haunts. Old stories. Maybe a few old friends. Portrait of the winger as a young man.

So, he gives me the slip.

'I'm getting in on Friday. I'll give you a call.'

I've just woken up. I'm thrown. Footballers never call your house. Ever. I think it's a PFA rule or something. In my shock, I have failed to get a Dublin number for him. Or a mobile number. On the other hand, I think, blowing at a convenient dandelion, he's called once, of course he'll call to arrange the interview.

Of course he will. He loves me. He loves me not.

And that's how the moment slips through my fingers. That's how The Big Interview ends up being ten minutes at the airport hotel and an hour on the phone. That's how young guys like me learn never to trust again.

II

Trouble in the Field

FIRST SERVANT: Let me have war, say I; it exceeds peace as day does night; it's spritely, waking, audible, and full of vent. Peace is a very aploplexy, lethargy; mulled, deaf, sleepy, insensible; a getter of more bastard children than war's a destroyer of men.

SECOND SERVANT: 'Tis so; and as war, in some sort, may be said to be a ravisher, so it cannot be denied but peace is a great maker of cuckolds.

FIRST SERVANT: Ay, and it makes men hate one another.

THIRD SERVANT: Reason; because they then less need one another.

Coriolanus, Act IV, Scene 5

Sunday, 14th April

I am losing it. Whatever it is, I am soon to be without it. The stress, the tension, whatever. This week I found myself badgering Malachy to give me work at the weekend. I never do this.

Some years, when there are no World Cups or Olympic Games taking place, weekend work at GAA games is the staff of life. You get up, you get into the car and you drive to a provincial town to watch a do-or-die championship game.

And you know what, it's the best thing about the job. Leaving the city, listening to other hacks blathering on the Sunday morning radio shows and finally getting through the almost impenetrable traffic congestion near a provincial ground. You flash the yellow NUJ card with as much pizazz as you can muster and hope to be waved through. On and on the journey goes till you are ensconced with friends in the press box and gathering gossip. Love it.

This week it struck me, though, that I am going to miss at least half the GAA season. So a little baffled and suspicious, Malachy has let me head off to Thurles today to watch Clare and Limerick, two of my favourite hurling sides, play a league quarter final.

When I was a kid, Limerick were a big deal in hurling and I developed an attachment to them that remains to this day. Clare, on the other hand, are a recent enough flirtation, but I have stuck with liking them even in the years after my media comrades decided they had had enough of the Loughnane revolution.

Today is a disappointment. Neither side looks as if there will be anything to stop them taking sun holidays in July. I always go to Clare games hoping that they'll have found a forward to match Jamesie O'Connor, who has been carrying them for years. Today, it looks as if Jamesie's decline might have started before Clare's auditioning process is over. Lots of Clare's parts seem to be arthritic.

Limerick, on the other hand, aren't creaky or aged. They are young and finding their way and are having troubles on the side-line, but give the impression that it will be a season or two at least before they get there.

Thurles is a nice day out, but spoiled always for us *Irish Times* journalists by the fact that Semple Stadium is not five miles further away. If we travel 100 miles from base, we automatically qualify for an overnight allowance. Thurles, like its accursed northern sister Clones, is just the wrong distance from Dublin. Still, they let you park your car in the shadow of the stand and they give you tea and sandwiches at half-time and the welcome is always warm and friendly.

Afterwards, we stroll across the pitch to gather a couple of quotes. At this time of year, it's a pleasant duty. Doors are open and you can sit down on benches and chat to players just like grown-ups would. Come summer, they'll be ducking and diving, and through uncanny bad luck, even if you call their number twenty times in a day, you will always have just missed them.

I drive back to Dublin content however that I have made the journey.

In 1995, when Clare won the All Ireland, I made the trip back to Clare with them on the Monday night. Every sports journalist makes a trip like that sometime, imagining he or she is the first ever to do so, but the effort is worthwhile. We don't get out of the press box often enough to sample the way people feel about occasions like that. Seeing the bonfires burning on the road into Clarecastle and the people of the parish coming out and claiming their boys from the bus so that they could carry them on their shoulders to the centre of town – that was a night.

In these times when sport is packaged and sanitized for us, when professionals form their own gated communities and teams mean less and less to the people who follow them, hurling and football are among the few sports that are truly worth writing about.

Real teams, real places and old-fashioned motivations. There's little enough hurling in a summer without a World Cup filching most of it.

Chalk it up as a good day.

Wednesday, 17th April – daytime, the Four Courts

Heavy morning rain hoses me down the quays and sweeps me into the Four Courts.

Today is the big day. The case. Drowned rat is precisely the sort of look I had hoped to put across in the witness box.

No settlement has been reached in the month since we met the lawyers. To be honest, I have been half-expecting that Jim Bolger will drop the case. When big problems loom in my life, I tend to tell myself courageously that they may never actually happen. That will be my last utterance on this earth. Sure it might never happ—

I don't know why I am surprised to be here on this morning. If Jim Bolger has been thinking of litigation for all these years, he's hardly likely to drop it at the final minute. Yet I thought that, maybe, he'd root out the piece one morning and look at it and wonder what all the fuss was about.

We assemble in the rotunda of the Four Courts. Mal, myself, Eoin McVey, the paper's Managing Editor, and an expensive-looking posse of lawyers. We are down for some action today but, over coffee, it transpires that the lawyers don't think we'll even get on the pitch. It would be rude to ask, but I can't help wondering how the meter works for these things. Does it start whirring very quickly once a lawyer stands physically inside the courtroom, or does drinking coffee and being available to stand inside the court also occasion whirring?

John Waters, a colleague in *The Irish Times*, is suing the gossip columnist Terry Keane today. Gareth Cooney is representing John Waters and, as we sup coffee, I can see the two of them in discussion. The speed at which the court will get to our case is a function of how quickly it deals with the *Waters* case, which will be high profile enough and juicy enough to sell tickets to.

We sit in gloomy mood in the cramped restaurant in the Four Courts as people in wigs and gowns scoot busily all around us. I'm asked what I think of the idea of making a settlement out of court.

It's nice of everyone to ask really, because this case doesn't have any big journalistic principle involved in it. Even I can see that, and while I reserve the right to my passionate insistence that I wasn't referring to Jim Bolger, for the paper it's just a clunkily phrased paragraph that we got caught out on. And, more importantly, in a time of scant resources, it's not my money. I hate and detest the thought of it passing to Jim Bolger, even a penny of it, but going into court with everybody's meter running furiously means that we could end up paying perhaps the same amount of damages as we might be able to settle for now but massive, massive costs. We don't have that to play around with. I say I'll go along with whatever is best.

The lawyers and Eoin point out an additional benefit. If we settle, I won't have been sued. There'll be no question of the journalistic equivalent of having a police record. Nothing marked into the loss column. My integrity, whatever a decade of it is worth, won't have been impugned or diminished. I can still trade on it.

This depresses me. Somehow, it had never really struck me that my integrity would be questioned, or could be questioned. It never occurred to me that people would consider that I had done something wrong or that I had become less reliable as a journalist. That, though, is what we are here for.

I had pictured *Mr Smith Goes to Washington*. Myself, suddenly as learned as my learned friends, earnestly arguing points of logic and inference with Gareth Cooney and, afterwards, a jury in the worst-case scenario saying to themselves, 'He's a good man but, inadvertently, he has caused hurt, it is with the greatest reluctance that we find for . . .'

At about 11 a.m., our lawyers establish that we won't be getting to court today. It could be weeks, even next term, before we come up. Meanwhile, they might attempt a settlement.

We head out into the rain again. I know now that, sometime today, I will get a call telling me that we have settled with Jim Bolger. I can feel already that it will hit me like a death in the family.

I stand outside on the quays staring into the boot of my car, having forgotten why I opened it in the first place. I wish now I had been talking about Jim Bolger. I wish I had got my money's worth out of this. Instead, I feel like I've been mugged. Something has just swung at me from out of left field and left me confused and sick.

I hear a voice from the traffic behind me. 'Still haven't found what you're looking for?'

I turn around. Mick Wright, an old Offaly footballer, a journalist and one of the nice guys, is stuck in the molasses beside me, leaning his head out of the window into the rain. I haven't seen him in a few years.

'Bad day, Mick,' I say.

'We all have 'em,' says Mick. 'We all have 'em.'

I'm about to tell him my specific woes, when something else stirs in the back of my memory.

'Did I hear you were sick recently, Mick?' I ask.

'Yeah,' he says. 'Leukemia. Almost a goner there for a good while, but I'm back.'

Jesus. I had no idea. I shake Mick's hand, tell him it's good to see him and go back to looking into the boot of my car. I find what I'm looking for – a shred of perspective.

There are worse things than Jim Bolger and his solicitor.

Just before tea-time, Malachy rings me on the mobile and says we have settled with Bolger. It has cost about a year's wages for a journalist and the same again for legal fees.

With regard to Jim Bolger's good name, there is no requirement to publish any apology, clarification or report on the matter. I tell Mal that I don't mind if we do. I don't feel as if I've anything to be ashamed of.

And that's it. I head to Lansdowne Road. I feel beaten and bruised but very glad that I met Mick Wright today.

And nobody from the paper ever mentions the case to me again.

Wednesday, 17th April – evening, Lansdowne Road

It has rained all day. Rain of biblical proportions. They seem to have given up on Lansdowne Road, just let it take whatever falls and hope for the best. There isn't even a man out making holes in the ground with a pitchfork.

Ireland beat the USA. No big deal except the Americans like their friendlies and take them seriously. Afterwards, we sort of embarrass ourselves in the press conference. There being no American media present, we force the American manager, Bruce Arena, to speak about us and only us.

We have only one thing on our mind here. Filler. We just wish to make statements and have them confirmed for attribution. The older guys used to make up quotes or, at best, bowdlerize them into press lingo (the most celebrated example is the Bohemians' player Gino Lawless being quoted as saying that he felt his tackle 'was injudicious but scarcely malicious'). Occasionally, you still see the odd English tabloid operative in full swing. Once, in the Czech Republic, I saw Karel Poborsky, the former Manchester United player, being approached by one such. They spoke for a couple of minutes, catching up sort of talk. The tabloid operative came back and asked us all the same question, 'You saw me speaking with him, didn't you?'

'Yeah.'

'Well don't be surprised at what you see him saying about Alex Ferguson later this week.' Poborsky, of course, had said nothing of what he would be reported as saying.

With Bruce Arena, the game is to stockpile handy stories. The Americans have just played Germany who will be World Cup opponents. This offers the chance to write both an 'Arena Fancies Irish' story and an 'Arena Has German Doubts' story.

Most coaches just wearily co-operate with this nonsense. Bruce Arena just seems baffled. 'I'm disappointed we didn't walk off the field with a point here tonight,' he says. 'Give Ireland credit for the second goal. They are a good team, strong physically, two headed goals, strong defenders. Obviously with Roy Keane back, they'll have a good midfield and with Duff at front – he's a handful.'

'How would you compare us with Germany?' he is asked.

He answers without reference to annexations. 'I don't think comparisons like that are valid.'

'Well, would you see Ireland doing well against Germany?'

'What's your definition of doing well?'

'Drawing?'

'I think Germany will surprise a lot of people.'

There is a brief diversion as Mr Arena makes so bold as to comment on his own team. We shut him up quickly. Now, back to us. Are we more physical than, oh let's just say, for example, Germany?

'I'm not sure too many teams will be more aggressive than the Germans. As big as the Irish are, the Germans are dominating. I think they'll be a real handful.'

We are growing impatient with Mr Arena's flagrantly intelligent carry on. Nobody asked him for considered opinions. If he doesn't say something bland and meaningless about us soon, somebody will headbutt him. Or write an 'Arena Slams Irish Hosts' story.

Fortunately, Mick McCarthy arrives. First time in his life that Mick has been responsible for lowering the tension levels at a press conference. Mick is hap-hap-happy. So damn happy, he forgets to be rude to us.

Bolger. All this rain. Mick being nice to us.

The world must be ending.

Wednesday, 8th May

Less then a year ago, I expected that somebody was going to take me away from all this. Make me rich and a little bit famous. Give me a new life.

Last year, I had a couple of little tryouts for *Sports Illustrated*, the American magazine that sells in its lucrative millions. The week that David Duvall won the British Open, I wrote the cover story. Everyone seemed pleased. In my modest way, I was dizzy with excitement, brimming with myself.

I sat at home and waited for the call. I could remember talking in the mid-1990s to Michael Bamberger of *Sports Illustrated* and quizzing him crassly about wages at the magazine. He threw me some numbers and told me that it was a lot more money for doing a lot less than you do on a paper. I liked what I was hearing. He also said that you have to do it all a lot better than on a paper, but by then I was just murmuring the numbers he'd quoted over and over.

So when I wrote the David Duvall piece, I sat in for many evenings working out just what inflation would have done to *SI*'s wages in the intervening years. It seemed likely that the family would be forced to live in a large apartment in Chicago, or maybe New York, and retain just a modest summerhouse in Maine or Cape Cod.

I braced the kids for a return to America. And never heard from *Sports Illustrated* again.

I'd almost forgotten about the failed audition until last week when they rang and asked if I could do them a favour. Run across to The Belfry in England and interview Jos Vanstiphout.

In fairness, I had brought Van Stiphout to their attention a year previously. I had spotted him at the US Open in Tulsa, where, in all honesty, he was hard to miss.

He was wearing sunglasses in which you could see your reflection and sporting a white shirt so clean that you might dine off it. If he looked like an elfin Belgian pop star from the early 1970s, still working under the same hairstyle, well that's because he was.

And is. On the balconies and porches, though, he was talking the talk to the folks from IMG. They were all jumpy about their kid, Retief Goosen.

'Ho! Don't worry, my friends,' said Jos to the IMG suits. 'Don't worry! He'll win big time. Don't you worry. He's going to win, win, win. Big, big time.'

That was the scene. Goosen is about to win the US Open. Jos Vanstiphout is about to become the hottest mind-guru in golf.

Later, I come across him in Lawrence Donegan's wonderful book *Four Iron in the Soul*. Paul Kimmage had interviewed Vanstiphout and now I was getting a little commission to go and see him myself. Very rarely do you get days in sportswriting that work out perfectly, but I note this day down as one of them.

Good parking spot at Dublin Airport.

Remember to remove keys from pocket before walking through scanning machine.

Quick hop to Birmingham.

Straight into hire car. Big hire car.

Drive out of airport and onto motorway without seeking directions or looking at map. By dumb luck, drive straight to The Belfry.

Asked to park just outside credential centre. Thank you.

Large fuss made over me because I seem to be from *Sports Illustrated* who don't usually cover the Benson & Hedges International Open.

Have no arrangement to meet Jos Vanstiphout, but literally bump into him as soon as I walk to the practice range. Interview for eighty minutes. Great quotes.

Like the calls to his brother.

Call One: Jos announces he is packing in business and becoming a golf-guru on the basis of a golf book he has read.

'Are you mad?' asks his sensible Belgian brother.

'No way,' said Jos, 'no fucking way. I know you think I'm crazy but I'm going to be number one in five years. Number one man.'

Call Two: Jos has been trailing after the tour for some time when he meets Retief Goosen. The South African is just another harmless milquetoast filling up the beds in the tour hotels. But a light goes on. Jos calls his brother. 'The moment after I spoke with Retief in Switzerland for the first time, I called my brother at home and I said, "That guy is going to make me fucking famous." That's what happened. His talent I saw that. God-gifted talent. That's one thing, but up here,' and he taps his temple, 'was easy to fix. Well maybe not so easy, but I knew I could handle anything up there.'

I'm done interviewing Jos and it's still not noon. Swan through press tent saying hello to hard-working Irish and English colleagues. Slight American accent affected.

Passing the scorers' tent when I see Retief Goosen enter.

'Retief,' I say, 'quick word?'

'No,' he says.

I wait for him to come back out.

'Retief? Just two questions. Puh-lease.'

'Two questions, max,' he clips.

'Describe in detail the circumstances of your first meeting with Jos Vanstiphout.'

He begins to tell the story and then says, 'Wait a minute, that's not a bloody question.'

'So I still have two then, do I?' I ask.

He laughs and gives me about ten minutes on Vanstiphout. That's all I need.

I go for lunch, call Aer Lingus and arrange an earlier flight home.

I'm back in the house for tea.

And I like the story. Not often you get to meet a chain-smoking Belgian pop star from the 1970s who is making a living fixing the heads of top golfers. I write the story that night before I go to bed.

I wish there were as many that are as easy.

It even finishes well. Imagine a small man, with cigarettes, a centre parting and a voice from Radio Luxembourg.

Is there anyone he yearns to work with?

'Ho! For the moment my hands are too full! Not even Tiger Woods. Thank you very much.'

Anything he misses about the old life?

'This is more fun in life than pop music, my friend. Hey, to be getting as many girls as you can without doing anything, it's OK, but not when you're fifty-one. I'm good, but I'm not God. Every night a different woman? Please no. Not now.'

And he sucks the last life out of a Marlboro and strides off in his mustard windcheater and blue jeans.

Home. Home on the range.

I sleep the sleep of the just.

Wednesday, 15th May

European Cup Final.

For some reason, Glasgow always reminds me of Brooklyn. One of those places endlessly sentimentalizing about its own boisterous youth. A beautiful woman with a busted nose and grey hair, showing you how once she could dance. Liverpool carries the same look. The present is dishwater grey and somehow arthritically hopeless, but the past, well baby, you should have seen us.

I'm in a sports shop on Sauciehall Street, killing time. I've been here in Glasgow since yesterday, having attended a couple of stultifying press conferences and listened to many people whine about why the Real Madrid team were so rude when they came through the airport. The reason is that they live in another world, a world so far away from Sauciehall Street and from Glasgow's past as to be uncharitable to us mortals.

A mother has brought her two sons to the sports shop for a treat. She is buying them a couple of Irish World Cup jerseys, not the official Umbro shirts but a couple of knock-off replicas with shonky logos and extra stripes. They cost £10 each and the woman is haggling with the spotty assistant. She wants to pay £15 for the pair. The kid at the counter is saying no, but his crusty face is traffic-light red.

'I cannae.'

'Not good enough for ye?'

'I cannae do it.'

'Ye'er turning up yer nose ay?'

'Nay. I jes cannae.'

And I'm thinking that once in the backstreets of Marseille, Zinedine Zidane might have identified with this scene, but today, this isn't part of his world. That's why rich people sneak through the back entrances at airports. The smell of our ordinariness offends them.

This week seems like a series of missed connections. Various worlds flirting with each other but not quite clicking. There are briefings for anyone interested in the progress of Ireland and Scotland's joint bid to host Euro 2008. Briefings and receptions and plentiful bumph to take away. It's a little poignant. A personal ad nobody will ever reply to.

If you peep over the glossy brochures and turn your head away from the fine stadiums of Glasgow, you see why. Pretend for a minute that you are a European football administrator. You see a cramped, dirty, muscular city around you. You see churning grey skies and stern, ruddied faces and all the talk is of parochial hatreds and traffic jams. Pretend for five minutes that you are a UEFA man in your bespoke suit and cloistered hotel and imagine how scary and alien Glasgow is to you. Like so much north of Watford, the world that Margaret Thatcher razed has been only half rebuilt.

Pretend for five minutes, and you will appreciate that Scotland and Ireland have no chance of hosting Euro 2008. That's even before you start considering just how comical the distinguishing features at the Irish end of the bid are. If Glasgow has a busted nose, Dublin has a clown's red nose.

I'm staying at the cheap, and defiantly cheerful, Central Hotel where battalions of Irish fans billet themselves when they travel to Celtic games. Every taxi driver I meet tells me this. 'Ye'll be a Celt then,' they say. Travelling to the Central Hotel marks you out as a Celtic fan as surely as wearing a green-and-white hooped jersey.

There's no point in denying it either. I've always liked Celtic. Liking Celtic is part of the national obligation, yet the nearer to the epicentre of Celticness I get, the queasier I always feel. The tedious sectarianism, the mendacious stoking up of old hatreds, by people several generations and many miles removed from real trouble, seems more ugly and tasteless here where remove should provide an excuse. That Glaswegians seem willing and able to keep the ancient sectarian virus alive, regardless of the environment around them, is a singularly depressing thought for anyone interested in a cure for the neighbouring island.

I can't find any other media people around the Central Hotel, but the place has the virtue of being attached to the main railway station and of being, well, central.

Today is match day and it's an expensive day too. I have travelled without the electrical connection for my laptop, an omission that involves a taxi trip out to a computer centre in Finniston, there to spend nearly £100 on getting the right replacement. The taxi driver is a Rangers fan. Dyed-in-the-blue-wool about it. He tells me nothing personal, but he hates Celts. By way of showing how reasonable he is, he tells me that he hates Aberdeen fans just as much though. I adopt a policy of sunshine diplomacy and start giving him the bits of souvenir tack that came in the goodie bag we got at the accreditation centre. He's baffled, but feels obligated enough to wait outside the computer centre. Now he has to hit the traffic on the way to Hampden rather than go hame to his tae as he'd been threatening.

The traffic is a nightmarish vision of what Glasgow might be like if it were hosting the European Championships. Along Cathcart Street and up past the Mount Florida church, the city is choked with smoke-glassed people carriers. And luxury coaches. And sponsors' cars.

It seems as if the sanitized, corporatized world of football had come to taunt Glasgow one last time. This is what the city will never have. More poignantly, if you love football, Glasgow is what football has lost. Glasgow, the city that once sent out eleven of its own sons – a Celtic team all born within a ten-mile radius of each other – to win the European Cup. Those boys would scarcely recognize what the game has become. The Lisbon Lions would scarcely be able to identify the corporation that is Real Madrid as a football club . . .

Hampden Park is cosy and modern these days, no longer the grey monolith to working-class passions that it once was. The organizers have produced a replica of the programme for the storied 1960 European Cup Final that was held here. The detail on the teams from Eintracht Frankfurt and Real Madrid is vague and sketchy, but the beauty lies elsewhere. The programme notes, helpfully, that the ball to be used for the night would be 'the Thomlinson Improved T Ball'. This wonder of leather and stitching would be 'supplied by the Sportsman's Emporium, 103 St Vincent's Street, Glasgow'.

Furthermore, the T Ball, locally made and ever improving, was the ball 'used in more international matches than any other football'. And not one Asian child exploited in the process.

The ad for a local drapers on the back page of the programme promises that a man can 'dress the family out of income and leave the holiday savings intact'.

Innocent times, but an era when at least football was still plugged into its hinterland. In 1960, there were ordinary Glaswegians swaying on the terraces as those eight goals were scored. Tonight the only ordinary Glaswegians here are asking if we want chips with our burgers.

On the hills above Hampden, large, white temporary edifices have suddenly appeared like alien craft bearing the logos and brand names of UEFA's spangling array of Champions League sponsors. Little rows of houses behind the ground have rented their gardens to TV companies to help bring the pictures to the homes of the sponsors' market.

These brand names have borrowed the lustre that should belong solely to men like Zinedine Zidane and Luis Figo, and they have filched a bit of the tradition of Puskas and Di Stefano. Tonight there are no hard-bitten Glaswegians pouring towards the ground half bent against the elements, hands in pockets, caps slung low. Tonight the kids are out getting free stickers, which sponsors are dispensing from shiny vans. The kids wear self-adhesive logos on their shirts that say MasterCard and Amstel. Meanwhile, their parents are standing at their garden gates watching another world have its fiesta.

Football has inflated itself, but by becoming bigger and bigger, it has somehow made itself smaller and more disposable. Ordinary people gather to watch the crowds instead of being part of them. Football is a TV entertainment. Just the other day, Alex Ferguson, reared in nearby Govan, spoke of attending the 1960 final as a young man, a few years older than those economically and socially barred from last night's spectacle. Ferguson was one of 130,000 to be shoehorned into Hampden that night, most of them from the working-class districts that give this hard-faced, old city its raucous character.

This week in Glasgow, there has been more than the usual amount of cheap sentiment for the old days, yet, amidst all the maudlin reminiscences, it seems to have gone unnoticed that football has abandoned places like Glasgow. Sure the town still has its two enemies living cheek by jowl, but Celtic and Rangers are a sad little Punch and Judy sideshow. It makes little difference if the European Championship of 2008 comes here or not. That competition will take place in a hermetically sealed bubble. The usual suspects will make out like bandits and the locals will be told they are the best in the world. Their kids will get free stickers.

Today, several people told me that they would be bringing their children into the main square after the match because this, they felt, was a bit of history. And what about the matches? I asked. They stopped being able to afford to go to Celtic or Rangers matches some time ago. One man had brought the kids to the airport to see Real Madrid arrive on Monday. There were perhaps 1,000 fans there. Real Madrid escaped through a back entrance.

And no chance of a ticket for the game itself? A German had offered two for £500 and the man had put them in the way of a regular customer in his cab. Too many other things that he himself could do with £500. Otherwise, tickets were as rare as hen's teeth. The occasion, like Hampden itself, has become diminished and corporatized.

The closest we get tonight to a people's game is the limp hilarity of the streaker. White like a lump of freezer meat, he dribbles away with the match ball and slots it past Butt in the Bayer goal.

Back in 1960, Eintracht Frankfurt were making their novel first voyage into Europe, having done the hard thing by actually winning the German league the year before. Tonight, Bayer Leverkusen arrived in Hampden unfestooned by the ribands of champions and playing for all intents and purposes in the shop window. Next year, they will be an asset stripped by the big boys. Ballack is already on his way to Bayern Munich. The Leverkusen adventure, a freak of circumstance (and fine management by Klaus Topmoller), will be consigned to the sort of oblivion whereby a team becomes the answer to a trivia question.

Meanwhile, the G14, that self-interested convocation of Europe's top clubs, have been meeting like the mafia families to discuss matters of mutual interest. The issue of capping players' wages is on the table. Of course, they should do this. Having driven the game into this cul-de-sac, they should initiate the escape plans. If not, even the Bayer Leverkusens will cease to exist. Football will implode.

Still, at the heart of the pomp and celebration, this is a football game. Real have a maudlin following in Glasgow, but the real romance is with the German underdogs. UEFA or the G14 can't change that. Eleven against eleven.

Early on though, it looks, disappointingly, as if the Germans are going to content themselves with roughing up the Real Madrid side. The skirmishing ends after nine minutes though, when

Roberto Carlos hurls a long throw down the left flank and Raúl turns like a darting fish. The German defence come over all Keystone Cops. Raúl slips the ball past Butt and into the far corner. Imagine, Raúl is a lesser light in this galaxy. A rout seems likely.

Leverkusen could make pretty origami out of oak trees so good is their improvization. They've been resourceful as boy scouts all season. Rub two sticks together and they'll make fire. Bernd Schneider ponders endlessly over a free kick, but still not long enough for Real to work it out. The Brazilian, Lucio, heads it home. He then celebrates by revealing a T-shirt that tells us that 'Jesus Loves Us'. 'Proddy Jesus or Taig Jesus?' someone asks. Whatever.

One all. Clear the floor for dancing if you please.

The ending is fraught, the journey to it flecked with moments of trouble, but Real get there with style nevertheless. On a night that demands redemption through a little poetry, Zidane gifts us a goal of epigrammatic brilliance to separate the teams.

On the cusp of half-time, another move down the left. Carlos, bald and gleaming, stabs a looped pass off his toe and over the head of stranded Sebescen. The ball falls in a sweet arc towards the edge of the area and, as it heads earthwards, Hampden gasps in pantomime fashion. It's him! Zidane lurks unmarked and wolfish. We wait for his genius to intersect finally with the random lines of the game. He waits too. He knows. We all know. He stretches his left leg balletically as the defence organizes itself under the din of sirens. Too late, too late. The ball moves as quickly and as unstoppably as a rumour towards the top corner.

A perfect goal. One of those frameable moments like Michael Jordan's final shot in a Bulls uniform.

On some nights you can almost forgive soccer anything. That moment of sublime beauty is enough for me to almost forget that, when Zidane scored, there were no kids in the house, no boys who would crystallize the moment in their imaginations and keep it there until some day they would chip away at the memory and hold it up as a thing of wonder for their own kids. There are no kids here to tell their own kids, like Alex Ferguson did this week, 'I was there.'

Anyway. Cue the fireworks and the Queen music. Again.

Half an hour later, while we are working at our desks and everyone is gone, the Real Madrid players come running back onto the pitch. A handful of their fans remain but, by and large, they just seem to want to savour the moment in private and with each other.

It takes hours of standing in the rain before a taxi driver can be inveigled into carting me back to the Central Hotel, but the thought of the millionaires on the pitch enjoying their own private party remains with me.

Friday, 17th May

Glasgow has taken its toll. Mean city.

Up all night trying to shake a cold and to finish a couple of features for the *Irish Times* World Cup magazine.

My Damien Duff piece is straightforward enough interview fare. The other effort amounts to a landmark exhibition of my own laziness. When a magazine was first mooted, I conceived a huge piece that would revolve around the Ireland versus Italy game of 1994. Not only would I interview all the Irish players who played that day, carefully assembling a mosaic of the entire momentous occasion, but I would dip into the world outside the touchlines. I would visit Loughinisland in Co. Down where people gathered in a pub to watch the match and were mowed down by loyalist gunmen as they did so.

I would interview a couple of the players who played in the Dublin versus Kildare Gaelic football game that was broadcast in bars around Manhattan that morning. I would talk to people in Little Italy, like my friend Dave Hughes who went there that very night in his Irish jersey. I would weave these short stories in and out of the narrative so that it read like the opening chapter of Don de Lillo's *Underworld*. It would be a work of genius. Form and content rising to match the momentousness of that occasion. The result that was heard around the world.

Sadly, Paul McGrath was missing when I called his house. Andy Townsend I reached on a busful of people singing 'Viva España' in a resort in Spain. Ray Houghton's number had changed sometime in the six years since I last called him, and so on.

Instead, at 5.30 a.m., what I send off down the laptop with profuse and heartfelt apologies but no valid excuse is a hangdog piece wherein Jason McAteer and Phil Babb remember the good old days. *Dos amigos*.

I hang this piece of flimsy on the ludicrous premise that the Italy game was their first ever competitive international game and hey, who knows, Steven Reid may travel to Japan and play his first-ever competitive international game there. Sometimes I produce hokum. Sometimes I produce hokum with raisins. I press the *send* button with a shudder and thank the stars that, if all goes well, I will never set eyes on my contribution to *The Irish Times* World Cup magazine.

Ninety minutes later, I have packed two large bags so that their aggregate weight exceeds my own bodyweight. At 7.30 a.m., I'm standing in the rain outside the polling station in Balrothery waiting to vote. It's general election day. Ten minutes later, I am in the back of Paul and Anne Kimmage's car. We are heading towards the airport and, after a few minutes, all three of us are too sleepy to speak. Thus begins the World Cup.

We're sleepy. Roy Keane is grumpy. Airports are usually a good place to ask him for an interview, but this morning you can tell at first sight that Roy is travelling with a personal entourage of demons. He looks at us as balefully as a vampire might survey the pending dawn.

He has taken a little stick for missing Niall Quinn's testimonial game, which the team played in on Tuesday night, and he doesn't like it. He is going off like a cluster bomb, hitting, in turn, the following journalists with shrapnel: Philip Quinn, Neil O'Riordan, Billy George and Paul Hyland. Casualties would be higher only Roy tells Paul that we are all scum and, scummily, most of us decide to keep out of Roy's way for a little while rather than argue with him over the generalization.

Roy's mood hasn't been helped by the scenes at Dublin Airport. Flights are late because of air traffic control problems. There is a reception for the players that drags on and on, while they kick their feet and Bertie Ahern (it's election day) squeezes their flesh. A mascot for one of the tabloids tells Roy Keane to cheer up. The mascot narrowly escapes the ritual disembowelling that would have cast a slight pall over the beginning of our World Cup adventure.

We haven't even got off the ground yet and we journalists are moaning fluently. Due to our straitened circumstances in *The Irish Times*, the a capella Whining Group has been reduced to a duo. At Italy 1990, we had four journalists. At USA 1994, we had four. At France, 1998 we had four. This time, there's just myself and Emmet Malone, the football correspondent.

Emmet and I might reflect that we met in college in the 1980s where we became good friends, and that he managed my rather feeble campaign to become president of UCD Students' Union – indeed a campaign in which we were placed third behind a joke candidate and a man who is now a big hit on local radio in the midlands. Third in a field of three, or last, as it is sometimes known.

And here we are, almost rehabilitated, and covering a World Cup for *The Irish Times*! We could gratefully reflect on that, but, instead, we are of the view that everything to do with our World Cup coverage has been and will be a disgrace. None of it is our fault. Frankly we're not going to take very much more!

The journey is like something from the Middle Ages. It goes on and on, and several of us catch scurvy. Scheduled flights all the way. Dublin to Amsterdam to Tokyo to the Pacific Island of Saipan. Only the Football Association of Ireland could have dreamt up such a schedule for their footballers, who are tired and haggard after a year's exertions.

Saturday, 18th May

Here we are. Saipan.

A ramshackle little airport with dancing girls bearing garlands to greet us. Nobody except Milo Corcoran of the FAI seems to appreciate the garlands, and the girls go around the little lobby like frantic dogcatchers trying to loop strays.

Saipan, for those of us who have bothered to check, is a tiny island in the Pacific, a three-and-a-half-hour flight from Tokyo. Search for it on the web and a site comes up called Saipan Sucks. Another site describes it as the whorehouse of the Pacific. The neighbouring island, Tinian, has one of the longest runways in the world. It needed one to enable the *Enola Gay* to take off on its way to obliterate Hiroshima. We are charmed.

For such a small place, the island has tons of horrible history. After World War I, Japan controlled Saipan and the Northern Marianas under a League of Nations mandate. The island was the site of a Japanese air base early in World War II and was then seized by United States forces in July 1944 after a bloody three-week battle. Forty thousand Americans stormed the place and 3,400 of them died; 27,000 Japanese also died, about a third of them in mass suicides. Chilling accounts from American soldiers detail the difficulty of getting landing craft ashore, because so many Japanese citizens had flung themselves from the island cliffs. The father and mother of one family of four, who were dawdling about there, were shot from behind by a Japanese sniper who then stepped out to his own death. Saipan then became a base for air attacks on the Japanese home islands.

Saipan and the other Northern Marianas voted to become a commonwealth in 1975 when, to help stimulate industry, the United States agreed to exempt it from federal minimum wage and immigration laws. That backfired. Soon there were 50,000 Chinese garment workers busily undercutting their American counterparts.

Until 1998, this dot in the water remained the centre of the sweatshop universe. Garment factories speckled the island. Rows of imported workers slaved robotically under dull fluorescent lights. They sewed, they ironed and they packed, and then they sent their produce off to American retailers like the Gap, Tommy Hilfiger and Sears Roebuck. In 1998, sales generated from Saipan were worth nearly $1 billion. Most of the garment factories which emerged were foreign owned. The workers came mostly from China, Bangladesh and the Philippines, brought in for one or two years, and were paid $3.05 an hour, compared with $5.15 in the United States.

So, three owners (Spain, Japan and the US) in the last century, mass suicides and a shocking death toll during World War II. Then the cheap labour era and a reputation as the knocking shop of the Pacific.

What's not to love?

Some traditions have continued. The hotel we media are staying in, the Dai Ichi, gets plenty of mentions in union records, having sacked all its Filipino workers when they became interested in joining a union. The place is staffed now by cut-price Nepalese instead. So it's come to this, Sherpa Tensing. Bring my bags to my room and no, don't use the lift.

We can hardly wait. We're tired and cranky. We left shortly after 8 a.m. on Friday. It's almost twenty-four hours later, mid-afternoon on Saturday, when we leave the airport and board the bus to the hotel.

We bounce along the dusty roads and, as we travel, Ray Treacy gives us a sunny commentary on the history of the island. Ray is a dubious historian and he thinks little of our academic attainment anyway. I'm dozing as I hear him point out the local hotspots.

'That's the local bike-hire shop. Good way to get around the island and probably the only ride most of you losers will get.'

Groans.

We pass a huge new building, a shopping mall.

'Genuinely lads,' purrs Ray who regards this as a prime titbit, 'in there, that is pure duty-free shopping. Lit-er-ally duty free.'

'Ray,' says somebody from the back, 'we've done twenty-three fucking hours and come through four fucking airports for a duty-free mall. Literally Ray, shut the fuck up.'

We hate Ray right now.

The Ray Ballad starts up.

'Ringsend Ray

Con—
De—
Scending.'

We drive on through the streets that, literally, as Ray would say, have no names. We see an old American tank stuck in the clear, blue water just off a golden beach. The whole place has that eerie feel of tainted, cursed beauty.

We get our heads down for our first night on the island of Saipan. We are tired and short-tempered and full of airplane food. It's the best part of the week. Soon the 'certain people' call will come from Mal.

Sunday, 19th May

This morning we had our first World Cup press conference. Usual shambles. The show has just transferred its run to the Western Pacific area. It's a chronicle of a bad time foretold. We gathered after some hoo-ha in a little restaurant in the media hotel. Mick came among us and filled in the gaps in our knowledge of the epic journey we had all made together.

Nobody had jumped out of the plane.

Nobody's chewing gum had lost its flavour on the bedpost overnight.

Nobody died.

It's a housekeeping press conference and it finishes with a discussion of how things are going to be for the next few weeks. Not good.

Every day we will get the manager and three players who will operate off a rota. This sounds a whole lot better than it actually is. A few of us are concerned about the proposed midday start to these press conferences. This schedule suits the *Evening Herald* perfectly because it's the middle of the night back home. It suits the radio and TV people. It suits the wire services. It leaves nothing for those of us whose papers won't be coming out until the next day.

We ask Brendan McKenna, the FAI press officer, to ask Mick if separate conferences can't be organized for the Sunday and daily papers. Perhaps the odd feature-writing opportunity. We approach Mick together. Brendan pops the question and says timidly, 'You don't have to, now, Mick.'

So Mick rejects the idea out of hand. Excessive exposure to the press might cause him to catch some debilitating disease. 'No way,' he says.

I am furious. We have each paid over ten grand for being here in this crummy hotel and most of the papers (except us, it should be said) have paid another couple of grand into a team media pool for the right to access. Now the team won't organize their press responsibilities in an adult way.

This is my third World Cup and I'm feeling old and curmudgeonly. And why not? Our press operation is like an arm of the Official Secrets Act. Only the English and Irish sides bother with the players' pool stunt. This time, I think the players plan on giving the lot to a charity. Generally footballers believe that, if Hitler had annexed Poland for charity, it would have been fine. But the principle remains the same. They want cash for clichés. Several of them have made arrangements to do ghosted columns for papers that they have already broken. There are horror stories circulating among our ranks about journalists being left waiting for three or four hours on their first ghost dates.

There is a genuine belief among the squad, I think, that we wretched hacks are here to get our jollies by just being around the team and sucking in the same air, and that's more than we deserve.

The response to this is necessary. We're here as a surrogate presence for the people the team represents. We're here to get the team's thoughts and words out there, because the way in which the team represents the country is of huge interest to the country. Contrary to what he often says, it's not Mick's team. It's our team – the national team. And if we just take the express lift from the high moral ground to the bottom line, the fact that we're here creates the hype, which creates the excitement, which creates the endorsement deals.

It's a mystery why sports people in this neck of the world are the last to appreciate the way this works. Nearly 100 years ago, ball clubs in America began paying journalists to accompany them on road trips. Then the papers wised up ethically and commercially and realized that sending the scribbler along was a worthwhile venture in its own right, and freeing him up to write honestly worked even better. Every other team at this World Cup, including the English, who have five press officers with them, will have this routine down as a matter of course.

Here, it's still an imposition. Mick's attitude is especially aggravating. It's well known that he's not especially well paid by the FAI and the difference between his wage and a Premiership wage is made up by endorsement work and paid appearances. All this is media driven, media generated and media dependent. Yet his exaggerated sense of grievance about the small percentage of harsh words that come his way, amid general showers of praise, just eats away at him.

Still I have a sort of friendship with Mick that dates back to a fly-on-the-wall documentary I helped out with during his first campaign as Irish manager. Apart from the fact that he's a paranoid loon with absolutely no respect for what I do, I think that Mick's a good guy. I let the issue go. We have weeks ahead in which to iron things out or to work around the system. No point in starting with strife.

Anyway, tonight has been designated a special night of bonding. Under the palm trees, the journalist and the footballer shall be friends and verily the choirs of angels shall sing.

As it turns out, tonight will become the sort of landmark night that would be a cause of sensation if English players had partaken in it. It will be the sort of night that would have generated acres of tabloid outrage and volcanic rivers of hot poured scorn. There would have been a chain reaction of bad feelings and sackings.

We are Irish though, and we do things differently. All the night provokes is hangovers. The team have hosted a barbecue on the beach over at their hotel, which is perhaps 100 yards away from us geographically and three stars away from us service-wise. As usual, we will be spending our days milling about their lobby like pests.

Anyway we have trudged across the beach to chomp spare ribs and slurp beer. A few of us are uneasy about going, it doesn't do to socialize with players, and it's obvious we're being buttered up. Instead of leaving a wooden horse out as a gift, they are dangling a few spare ribs.

On the other hand, we're 2 million miles from home on a little island in the Western Pacific and the local big wigs are to be in attendance. It would be rude not to go.

The barbecue is what might be termed a qualified success. We media, about twenty or so of us who have made the journey to Saipan, sit at our tables. The players sit at theirs. We eat. They eat. We make some conversation with locals. The cool-looking guy in the denim shirt and the Tom Selleck moustache at our table, it transpires, is the local judge. All the while these wild cats, who are as skinny and as emaciated as heroin addicts, circle the barbecue patiently waiting to get among the scraps.

We make small talk and we keep an eye on the players. The politics of these things are always interesting. Who sits with whom? Who ignores whom? Who drinks? Who doesn't? Who is outgoing? Who is plainly nervous? What's the pecking order?

Mostly, of course, we watch Roy Keane. We are humming with updates on his mood. The 'Snubbed Taoiseach Incident' at Dublin Airport yesterday morning has already hit the papers. The suicide bomber who asked Keane to cheer up has been identified as a leprechaun operating in a promotional capacity on behalf of one of the tabloids. Yikes!

Keane sits with a few senior players and passes the odd comment out of the side of his mouth as if he has lockjaw. Not his scene but, like us, he's here for appearance's sake and because there would be a fuss if he wasn't.

When we're done eating, and when the conversation has petered out, an MC bounces on stage and makes some awful jokes that reverberate in the silence. He calls on Mick McCarthy to say a few words.

Mick compliments the MC on his Hawaiian shirt, but adds that he can't say the same nice things about the poor man's wig. Gulp! It's true! He is literally a local big wig.

The poor old sad sack is wearing the world's worst rug, a red-thatch job with a little ponytail at the back. Why Mick chooses to mention it though is a mystery. The man blushes scarlet and there is an embarrassed silence before he retrieves the microphone from Mick and ploughs on.

There then follows an hour-long exhibition of native dancing. Three women and three men performing various slappedy-doo numbers from various local islands. I say an hour, but I mean an eternity – it's dull as cabaret. The men wear grass skirts and Y-fronts underneath. The women wear wraparound skirts and half coconuts instead of bras. It's a look that wouldn't be very practical for tennis or badminton, but who are we to impose?

Somehow intercepting the lowest thoughts of the shipwrecked Irish crew, the MC lets it be known that the prettiest girl, the one who appears to be wearing Wonder-coconuts, is only thirteen years old. More gasping. We are either ashamed or we are thinking that people would understand our bad thoughts. The judge narrows his eyes and takes a good look around.

As revenge for our leering, the women start to pick on us. Journalists and players are forced, at coconut point, to get up on stage and take part in a belly-dancing exhibition.

Straight up I have the sort of belly that is designed to be danced on rather than with and, fortunately, I am spared. Roy Curtis of the *Sunday World* and Philip Quinn of the *Irish Independent* aren't. They are plucked from our midst to represent the scribbling community in one of the most obscene displays of wobbling and jiggling ever witnessed.

First though our host insists on showing us his prowess in the art of cutting coconuts in half with a sword. He makes a considerable show of swinging the sword around near Philip Quinn.

'Cut his head off!' shouts Roy Keane. All heads swivel. Roy is grinning. Despite recent differences, he quite likes Quinner and the joke dissolves a lot of the tension in the air.

The sword swishing resumes. To be honest, we suspect there must be easier ways of doing this. Our host draws back the sword and begins hacking away. Not a Kodak moment.

Then, after a fill of food, we are asked to watch the lads shake their ample boogie down. Roy and Philip do their best but I think I speak for all who were present when I say, 'Yuck.'

Robbie Keane keeps the players' side up with some lithesome bump and grind gyrations that are so salacious as to still be illegal in most American states.

When Robbie is finished, the MC sucks up to the young

millionaire and chooses him as the best hog in show. Robbie gets garlands and a kiss from the thirteen-year-old. The MC shakes Robbie's hand.

'Thanks very much, Mr Strachan,' says Robbie.

It brings the house down. The man with the rug looks exactly like Gordon Strachan.

Now that the dancing is done, the players make a big deal display of heading off to bed early. Keane slips off by himself into the darkness. From the rest of the team, there is so much theatrical stretching and yawning and nighty-night now stuff that it sounds like the end of *The Waltons*.

We dissolute hacks wander around mooching drinks. Paul Kimmage and myself have a couple in the team hotel. Then Ray Treacy arrives.

Ray is in sociable form and we have a question for him, which we ask almost in unison. 'Why Saipan?'

'Well,' says Ray, 'that's a story.'

One day Ray had just finished loading a long, long line of his punters onto an airplane, when a man he'd never met before approached him and said he'd heard that Ray was looking for a World Cup base.

'Yes,' said Ray.

'Saipan,' said the man.

Ray made a note. Forgot all about it.

He went home to his bed that night and, before climbing in, realized that he'd scribbled the suggestion from a punter on the top of a cigarette box. He fished the box of fags from his trousers. There were the words. Saipan. John White.

He let that percolate in his brain for a few days, then pulled down the relevant internet pages. He was intrigued. More so than with anywhere else that had been touted. He mentioned this to

Mick McCarthy who agreed to fly all the way just to see the place. Ray and Mick played golf, Mick shot a seventy-four.

Love Saipan? Again, what's not to love?

Ray persuades us to have a quick one at a bar up the road where he has agreed to meet somebody, so we dander to a bar called The Beefeater for a late sup. The Beefeater is Saipan's English-style pub. Peeling and unpromising on the outside, it's a badly lit plastic-and-leatherette place inside. If you imagine a venue where sailors might gather to drink and to fight when on shore leave, well that's The Beefeater. Pool table. Jukebox. And that's it for frills, or things that might get broken.

When we arrive, about half the Irish World Cup team are inside already. So are most of the Irish media. We have a strong inclination to leave, but we opt to stay for a quick one and then escape. Myself and Paul are taken by surprise to find such a mixed gathering in the place. In ten years of covering the Irish side, I don't think I've ever been out for drinks with any of them. Naturally, I, personally, have been swamped with social invitations, but the players have gradually learned to respect my privacy.

It emerges that a *détente* has been reached between media and players. For one night only, everyone drinks together and nobody squeals. This is the last night of liberty for the players and, having ingeniously tried to give us all the slip with the comedic yawning and stretching routine back at the barbecue, they are resigned to sharing the bar with us.

In the old days under Jack Charlton, there was quite a bit of fraternizing between media and players and some competitive sessions of drinking each other under the table. I arrived on the scene too late for that. Which is a good thing. There's nothing sadder than seeing hacks trying to get into the social whirl with players.

They are players. We are journalists. Different species. Getting all close and pally with a player is fine, but the next time he has a howler and you cover for him, you should have a little disclosure at the end of your report: 'The Journalist Drinks With Several Members of the Beaten Team. Copy Content Has Been Written With a View To Continuing This Arrangement.'

That's my theory anyway.

In reality there's a symbiosis there that neither side likes to acknowledge. We need them. They need us. In an awful way, we are fascinated by each other. We, especially us feature-writing geeks, like seeing what makes certain players tick. For their part, they enjoy quizzing us about this and that. Every player will have some hack who he thoroughly despises and wants to make an enquiry about. Inevitably, the hack will have stitched the player up sometime in history and the nature of your response will determine the player's attitude to you.

So, it's best if we watch each other from a distance.

And players are obsessed with, of all things, those dopey player ratings that some newspapers tag on at the end of a match report. Most professional footballers will, in time, get over being accused of rape, pillage and wearing a mullet, but give them four marks out of ten on a day when they reckon they've done well and you've made an enemy for life. Somebody told me once that, when required, Brian Glanville would reluctantly supply ratings but would give everybody seven and let the desk sort it out. Eminently sensible.

Things are merry tonight though. Ten out of ten for the merriment. The festering resentments which exist between players and journalists are laid aside. There's music playing and practical jokes going down and hard drinking on a grand scale. The players are bowing out in style.

It's interesting that they voyage around Roy Keane in just the same way as we do. In Tokyo Airport on the way here, we had a stopover of an hour or two wherein we were brought to a special lounge. As we all sat around drinking coffee and looking awkward, Shay Given, a little giddy perhaps from just having signed a new deal with Newcastle United, popped up and slipped a tape into a large ghettoblaster that was sitting on a counter. For a second, there was horror on every face. The tape was highlights taken from Today FM's occasionally brilliant Radio Roy pisstake in which Keane's customary air of menace is replaced by a sort of comic goofiness which shouldn't come off but does.

The tape played and the place went silent while everybody glanced over to see how Keane would react. We half expected Mick Byrne to dive on the ghettoblaster in the manner of a bodyguard taking a bullet for his boss. 'Noooooooooooooooo!'

Roy loves it though. He's heard about the pisstake but never actually heard it. He sits there laughing his old head off and the sense of relief is so great that the other players laugh along louder than is strictly warranted.

In the bar tonight, Keano's mood is the subtext to nearly everything the players say to each other. The players' training gear has been late arriving from Dublin and there is speculation that Roy is unhappy with this. Some of the lads have composed a song to the tune of Rod Stewart's 'Maggie May':

> 'Wake Up Mick
> I think I've got something
> To say to you
> The gears not here
> And Keano's fucked off
> Says it's not like this
> At Man U . . .'

*

The bar is owned by a guy called Carl, who is a brother of the former American Olympic swimmer, Debbie Maier, who won three gold medals at the 1968 Olympics. Carl is a nice guy, but when it comes to getting his bar emptied at the legal closing hour of 2 a.m., he is a complete amateur.

There are various birthdays that need celebrating. We enter agreements to pay over the odds for drink. We make solemn promises to make this one the last, the very last. And now Carl, before we go, we'll just have the one we came in for.

Carl has never seen a night like it. Unwisely, he's trying to keep up in the drinking stakes and this is eating away at his resolution. The time slips past 5 a.m. and it starts to get bright outside. Carl is still attempting to close his bar.

Little snippets from the general clamour interest me. It's amazing how much the players resent the media coverage that led to the end of Phil Babb's career. It's interesting how much they generally resent certain journalists and certain papers. The *Evening Herald* seems to be getting a good going over.

It's not very satisfying to know that I am getting through the night unscathed. Not many of the lads read *The Irish Times* and those that do don't take it seriously. Tabloidese is the lingua franca of their profession.

Snapshots.

A competition organized by Gary Kelly where everyone draws a horse on a napkin. For some reason I won. Ian Harte is disqualified for letting somebody else see his horse. Robbie Keane is disqualified because he's from Tallaght where whoa means the opposite to giddy-up. And so on. I win and Gary keeps shoving a big pile of money my way. Eventually, we give it to Carl, who sets them up again.

Then there is the spoon game. My friend Mr Paul Kimmage,

the eminent journalist, stands with a spoon in his mouth. He faces Steven Staunton, the famous international footballer, who also has a spoon in his mouth. Both men have their hands clasped behind their back. They are going to go spoono a spoono.

The famous footballer bows his head first with oriental solemnity. The eminent journalist then attempts to hit the footballer on the top of the head using the spoon, which he, the journalist, holds in his mouth. Paul pulls his head back and swings the spoon down but his teeth have little purchase on the spoon and it bounces off Stan's hair.

'OK,' says Stan, 'my turn.'

So the eminent journalist smiles thinly and bows his head. Suddenly, racked with suspicion, he glances up, but Stan is standing there with the spoon in his teeth and his hands behind his back rolling his head as if he were loosening his neck muscles.

'You're either going to play the game or you aren't,' says Stan from between the teeth that hold the spoon.

'OK,' says Paul.

He bows his head again. And then Stan's accomplice, call him Discopants, leans across and whacks Paul mightily on the top of the head with a heavy spoon which he has concealed in his hand.

'Jaysus,' says Paul straightening himself up and rubbing his aching nonce. 'You're good at this Stan. Give us another go.'

So it continues till Paul's head is thoroughly re-contoured.

And Roy Keane is asleep in his bed across the road not knowing what he is missing.

There's a long, drunken and complicated competition where even myself and Emmet, by far the two most politically correct people on the island, find ourselves turning to the person beside us and, in the manner of Daniel Day Lewis playing Christy Brown but with the twist of a Welsh accent, wish our neighbour good luck and all the best at the World Cup. I wish I could tell you that we had the spine to object to such carry on but the shots of rum, tequila, Jameson and Jack Daniel's, which were punctuating the flamboyant beer drinking, were having their effect.

Songs were sung. Yarns were told. Some scores were settled. I have a pleasant memory of Robbie Keane and Gary Kelly, both good singers, harmonizing on a country song called 'I Thought You Walked On Water', to which they had only to slightly alter the words in order to turn it into a savage pisstake on Niall Quinn. Niall, in fairness, loved it.

Robbie Keane has begun to fascinate me. I've had a few little slices off him in columns in the past and his agent once offered me the chance of flying to Leeds for a whole five minutes of one-on-one time with Robbie. Nothing I've read or seen about Robbie has led me to expect that I'll actually end up liking him. Around the media, he's always seemed hostile and on edge. Tonight though, he's relaxed and funny.

The players call him Whacker, which catches a good deal of his quintessential Dubness. He grew up in Tallaght, near his friend Richie Dunne, and here are the two of them at the World Cup together enjoying themselves like a couple of millionaires in their early twenties. Did you evah?

Keane is still only twenty-one but he carries himself like a guy at least ten years older. In the media, we have always said that Keane is in thrall to his agent and that he seems to have to ask his agency every time he wants to go to the toilet. Maybe he's just being cagey, finding his way in the world though. Here in Carl's bar, he's witty and brash with a confident way of carrying himself that I've never seen in a twenty-one-year-old before.

And besides, he's a Leeds United player. I remind myself a few times that here sitting at the bar with me are three Leeds

United players. This is what being a fan with a typewriter is all about.

See, I developed an attachment to the wrong team after the 1970 FA Cup Final that Leeds United lost to the London club Chelsea in a replay. It was the wrong club in so far as the school I attended at the time was in London. In fact, it was a Chelsea fundamentalist school. And I fell in love with Leeds United, a love that dared not speak its name. That is until, at a birthday party, my parents presented me with a full Leeds United kit, including the Number 8 jersey worn by my hero Alan Clarke. Try explaining that away, Salman.

With my secret out, I grew strangely reckless. Soon afterwards, the nuns who ran the school invited us to contribute a penny a week towards the rearing of what were generically known as 'black babies' somewhere in Africa. We weren't told where in Africa these 'black babies' lived but, for our penny a week, we were each allowed to christen a baby. I called mine Alan Clarke and can remember being upset when I wasn't allowed to include the player's nickname 'Sniffer' as a middle name. This decision on the 'Sniffer' issue seemed especially harsh and vindictive, as most of the other kids in the village (or indeed in Africa for all we knew) were given the Christian name Chopper by my schoolmates, in honour of Ron Chopper Harris, the psychopathic Chelsea full back.

Anyway, by 5 a.m., or some time thereafter, we are a rabble. Suddenly, there are growling recriminations and nasty hisses as the gathering breaks up into smaller groups. At one point, Neil O'Riordan from the *Sun* tells Niall Quinn that the team should be embarrassed by their performances in the qualifying campaign for the 1998 World Cup. There follows an awkward silence. Don't hit us, we tell the players. We wear glasses. We'll have to write about it tomorrow. Please.

Suddenly we can't get out of there quick enough. Emmet has

decided that it's five in the morning and he is Marshall McLuhan. He is reaching out to the young and enquiring mind of Richard Dunne. Sadly, Richard has chosen the wrong subject and the wrong man for an argument. Emmet is dwelling on the nuanced and complex relationship that exists between players and media. Richard, forgetting perhaps that he has been drinking for several hours, is asking Emmet why journalists feel they can ask questions about his 'lifestyle'. Emmet is red in the face trying to explain. En passant, as it were, Richard Dunne announces that he is going to hang Emmet from a rope.

Ian Harte, who has been quiet all night, is appalled by the sudden turn of events. He is leaning across to Carl the barkeeper offering some advice, 'Carl would you ever throw us all out for God's sake. Please Carl. C'mon. Just throw us out of here.'

One sane voice.

In the end we throw ourselves out. We go off to bed and soon it is bright in Saipan. Emmet is still banging on my door as I fall asleep. He's pissed that nobody understood the breakthrough he was about to make with Richard Dunne. I'm too tired to walk to the door to tell him to go away.

Monday, 20th May

When next we see the players, there are sheepish looks and rolled eyes exchanged. Monday is lost to most of us. Sunday recedes like a fog. Not a bad bonding exercise all in all though. When my head stops hurting, I count up the number of players I am now on better terms with. Even if I am about to vomit my pelvis down the toilet, it has been worth it journalistically. That's the stuff they don't teach you at journalism school.

What little of the day that's worth remembering involves tender attempts to lift my head from the pillow and the insistence of Mother Nature that this is precisely the wrong thing to do. For doing a drunken impression of Christy Brown, I have been punished by paralysis.

I know that, in the afternoon, the phone rang. Malachy with his traditional 'bylines' rallying call. Leaving Dublin, Mal has told me that he expects a column from me, arriving Sunday for Monday (done, and what a side-splittingly funny *Lord of the Flies* pastiche it was too) and then nothing till I hit him with – ta da! – 'The Big Feature' for the following Saturday. I have nodded earnestly. He has sworn to forego the mandatory bylines call. But now . . .

'Tom,' he says.

'Uh,' I say. 'Mal?'

'Tom. Mal,' he says.

'Mal,' I say. 'Tom.'

'Listen Tom,' he says, 'what have you got for me for tomorrow?'

'For tomorrow Mal?' I say.

'Yeah,' he says, 'what sort of a piece will you be filing?'

'Eh,' long pause as head clears. 'Well I won't be filing anything. You said to do the column for Monday and to come back in then on Saturday with the big feature. I'm still hoping for Keane.'

'Hmm,' he says, 'I really do need to start getting bylines into the paper.'

'But I'm trying for the Keane feature. There's nothing else happening and two of us covering it.' I'm crossing that invisible line between explanation and whine now.

'I know. I know,' says Mal reaching for his trusty anti-whine device, 'but certain people here see yourself and Emmet off on that island and they wonder why has Mal got two of them there. So I need bylines.'

'Well, tell "certain people" to give me a call if they're wondering. I don't know why we're here either, but I know that I shouldn't lift my head off the pillow. I didn't get to bed last night.'

And Mal gets grumpy. I promise to do a 'Saipan letter' on Tuesday for Wednesday and attempt to go back to sleep. It's not happening. My stomach and head are rioting. I have a feeling I should be stalking Roy Keane.

Tuesday, 21st May

It's already time to deliver the damn letter. I wander down the beach to the team hotel. Saipan is an odd cocktail of stunning beauty, poignant history and enthusiastic bad taste. If you walk down the street to the team hotel, you have to make your way past the massage girls and the hookers offering their various specialities. Walking down the beach to the team hotel means you can paddle in the clear, blue water and listen to the gentle roar of the jet skies.

I sit strategically placed in the lobby of the team hotel. We hacks are masters of strategic lounging. You sit somewhere visible enough so that every player who emerges from the lift can see you, but far enough away so that it looks as though the last thing you are interested in is football players. Then you order a drink (conspicuously non-alcoholic to counter the stereotype) and glance up in complete surprise every time you think you hear a player passing or a lift door opening.

Gary Kelly and Ian Harte come over to discuss The Beefeater and all that went on. They trained hard in the broiling sun yesterday and my eyes water as I think of just how much I admire them for doing that.

Through the lobby then comes Ian Evans. Same old routine. Toting bags of balls and bags of bibs. The Irish bring an odd and reassuring permanence of ritual to their business. Joe Walsh and Johnny Fallon come through the lobby next. More gear. Drinks. Medical stuff. The quartermasters in this small sporting army on the move.

Finally, some time later, moving leisurely like cattle, the players begin padding through. Tony Hickey escorting the team. Mick Byrne trailing along as usual with his jokes and mischief. Their society is broken down into the familiar groupings. Senior players together. Goalies usually together, but they've left early today with Packie Bonner. Youngsters, the DVD-and-video game set, all together. The old ones roll their eyes these days. There aren't enough card players to make up a decent poker school anymore. There isn't enough money you can take off young players that will make a difference to them. Time was when you served your apprenticeship in a lesser poker school and worked your way up through the squad. Permanence of ritual, you say?

Then bingo! Steve Staunton and Roy Keane are passing through the lobby sharing what appears to be the greatest joke ever told. Regardless of the fact that I may be the butt of that very joke, I approach at pace.

'Stan,' I say, nodding at Staunton.

This is the first time in my life that I have ever called him Stan. Most sportswriters need only the briefest acquaintance with somebody before they will start using their nickname, but it makes me feel more fraudulent than ever. However, I have drunk with Stan and watched himself and Niall Quinn reshape Paul Kimmage's head with a spoon. That's as much intimacy as I have ever enjoyed with a footballer. Stan it is. And besides, no harm in showing Roy that I'm one of the boys.

I turn towards Keane now. He's helpless. I have him.

'Roy,' I say.

He nods at me. And he keeps walking as if I've come beetling towards them at top speed merely to utter the words 'Stan' and 'Roy'. He must think I've been in speech therapy.

'Any chance of a quick word, Roy?' I call after him. (Somebody once asked the same question of Kenny Dalglish, who replied tartly with a quick word: 'Velocity.')

He stops.

I blurt out that, yes, I understand I may be still on his personal death list since the time I got all fast and loose with his phone number, but right now it's my solemn duty to ask him to sit down and do another interview with *The Irish Times*.

Keane stares at me for a second. Staunton looks at me with some distaste as if he'd never spotted before that I am actually an invertebrate.

'Yeah sure,' says Roy. 'When do you want to do it? Today is it?'

'Not today,' I say firmly. Sorry to disappoint, but I haven't actually got a question in my head. Roy mentions that he's also doing an interview with Paul Kimmage. I'm not sure if he is implying that, maybe, I would like to read that interview instead, but I act surprised and request that he just fit me in.

Realizing that I am pathologically incapable of making a decision, he instructs me to come along to the training session, which is due to start in about half an hour, and to wait for him at the fence at the end of training. By this time, he will have ascertained his schedule for the next couple of days and we can set a time. Roy is in fine form. So, suddenly, am I. I have a date.

The training ground has been built by the locals specifically for the visit of the Irish squad. It's one of those gifts where you have to keep reminding yourself that it's the thought that counts. No dressing rooms. One set of posts. A little home-made shelter for players to sit in away from the sun and a viewing area right behind one of the goals, which means the players can whack footballs at journalists' faces all afternoon.

The pitch lies a few miles away straight up the coast road; azure sea on one side, parched fields and shacks on the other. I arrive early in the session having rung *The Irish Times* to leave a message on Mal's machine. Only the slightest whiff of the heroic martyr about it. Yes I will send a Saipan letter, but really, I'm busy preparing for the Roy Keane interview that I have just secured.

Irish squad training sessions are pretty much the same every time you watch them. After a while, only a trainspotter could tell the difference. Stretches. Jogging. Shortsided games. Sportswriters watch for the interaction between players, to nick little cameos for features and generally just to give the inside guff. Mostly we don't watch at all, we just stand and talk.

Today's session though, this one will turn out to be historic.

The sounds of training are as usual. Taff Evans with his drill sergeant's voice driving the proceedings. 'All right, all right, all right. *WHY DON'T WE JUST GET ON WITH IT INSTEAD OF MOANING LIKE LITTLE OLD LADIES THEN.*'

And the nicknames called out into the soupy air. The tags make their own poetry.

Carso and Keano
Stan, Whack and Quinny
Breeny and Dino
Duffer, Trig and Finny.

When Damien Duff needs a pass to latch on to, as a prelude to one of his happy-footed runs, he roars, 'Send me, send me!' Like a sixties hippie.

When Roy Keane loiters thoughtfully on the ball he hears the same chorus every time: 'Keano Wide. Keano Wide.'

And when Gary Breen makes a run forward in training, he hollers the same thing as he goes in search of the free header, 'Dink It! Dink It!'

We write this down. Dink it! Send me!

They have it easy today, or as easy as you can have it given the humidity and the still, soupy air. They make little lay-offs and whack shots at the goalies for half an hour. Then Ian Evans announces a game of one touch. Nine-a-side to round off training.

'No keepers,' says Evans.

'No fucking keepers?' screams Roy suddenly.

The keepers had been down here to work out before the rest of the squad arrived. Now, they're tired. Roy feels that tiredness is the correct state of being for anyone on the cusp of a World Cup. He screams this view at Evans, who blows the whistle and gets the nine-a-side game started.

Roy plays furiously, but not furiously enough for his anger to blow over. As soon as the game peters out, he's off. He has a go at Packie Bonner, the goalkeeping coach, and though we can't hear what is said, he throws his water bottle away in disgust.

Meanwhile, incongruously, it is kiddies' day at Irish training. John White, the guy from Summerhill in Dublin whose name Ray Treacy scribbled on that cigarette packet months ago to get this whole trip in motion, is herding kids towards the players.

Roy is finding the white-hot centre of his inner volcano as perhaps twenty-five toddlers are being ushered past to meet the rest of the team and play keep ball with Niall Quinn, Damien Duff, Mick McCarthy and other soft-hearted squad members. Roy doesn't even see them. He is screaming at Alan Kelly the reserve keeper.

Alan has made the mistake of engaging Roy, telling him that he's tired.

'What do you want – a fucking medal? We're all fucking tired,' he screams. 'We're supposed to be preparing for a World Cup and you're all fucking crying that you're tired. What do you think I am? We're supposed to be fucking tired. You won't be too fucking tired to drag yourselves out for fucking golf tomorrow, will you? Poor fucking things.'

'Calm down,' says Kelly.

'Are you going to make me calm down?' screams Roy. 'Are you going to fucking come over here and make me calm down?'

All this while I'm standing by the fence, right near the team bus as instructed. I'm afraid to leave, in case Roy accuses me of breaking the arrangement. I'm afraid to stay, in case he thinks I'm hassling him. I'm afraid to take my eyes of him, in case I miss something. I'm afraid to look at him, in case I meet his stare and do something dumb like roll my eyes sympathetically. Everyone Roy looks at now, he burns holes in.

Roy is wringing out his sweat-soaked vest. He gets tired of this and flings it away. He throws a few more obscenities at Alan Kelly, who has changed tactics and is staring fixedly ahead now at something in the distance.

Then Roy heads my way. I try to make myself as small and insignificant-looking as a six-foot-three galoot can be. No need. Rage has blinded him. He steams past, straight onto the bus.

Then there is an interlude of dark comedy.

A young kid cheerily marches on board after Keane. He has a football that he wants signed.

Oh God! Everyone looks in horror as if the kid has just paddled into shark-infested water. It's just that it's too dangerous for anyone to wade in and get him. Please let him be all right in there.

Really, being nearest the bus, I should tell the kid to stay out, but I'm in another world right now. Anyway, I've seen Keane with mascots and other kids and he loves them. Perhaps there won't be a tragedy.

The kid is gone an awful long time, but none of us will go and investigate what is happening beyond the smoke-filled windows. Finally the kid gets off, with his ball signed and he looks none the worse for wear. There is some sort of protection that God offers to the foolish and the innocent.

And that's it. Presently, the team file onto the bus. Emmet and myself take a cab back to the hotel, swapping Keane stories. My interview is slightly in limbo now until Roy cools down. I have also forgotten about the Saipan letter. When we get back to the media hotel, I decide to wander down to the Hyatt, to find Keane, for better or for worse.

I find him straight away. He's at a table in the grounds of the hotel with Mick McCarthy. I dawdle for a while hoping that their meeting will be brief, but Mick spots me and gives me a black look. I pass on and head back to the room to write the Saipan letter for Mal.

This is trickier than it should be. All things considered, I decide to leave the lurid description of Roy rage out of the piece for the moment. It's a small enough incident anyway and the *Herald* will possibly have it in late editions today. The *Indo* will probably have it tomorrow. Whatever happens, the accounts will be widely circulated by tomorrow and the whole thing will be vastly inflated from what it was. I don't want to jeopardize whatever chance there is left of an interview by making more out of a training-ground row than it merits.

Anyway, hopefully, there will the opportunity to ask Roy Keane about it all.

Make check call to the office to make sure they got the stuff. Call home. Turns out it's my birthday.

Wednesday, 22nd May

The team are due to go training around 10 a.m. First, though, an early-morning press conference. We are 100 per cent taken by surprise. Mick McCarthy takes out his slingshot and hits us with the pellets straight between the eyes.

Bam! Until a little while ago, Roy Keane was on his way home.

Bam! Colin Healy, the Celtic midfield player, had even been summoned as a replacement.

Bam! Matters were only resolved early this morning as the sun was coming up.

We sit in the little restaurant stupefied, working out by exactly how much time we have missed the last editions. For Emmet and myself this is a nightmare, it's past midnight back home. It will be nearly twenty-four hours before the paper runs again. Having sent two of us off to this sleepy island, the biggest story has broken at precisely the wrong time. The best we can hope for is an authoritative follow-up tomorrow and, hopefully, the Keane interview for Saturday, but right now that seems a slender hope.

'He said he was going to go,' continues Mick McCarthy. 'We had a number of discussions last night. He spoke to other people back at home and, through these talks, it came to be resolved. Now there's not a problem.'

Not a problem. Speak for yourself mate! We have all day today to play catch-up and nobody to play it with.

Keane has, apparently, told Mick that he had worries over his lingering knee injuries, that he had personal problems that he needed to deal with. Little wonder Mick was shooting dagger glances at me as he sat in the hotel garden with Roy.

Yesterday was the last day upon which it would have been possible to summon a replacement for Keane, and Roy was, apparently, eager to allow McCarthy the room to do this. For a period, McCarthy and the team thought they had lost their captain, midfielder and one true star.

'We had extensive discussions around tea-time yesterday,' says Mick, matter of factly, 'and again in the evening. Preliminary arrangements were made for Roy to travel home.'

Meanwhile, we'd slept like babes 100 yards up the road.

Mick's press conference finishes. The need to go training brings the questions to a natural end, but, the truth is, we are too surprised to even come up with a series of penetrating questions. Most of what we ask is why? We need a more forensic examination of what was said, when it was said, what the precise sequence of events was.

It's an odd story. This morning, as we get first wind of it, the business is already done and dusted. Keane was going, now he is staying. There's no breaking news beyond that. We've just got to follow up on what we missed.

We stand around in the corridor collectively digesting the implications.

Nobody is sure what to make of it. All week there has been speculation that one of the Sunday tabloids is about to perform a stitch-up job on Roy Keane's wife, or on Roy himself, at the weekend. We discuss this rumour in the oddest way.

These things happen in the media and we all react as if we aren't part of it, as if these stories are just acts of God that we must all endure. Even the tabloid guys are shaking their heads sadly at the thought of the pending atrocity about to be perpetrated on the Keanes.

And there is speculation about drink. We widely assume (although there has never been confirmation) that Roy has a drink problem or that, at the very least, he struggles with the stuff and goes hard on himself if he breaks his pattern of general abstinence. Maybe he's struggling. We don't know. There are twenty opinions and no facts.

I'm not sure about the drink thing. The theory I've been nurturing is that Roy gets depressed. Black, coalmine depressed.

It's getting on for 10 a.m. Now or never. I walk across to the team hotel and just catch the team gathering to leave. The bus is late and most of the players are milling around in the sun outside. A few of them give me knowing little nods. They know what I've come for. Picking over the carrion.

Once again, Roy Keane is walking across the lobby. Last of the bunch. Tony Hickey, the security man, is shadowing him in case he's bothered by somebody like me.

Keane's in a good mood though.

'Ya still want to do it?' he grins.

'Yeah, well OK.'

He's still committed to talking to Paul as well. He proposes doing both of us this afternoon while the rest of the team go golfing. He asks if I want to go first or second. Luckily, I've thought of this.

'Second,' I say.

When I started out interviewing people, Paul Kimmage and David Walsh were the big stars of the sports feature-writing business. Still are. Occasionally in copy, one or other of them would include a sentence like 'in the course of a four-hour conversation, he gave no indication of . . . being a werewolf.'

I've had meaningful relationships that lasted less than four hours. Besides, I know Paul to be a grittier interviewer than me. If Roy is reluctant to talk, Paul will soften his cough better than I can. All week, despite the fact that Paul and I are good friends, I have been worrying about finding myself sitting with Roy for half-an-hour or so and then hanging around the hotel lobby for hour after hour knowing that Paul was somewhere doing the definitive piece as Roy lies on the couch weeping and wondering why he has never had the courage to say all this before now.

Ostensibly, I have the advantage here. I work for a daily paper and Paul works for a Sunday one, so I will get into print on Saturday. Fine, if my piece is better than Paul's. However, if Paul goes second and gets an open-ended amount of time with Roy and comes up with one of the pieces he's capable of producing, I'll just look like a fool.

I imagine sitting in my room in the media hotel racking my brains in order to come up with a way to stretch my little Roy interview to 2,000 words and, in the distance, down on the beach as the sun is setting, I can see Roy and Paul walking. Roy is off the couch now, filled with new perspective and ideas. They are just two shadows, but Roy and Paul are gesticulating, nodding, arguing, jointly baring Roy's soul.

Paul is capable of it. He's a great interviewer who uses silence and aggression as weapons. And he's a former pro sportsman himself. Lots of the players have read *A Rough Ride,* his matchless book about his cycling career. That personal history gives him an edge. Professional sports people respect him because they know that he knows what it's like.

I'm just a fat geezer with a tape recorder and I could get filleted here this week. I arrange with Roy that Paul will interview him from 3 p.m. to 4 p.m. and then I will take over the inquisition. Fingers crossed that Paul won't throttle me when he hears this. We're already uneasy around each other this week knowing that we're hunting the same prey.

It's 2.50 p.m. Paul has booked Room 311 upstairs for the interviews. We're sitting in the lobby, tense and grumpy with each
other. Roy Keane is always early for these things, so we've been
here for a while saying nothing.

When Paul disappears upstairs with Roy, I start to panic. Not
about the questions I'm going to ask, but about what I'm wearing and what I'm carrying. I have rules about interviews. Never
wear a watch. When you have your fist propping up your chin,
the hands of the damn watch will be all that the subject will be
looking at. Never wear anything that isn't nondescript. Right
now, I'm wearing a T-shirt that suggests rather loudly that 'I'm
a prat'. And I haven't got spare batteries for the mini-disc
recorder.

By the time 4 p.m. comes close, I've been running up and down
the row of little shops outside the team hotel for the best part of an
hour. I'm now wearing a souvenir Saipan T-shirt, which has a
large whale logo depicting a playful whale wearing sunglasses. I
regret this T-shirt already. On the other hand, I have enough spare
batteries to meet the energy needs of small town.

On the way back through the team hotel, I meet Mick
McCarthy. Mick is in his cycling gear. He has been out cycling on
the mountains, something he's been doing a lot of this week. We
chat briefly and I tell him that I thought he handled the whole Roy
business the day before quite well, especially the prompt and
straight-up morning press conference. Mick seems pleased and I
tell him that, as a matter of fact, I'm off to see Roy now.

'Ay? Well, good luck,' he says.

At 4 p.m. exactly, I'm knocking on the door of Room 311.

The interview runs fine. I have the news instinct of a three-toed
sloth and what fascinates me the most during the conversation is a
digression he makes to speak about how uncomfortable he felt in

University College Cork recently on the day when he was presented with an honorary doctorate. I mean to return to the issue, but he wanders off into other areas and I forget about it till it's too late. As soon as we wrap up, I start to regret not exploring the issue of why millions of pounds and the captaincy of Manchester United still can't close the gap for Roy between Mayfield, where he grew up, and UCC.

This seems like a big opening to have missed. That refusal of Keane's to evolve and to change from being the kid from Mayfield seems to run to the core of his being. It's what makes him so hungry and so hard. He's answering to his home place all the time. Trying to retain it as one last spot he can feel comfortable in. It's what makes him despise all those around him who have settled for life in the comfort zone without first mining their talent and energy till there's nothing left.

That's my theory anyway.

There are several million theories as to what makes Roy Keane tick. Mine is no more valid than anyone else's, and one thing is for certain, once you produce a theory for Roy and attempt to place it like a rose in his buttonhole, he rejects it instinctively.

Today, though, Roy talks of his life in football and how, by choice, he has few friends in the game. For me, the best parts, the key parts, of the interview are when he speaks about his life after football, about the notion that, after a long while away from the game, he'd just be another face on the street, he'd be able to take his kids on holidays. 'Australia,' he says, and there's something poignant about it.

You can tell he's been thinking about these things. You can tell, when you look into his face, that he's paid a big price for being Keano, the mythical figure who grew out of Roy Keane from Mayfield.

Most of all, the interview seems to me to be a plain attempt to explain himself and what bothers him. He explains carefully again and again that it's not that he's come down on high from Manchester United expecting the world to smell of fresh paint and newly laid carpet everywhere he goes, it's just that he wants success so much, he needs other people around him to want it just as much. It's the shrugging of the shoulders, the laughing it off, that kills him.

I suspect, for the first time, that he's the only man in Saipan who truly believes that Ireland could win the World Cup if things were done properly and well.

We speak for an hour. It's not a bad interview and I am relieved that he has had no problem speaking about what has gone on here this week. My dread was that everything would be up for discussion except that. Apart from his useful critique of Saipan (a key departure from the official version), we've spoken about football and, generally, Roy has continued to draw upon the theme of all his interviews since the beginning of this World Cup campaign, when he stood outside the Amsterdam Arena and fumed that the draw we had just earned wasn't good enough, wasn't worthy of celebration. He raged then that people could be so easily pleased. That has been his theme song as he dragged the team through the campaign.

On the way downstairs, he's in good humour though. I'm working with Niall Quinn on his autobiography and Roy asks if we'll get much work done here or if I'll have to go to Calcutta to do interviews afterwards.

'You're some bollox,' I say to him, laughing as we get into the lift.

'Straight to hell is it?' he says and pushes the elevator button to take us down.

When we reach the lobby, Paul is waiting there. Roy excuses himself for a moment and nips to the toilet. When he comes back he asks myself and Paul if we wouldn't mind leaving out any negative comments he has made about Mick McCarthy in the course of the interviews.

'We've three weeks together and it's the World Cup,' he says. 'I have to respect that.'

Roy asks me if he can see my piece before it goes into the paper. I tell him that we can't do that sort of thing.

'Yeah sorry,' he says. 'Listen I'll leave it all up to you. Use whatever.'

I gather he's already asked Paul about this earlier. It's not a problem leaving Mick out. I don't belong to the school of thought that says that once somebody says something in an interview situation, it's not retrievable, that they can't clarify or change their mind about saying it or that it can be printed without context.

All that Roy has said to me about Mick is that he feels that the manager should take responsibility for the mess here about training grounds and training gear. Mick says he was let down by people. Roy feels that's not good enough. Roy's sense of disappointment is clear enough though throughout the piece without mentioning Mick.

Roy vanishes in the direction of the hotel gym. Paul's face is dark and he has a cut off me immediately. He's annoyed that I knocked on the door of 311 at 4 p.m.

'Bad form,' he says, 'you shouldn't have done it.'

In one way, I know he's right and if it had been Jason McAteer or Richard Dunne or any other player in there with Paul, I'd have stood outside and waited. But this was Keane in the week when he threatened to leave the Irish World Cup camp. No risks.

'Well, sorry about that,' I say to Paul. I'm not entirely sorry but not entirely in the right. Not quite eager to argue over it either. And we leave with sourness between us.

It's early morning at home and it will be an hour or two before there's anyone in the office even. I begin transcribing the interview word for word on the laptop. I always do this. It gives me a chance to listen to the whole conversation again and it prompts memories of what the mood and tone was like.

I realize immediately that I'm going to have to write the piece as a straight question-and-answer session as it comes off the tape. There's too much that I don't want to leave out, and the paper won't have enough space for the wordy paragraphs of description and setup that go in between.

I go and get something to eat and when I come back I call Malachy.

'How'd it go?'

'Fine.'

'Anything sensational?'

'No, not really.'

'Good enough though?'

'Yeah, you know Keane, he's always good.'

'So we'll run it big on Saturday, or is it strong enough to go tomorrow? It has more news value while they are still in Saipan.'

We discuss this for about a minute. Mal suspects that Paul might scoop us by running his piece in the *Irish Independent* tomorrow morning rather than hold it for his own *Sunday Independent* slot. I doubt it, but there's a certain appeal in getting the piece out of the way tonight.

We agree that I'll send over the question-and-answer session in a few hours when it's transcribed and then we'll make a final decision on when to run it.

I've already decided not to write the piece as a feature with colour and comment grouting the cracks between quotes. It'll be straight questions and answers. Verbatim.

It's about two in the morning in Saipan when I finish work. I send the piece across to Dublin and Mal gets back after a while to say that, yeah, we'll run with the piece in the morning.

It's getting on for 4 a.m. by the time the subeditors are finished with the piece and I'm released to go to sleep. By then, though, I've decided I'd better stay awake for a while and call Roy early in the morning just to tell him the piece is running on Thursday at home and not on Saturday. As soon as it appears, the other lads will be under pressure to ask him questions.

I go for a long walk on the beach and, at about 6.30 a.m., I call Roy in his room just to tell him.

'Sorry, did I wake you?'

'Yeah.'

'Ah, sure, you had to get up to answer the phone anyway.'

Little laugh.

'Listen, I thought I'd tell you that the piece is running today instead of Saturday. In case you were taken by surprise.'

'It's gone, is it?' he says.

'Yeah, 'fraid so.'

'Any chance that I could have a look at it,' he says, 'just so I can be ready for questions?'

'OK.'

I explain to him that the editions of the paper have gone now and there's no changing anything.

'Ah, yeah,' he says, 'no problem.'

We meet at 8 a.m. in the lobby of the Hyatt. I switch on the laptop and hand it over to him. He reads and reads and reads. His face dark all the while. Unreadable. Jesus.

'This is like bringing your homework in.'

'Ah no, don't worry,' he says

When he finishes, he gets up, hands the laptop back and says, 'That's grand, thanks Tom.'

Could have been worse.

He shakes my hand. Then he heads for some breakfast.

The team train at 10 a.m. without incident. Roy seems to be in fine form.

When we get back from training, I'm tired but I have work to do. On the way to the team hotel, I notice Roy being interviewed in the hotel grounds by Gabriel Egan from RTÉ. I hang around like a punter straining my neck to hear what's being said. It must be annoying for Gabriel, but I don't want everything that's in *The Irish Times* in the morning to be on RTÉ Radio too.

Roy finishes and gives me a quick wink and heads off to lunch. After lunch, I run into him again. He's been walking on the beach, one of those solitary walks he's made a habit of this week. We talk briefly. I wonder if the rest of the lads in the media hotel have been on to him yet with questions.

'Any shit?' I say.

'About what?' he asks.

'Anyone asking about the interview?'

'Ah,' he says, 'sure there'll be no shit about that.'

In the afternoon, I work on Niall's book with him. I've asked Niall to mention to Mick McCarthy that the Roy interview has run this morning. Just as a courtesy, so nobody gets ambushed. Niall has passed the message on but, frankly, he himself is not that interested in the piece.

'Has he had a go?' he says.

'Ah not really,' I say.

And that's it.

This first session with Niall is a disaster. Our first interview and, because I've been up all night working, I'm just a beaten docket. After about half an hour, I begin to feel sleepy. After perhaps an hour, Niall has found his rhythm and is telling stories about his early days in London. This is fertile ground in terms of how we want to define him in the book, but sadly, my eyelids weigh about a ton apiece now. I keep staring at him blankly, hoping that if I transfix him with my dopey gaze, my eyes will somehow stay open. I excuse myself a couple of times and go to the bathroom to put my head under the cold tap.

Poor Niall. He has an incredible memory for detail and every yarn he's giving me is good. It's a pleasure listening to him, unfortunately, it's also a lullaby. After maybe an hour-and-a-half, I am gone. My head is about to sink into my chest. I jump up suddenly and announce to Niall that we're done. That I should now do some sifting though these stories and get back to him with questions.

He looks baffled, but takes my word for it. I scurry off. My bed is calling me.

I run into Paul on the balcony corridor that links our rooms. 'I heard you ran a bit of the interview today,' he says. He looks depressed.

This is making his life difficult.

'We ran the whole thing,' I tell him.

'The whole thing,' he says. He looks shocked.

I invite him to the room so he can take a look at the piece on my laptop before he writes any more of his. I can hardly stand up now for want of sleep. Paul reads through the piece with a face darker than Roy Keane's this morning. I can tell he's appalled by me and my satanic deeds.

He puts the laptop down.

'Excuse me while I go and puke,' Paul says and walks straight out.

We've been friends for a long time and I want to go after him and talk. But the bed is there. I have a longer standing relationship with sleep. I haven't seen a bed for a while, so I lie down and drift away.

I'm dozing, and have been for an hour or so, when I become aware that the phone has been ringing incessantly. I smile to myself. Always happens when you interview Roy Keane. Everybody wants you on their radio show, their TV talk-in, whatever. Well, too bad. I unplug the phone and roll over.

Then within a minute there is knocking on the door. The hotel messenger, I presume, as I fumble towards the exit and fiddle with the locks. He must have a wad of messages, faxed interview requests.

Wrong. Instead it's the lads. A posse of them. A press conference has been called in the team hotel. Starting at 7.30 p.m. in the little Chinese restaurant, on the far side as you go in through the lobby.

'What's that all about then?' I ask.

'Keane's being sent home.'

Even as they speak the words, the lads are disappearing down the corridor, rousing other sleepers and miscreants.

Fuck! For a second I think I'm going to faint. I've no appetite for controversy. Fuck! Shit! Jesus!

First thought. This could be ugly. This could be my fault somehow.

Second thought. Hope that the kids don't pick up any negative vibes at school. Our eldest caught a little flack through the Michelle Smith controversy.

Roy Keane. Well he's a different dimension to Michelle. This will be big, big, big.

I grab my recorder and head after the lads. The lobby of the Hyatt is alive. Players are milling around in a state of shock. Hacks are whispering and conjecturing. The staff who look after the team are buzzing everywhere like sheepdogs with nowt to do.

'Well look what you've gone and done now,' says Jason McAteer with a big grin on his face. Jason would be there: some of the other players call him Taggart because he's always first on the scene at a time like this.

'Keep away. For the love of Jesus keep away,' says Gary Kelly making a cross with his two index fingers.

For a minute or two, I think that Roy Keane has been sent home specifically for doing the interview. This is sure going to make it hard to get other interviews. Whatever has gone on, the players are clearly reeling but getting over it all with humour. You can't grieve forever.

We file into the little Chinese restaurant. You can tell it's serious, none of the sponsors have their banners up behind the head table. The press conference is tense and odd. At the top of the room are Alan Kelly, Niall Quinn, Mick McCarthy, Milo Corcoran, Steve Staunton and Brendan McKenna. We get the news that we already know.

Roy Keane has attended a meeting.

Roy Keane has been asked about the interview in this morning's *Irish Times*.

Roy Keane has nuked the room.

Roy Keane has been asked to leave the building.

Some Roy Keane confusion here. Out in the lobby, the word was that Roy Keane stormed out. In here, Roy Keane was asked to leave. One thing is evident though, from now on, every sentence we write will contain the words Roy Keane.

The questioning is somewhat better this time. For the most part, we are brisk and to the point.

From Mick McCarthy tonight there is none of the usual snideness toward the media. These two Roy Keane press conferences have been promptly called, willingly given and well articulated. See, Mick does understand the function of the media as an intermediary after all. Roy should leave the building more often.

Everybody on the top table, except Brendan McKenna, speaks. The news is sinking in slowly. Roy Keane is out of the World Cup. Gone. Our best player. Our talisman. Our captain. It's a story so big as to be indigestible. One thought keeps recurring. I want to be back in bed, fast asleep.

Johnny Fallon is leaning against the reception desk. Johnny is the kitman for the team, but he's more than that. He's a friend and a valve. It's odd that the FAI hasn't thought to appoint somebody officially in this role, a sports psychologist who might listen to players and facilitate them. Anyway Johnny is quite close to Roy and, tonight, he looks pale. He echoes what several players have said. Never heard anything like it, but I can tell he's hurting too. There's not much about Johnny that likes confrontation and there's a big part of him that cares for Roy and knows what he's going through.

Emmet and I speak to Mal from a phone at reception. This is what Malachy is really good at, organizing people when there's a breaking news story. Almost always, we beat everyone else in these circumstances. He gives us his initial copy order. We're going with a blow-by-blow, word-for-word press conference transcript. A 2,000-word think piece full of thoughtfulness from, well, me, then a countdown chronology from me, a daft idea that I suggested myself believing that I would easily be able to fill in the blanks of Roy's last day with the squad. Emmet is writing page one and an inside piece. All sorts of other ideas are floating about in the office back home. A piece by a shrink. Pieces by various managers in other disciplines on how to handle a troubled genius.

We'll talk later.

Still, all I want to do is sleep. I count the nights since I came home from the European Cup Final a week ago. No sleep on Thursday, Friday, Sunday, or Wednesday. None tonight. I want some sort of adrenalin rush to kick in, but I'm too depressed.

I speak briefly to Mick McCarthy in the lobby.

'Well Mick. Sorry for bringing this down on your head.'

'Not you, Tom. It was what was said in the meeting. What Roy said.'

Mick seems calm and clear.

We get back to the sixth floor of the Dai Ichi and we work and work. At one point, I step out on the sixth floor balcony for some air. It's getting bright. Paul Hyland of the *Herald* is looking out at the morning smoking a cigarette.

'Harpo,' I say to him, 'I'm dead.'

'Jaysus,' says Paul. 'A World Cup, Roy Keane gone. We'll never work on another story like this. You've got to stay awake for it.'

I take his point.

Friday, 24th May – morning

Night has merged with day. All along the sixth floor of the Dai Ichi hotel, the doors have been open all night. Laptops humming, phone connections buzzing, offices called.

The snappers are on hot coals. They can't leave the island till Roy leaves, every newspaper in the world wants the picture of Roy

Keane carrying his own bags, getting ready for the seventeen-hour journey back across the world.

For my friend Dave Maher of Sportsfile, this is a delicate thing. Some time ago, Keane's mother contacted him, having noticed some exceptional photos Dave had taken of her son. She wondered if she might have prints of same. Dave, ever willing to oblige, ran off a sheaf of his best Roy studies and, the next time the team were in town, had them delivered to Roy's room. Unfortunately, Dave looks like, very like, the image of in fact, another photographer with whom Roy has had the odd run-in.

Roy took receipt of the photos for his mother and Dave was pointed out as having been the photographer who sent them to his room. A switch in Roy's head flipped. He flew into one of his Roy rages, genuinely mistaking Dave for the tabloid snapper. Dave was told if he ever came near Roy or any of his family ever again, etc., etc.

Several players went to Keane on Dave's behalf to explain the mistake he'd made, but he refused to accept it. Now, here in Saipan, Dave has not only been looking forward to the arrival of his tabloid doppelganger ('When Roy sees how alike we look well . . .') but now he is being asked to stay behind on a little island to get close-up shots of Roy on the worst day of the footballer's life.

Staying behind is a costly business. This morning, I'm glad the paper is broke. Myself and Emmet will be on the Continental Airlines flight with the rest of the party. Door-stepping Roy Keane in the Hyatt seems like the shortest straw.

Word is that Roy will be leaving the island not long after us. He'll want to get out before the tabloid cavalry arrives on the next flight from London. The snappers and scribblers left behind have the unenviable task of hanging around Saipan Airport to photograph Roy in his misery.

At just after 3 a.m. this morning, the snappers returned en masse to the sixth floor of the Dai Ichi. This is high-stakes stuff if you are a photographer. They had been to the airport, they had staked out the hotel. The porter in the Hyatt had been tipped handsomely in exchange for calling the sixth floor of the Dai Ichi if Roy Keane checks out.

When the lads get back to our floor, they are a little giddy. They have just been at the desk of the Hyatt making sure that Roy is still in his room. While the football world is in a state of apoplexy about Roy Keane and what he's thinking in there behind the door to Room 760, the woman behind the reception desk needs to have Keane's name spelt out for her so she can check the computer. 'Yes, he's still here.' At that moment, the phone at reception rings.

'Yes, Mr Keane,' says the receptionist and points to the phone. It's him! Keane has requested that no calls be put through to his room. He's calling now to change the orders. He asks for all calls to be put through to his room from now on. Then the receptionist says, 'And there are some people here to see you, Mr Keane.'

And the poor snappers have gone into a frenetic mime shaking their heads violently, stepping away from the desk as if walking on a minefield, mouthing the words, 'No, no, no.'

'Sorry, Mr Keane they don't want to see you anymore,' says the receptionist.

Nobody knows you when you're down and out, eh Roy?

There are hazy rumours flying everywhere about Roy's possible mode of escape. Will Manchester United send their jet? The airport is contacted. No charters or private planes due except the one the team are leaving on. There's a flight to Tokyo at 5 p.m., but will Keane want to hang around alone all day long while being door-stepped by some snappers and scribblers, none of whom, it is noted, has an especially good relationship with him? There's a rumour about a boat to Guam but it's hard to see Roy Keane standing on any deck that isn't burning right now.

The best available rumour seems to be that he might be on a scheduled flight for Osaka leaving Saipan at 8.20 a.m. We might all meet at the airport!

Myself, I finish work at 5 a.m. and begin packing for our 7 a.m. exit. I'd prefer to stay and try to grab a word with Keane, but the cost is prohibitive for our newly pampered employers.

At 6.45 a.m., I drag my bags downstairs and load them on the little bus that will take us to the airport, fully rested and recreated after our five days lazing in paradise.

There's some hilarity on the bus. Frasier, from Sky TV, has been getting under the lads' skin since he joined the trip. He's a nice enough guy but, perhaps, overly eager to integrate into what are hardened cliques. Every time he sees a group of Irish journalists, he seems to say, 'Alright lads, having a bevvie?'

The lads who quite often, believe it or not, aren't having a bevvie, were amused at first, but are now beginning to feel patronized.

Anyway, Frasier, presumably under orders left Saipan yesterday afternoon, apparently heading for Tokyo to get a headstart on things there. We are immensely consoled. Some of us have done good work, some of us have done bad work, but at least we were here when the biggest story of our careers broke.

Phew! There but for the grace of god etc., etc. . . . .

Players and journalists keep a respectful distance from each other in the tacky little souvenir shop at the airport. I bump into Steve Staunton who rolls his eyes heavenwards. I try easing his pain with a joke.

'Heard about my new service, Stan?'

'Nah, what is it?'

'Quick interview with me and I guarantee to get you home within twenty-four hours.'

He walks on quickly.

Paul and I have a cup of coffee in the waiting area, the training ground blow-up behind us.

Friday, 24th May – afternoon

Three-and-a-half hours of plane journey. For some reason, right at the start, the pilot decides it would be a nice idea if we circled over Saipan once or twice so we can all get a good look at where we have been. There is an excruciating silence. We press our noses to the windows and nobody notices the blue of the sea or the golden beaches. We're looking for the Hyatt. Roy Keane, our greatest player and greatest hope, is in his room there. Alone. His team have left the island without anyone so much as knocking on his door this morning.

Now we're having a pleasure cruise a few thousand feet above his head.

We sleep then. All the way to mainland Japan.

One hour of coach journey to the rural territory of the hotel in Izumo, where we will be staying for a week. Ray Treacy is at the microphone again. He is asking us to look at the gardens of the homes we're passing. Largely we are sleeping, but Ray is keen on this educational part of the trip.

'Out the back you'll see little monuments. Japanese families like to bury their dead in their own gardens.'

Silence on the bus.

A minute later we pass a regular-sized graveyard, full of memorials to the dead.

'What's that Ray? The Kennedy compound?'

Ray gives up.

Our hotel is small and modest and close to the little railway station. A party demonstrating chado, which means 'the way of tea', has been organized for us in the lobby by the local ladies. It is a tea party. We have to write. We have to file. Then, hopefully, we can find somewhere that devotes itself to the way of Guinness. We slope past the polite chado ladies and into the lifts. Not today, thanks.

There is a reception for the team at something called the Izumo Dome in an hour or two. Unless they are being presented with a surprise Keano, we are not interested. We go to our rooms and slam the doors shut. Then we open them again. The rooms are too small to be in with the doors shut. Dinky is the most generous description anybody can come up with. The pillows appear to be stuffed with marbles. And does anybody know how to file from these phones?

Later, there is time to explore. At the shops near the railway at Izumo there is a little home-made shrine dedicated to the pending World Cup and its spangling stars. One corner is dedicated to the team, who will be staying and preparing locally. Ireland and Mr Roy Keane. And there he is, with a Buddha's smile and a competitor's clench, appearing just as a head-and-shoulders shot, the small grin playing on his lips, coals burning in the eyes as usual. The man they voted off the island.

He dominates the shrine just like he will dominate the rest of Ireland's World Cup. We know now that Roy Keane will continue to be the dominant figure in Irish soccer until such time as he is either reinstated to the national team or retires. Until then, no Irish result will be complete without a post-mortem dealing with what might have been if Roy had played.

We get food locally and the unreality of our situation begins to sink in. Late last night, some of the players had dropped by Keane's room to say goodbye to him. For some of them, he has been a friend, somebody they drank with in lighter days and a guy whose rarely revealed warmth and humour could often be endearing.

Now they were leaving him behind on the edge of a tournament in which they had hoped to rely on him. The players we've spoken to found Keane calm and unrepentant and in oddly good form. 'Like a fella on death row, talking about the good breakfast you get.' And those dispatches from inside the room have only served to make the situation all the more bizarre. Could somebody of influence not have knocked on the door and talked reasonably?

Here we are in Izumo. This is where Keane's World Cup should really be starting. All night we talk about nothing else, teasing it out, playing around with it. Who is to bless and who is to blame.

One quote comes back to us from the Izumo Dome reception. Mick McCarthy on Roy Keane: 'That's history, that part of the trip I'm not going to discuss, anybody's opinion of it, criticism of it, analysis of it. I'm moving on. What I'm prepared to discuss from today onwards is the twenty-two players that I have got with me.'

Please Mick. Call my office and tell them that. Tell them it's all history.

Saturday, 25th May

Today, the team play Hiroshima. The Japanese have built a dinky little stadium specifically for the occasion of this harmless friendly. We are astonished. They think nothing of it. 'In future,' they say, 'we'll play practice games here.'

It's a lovely, easy day. No deadlines unless you work for a Sunday paper. Just sunshine and a languid game of football, in the course of which, Jason McAteer almost gets his leg removed by a Hiroshima player, a Cameroonian import called Bilong.

Afterwards, poor old Bilong is standing outside the dressing room holding his boots in a little bag in his hand.

Ian Harte comes out.

'Sorry,' says Bilong.

'Sorry,' says Hartey, 'wrong guy.'

'Oh,' says Bilong. 'You all look the same.'

Mick McCarthy allows no room for an apology. Several players tell the distressed Bilong to fuck off. It seems ungracious, but I suppose Jason McAteer's World Cup could have ended.

At the post-match press conference, there is a Japanese question that contains the words 'Roy Keane' in it. Mick doesn't allow a translation. He cuts in. No Roy Keane questions.

In a sort of Stalinist way, we are to wipe Roy Keane from history.

Sunday, 26th May

We've only been away for eleven days, but it seems like a lifetime.

It's lovely here in Izumo, tranquil in a way that I never expected of Japan, serene in a manner that seemed impossible while we lived under the volcano last week. This is rural Japan. Weather-beaten faces and a rural town veined by narrow aqueducts that flow to the plentiful paddy fields, those character-giving flooded rectangles that creep right up to the street corners downtown. Not a napkin's worth of land is wasted anywhere.

What must these people make of us?

Back home, the country is in turmoil. The Taoiseach is straining at his leash, eager to intervene in the Keane business. Arguments rage all day on radio and TV. The media are all over Keane's house like moths on a light.

We're trying to cover the story and we're trying to get ready to cover a World Cup and we're in the one place where nobody will talk about Roy Keane.

Emmet has gone to Kobe to watch Cameroon play England. This means just me on the team watch today. Training is at 9.30 a.m. at what transpires to be the rather splendid Izumo Dome, a wonderful half-moon that rises above the paddy fields and stands resplendent against the dark mountains. It's the biggest wooden structure in Japan, apparently.

It's non-eventful stuff. The highlight is watching Shay Given, who spends almost an hour saving shots of all manner and description from Packie Bonner. You look at Shay sometimes and think if you threw a handful of rice at him, not a grain would get past. When he is finished, he wanders up the field and gets a football and brings it back to the goal he has been working in. He places it on the penalty spot and then takes a penalty into the empty goal, raising his arm in mock triumph as the net ripples. And when he raises his arm, the two or three hundred Japanese who have been watching him burst into applause and cheering and Shay comes off with a big mischievous grin.

Otherwise, we take note of the absentees and grab a quote regarding same from Brendan McKenna, the FAI's press secretary. Then we mill around and swap rumours about Roy Keane.

I wander into the press centre and bang out a Monday column on how Roy really opened up a deep wound when he, in his now famous Thursday rant, questioned Mick McCarthy's Irishness. It's now become a matter of gospel fact that Keane called Mick McCarthy an 'English cunt'.

It's not a bad topic because Englishness is something that's never spoken of on these trips. The playing squad has plenty of English accents in it. Ditto the press party. We all rub along well together and nobody ever seeks to open up the issue. We never talk politics. Some of the English journalists refer to the team as if they were Irish themselves.

Yet when it was reported that Roy had questioned Mick's Irishness, a strange doublethink took place in every Irish conversation. We were appalled that such a thing had happened, that a man so intrinsically associated with Ireland as Mick McCarthy could have been questioned in such a way, but we were never comfortable discussing the issue with English colleagues. We kept away from it.

At the same time, almost every conversation had a moment in which one party sought to explain McCarthy's intransigence on the Keane issue. 'He's from Barnsley,' we'd say. 'He's a Yorkshireman.'

And somehow, until now, Mick has managed to maintain that duality. Proud of Yorkshire. Proud of Ireland. He overrode the racial divide in a unique way. That's how it should be, but others on the team aren't as confident, or as established in their identity, and they must be wondering if the view expressed by Roy was one that others in the team held privately as well. Eleven of the squad speak with English accents after all.

As a Monday morning topic, I am quite pleased with this. I've never thought of this stuff before, how delicate it is. How it needs to be unspoken. Thanks Roy.

I have lunch in a café beside the training ground, somehow managing to end up with fried chicken for the fourth meal in a row since coming here. It's always the same. There's a long gap between the time of us adventurously ordering some local delicacy and the time when the food actually joins us at the table. Much waiterly conferencing. Then some smiling and bowing.

And – ta da! – fried chicken.

Then I wander up to the team hotel to do some work with Niall on his book. I owe him a wide-awake session.

I tell him what I have been writing about and he stuns me by telling me that Keane never questioned anybody's Englishness. He questioned just about everything else and spread the insults like a slurry spreader, but the 'English cunt' jibe so faithfully reported elsewhere? Never happened.

Shit. Niall and I spend the afternoon taping more reminiscences about his London days. His impression of me has sunk even lower. The recording we made last Thursday on Saipan has for some reason not come out. I have three hours of blank disc.

Now, though, my mind is on the column, and I can't wait to get back and change everything. 'McCarthy Not In Cunt Slur Shock'!

I finish three hours' work with Niall and say a quick goodbye and virtually run across town back to the media hotel. First up, I rewrite the entire 'Locker Room' column and send it with the strap line 'Urgent Revision' to the desk. Phew!

Meanwhile, there are quiet rumours gathering that a deal is being brokered to get Roy back out to Japan. I have spoken to Niall about it and he has agreed that, if I ring him after 10 p.m. Japanese time, he'll fill me in.

I hold the rest of my work till then in case there is a major development. Unfortunately, Mick has come back from watching England play Cameroon in Kobe with his attitude hardened. Lots of other coaches he met there told him they'd have done the same. Earlier that day, Niall and Steve Staunton had spoken to Mick about reconciliation. Now Mick is feeling bolshie again. All diplomacy attempts are put off for twenty-four hours.

I file a training and injuries piece and report to Mal that nothing happened at the players' 5 p.m. press conference. He says that's good because he's pressed for space in the morning anyway.

Good? It's very good. Clean forgot to go to the players' 5 p.m. press conference.

Montueswednesday, 27th to 29th May – the longest day in the history of the world

Monday. New start. New week. Bring on the tranquillity.

For most of the day, it looks as if normality is reasserting itself. We go to training, work quietly in the press centre. Yes. It looks as if we'll be doing straightforward, training-ground and injury-news pieces.

Then, late in the afternoon, word seeps out that Roy Keane will be doing a TV interview tonight. I look ruefully at my bed. I won't be getting my head down on the bag of marbles that is the pillow tonight.

Bad news comes in convoys, of course. I get a look at the online edition of the paper. My rewrite of the Monday column hasn't been included, which makes me look like something of a fool.

An internal enquiry is launched. Baffling stuff. I'm told that the rewrite arrived in the office at around 7 p.m. and, by the time it got there, it was labelled, for some reason, 'Family Sausage'. There is no explanation for how this could have happened unless, of course, I dozed off and named the new piece after some long lost and much loved piece of domestic victual. Could be?

The bizarre thing is that nobody in the paper bothered to open the 'Family Sausage' file. We only have two people at the World Cup, where the biggest Irish sports story in years has been breaking and one of them files a story that, for some reason, is called 'Family Sausage'. The name of the author is clearly marked. It's a late-breaking, family-sausage story from the World Cup! You would think that somebody, out of curiosity if nothing else, would have opened the file and have a peek inside to see what's sizzling. But it sat there in the queue for hours and nobody bothered to open it up and see what 'Family Sausage' was all about.

More bad news. Mick McCarthy, who has refused to speak about Keane since last Thursday, has penned a column in the *Daily Mail* speaking all about Keane. Both Keane and McCarthy appear to be cashing in. Keane had a big piece in yesterday's *Mail on Sunday* for which he is rumoured to have received £140,000.

I'm in no mood for work. No mood for speaking with the office at all. It's unavoidable though. We're going to be in contact all night.

I wander down the hallway to buy some more of the little cards that enable us to file. Oddest thing. You buy a card, stick it into a little box on top of the TV, and it gives you an outside line on the phone and pornography on the television.

At a few minutes before 11 p.m., Emmet and myself finish up with the day's normal work and scoot to the Italian restaurant around the corner for some food to get us through the night. We've been more than adventurous about getting out around the town and eating the local cuisine. We've dined with our shoes off practically every night since we got here, but regardless of what we order, the locals keep giving us fried chicken. We've retreated to the Italian.

The plan for the evening is somewhat odd. Mal will have two people back in the office transcribing the Keane interview off the television. They will e-mail it to us. We will write pieces about it and then get a response from the powers that be.

We are to stay on high alert. Rumour has it that Keane is apologizing, or has apologized. There is a plane waiting to whisk him back to Japan. He could be joining us for breakfast.

On that basis, the saga could be ending tonight. We prepare some perspective pieces, some blow-by-blow, day-by-day pieces, and put down some thoughts on how it has affected our World Cup prospects.

Suddenly, it's the middle of the night. Keane is speaking to the nation. We the media are about to eat ourselves. A crowd of us gather in the bedroom of Mark Gallagher from the *Examiner*. It is rumoured that Mark will have the entire Keane apparition available on his laptop. We stand and wait. Mark is having no luck.

There are maybe fifteen or sixteen of us in his room plus a camera crew filming us all and our reactions. While Mark struggles with his obdurate laptop, Neil O'Riordan of the *Sun* phones his mother in Dublin. She holds her phone up to her TV set. We hold our tape recorders up to Neil's mobile phone.

This is surely the high point of the media circus. Roy Keane in Manchester giving an interview to an overwrought reporter that goes out on RTÉ like one of those grave addresses that cause the peasants to lay their scythes down in the fields and walk slowly towards the radio. This all comes to us via a television set in Dublin and via a telephone. We record it all under the eyes of a TV crew. We then go to write about it all in pieces that we send back to Ireland. And the TV crew show the footage of just how it was done.

And Monday night becomes Tuesday morning.

We work till dawn on this story of Keane's television appearance. We unravel and interpret. People run from room to room disclosing other titbits about what he said, how he looked, how people at home are reacting.

And at about 6.30 a.m., when we are finished, we realize that there is still time to get the FAI reaction. We gather in our hotel lobby and travel en masse across Izumo, a great raggle-taggle procession of bleary hacks. The locals, already confused by our ways, gaze at us with renewed suspicion.

At about 6.45 a.m., we are outside the Royal Hotel attempting to squeeze Mick McCarthy's response into the same news cycle as the Roy Show. Entrance to the hotel is politely barred. Finally, the FAI press officer, Mr Brendan McKenna, is woken by a member of hotel staff. We all love Brendan. He is the nicest man on the planet, but he's not who we want right now.

Brendan emerges with sleep in his eyes. He confesses that he knows nothing whatsoever about any Roy Keane TV interview. This is too bizarre for words. We fill him in, catch him up on the news and send him back into the hotel to get Mick McCarthy.

It's important now that we have Mick. The general word from home is that even though there has been no specific apology from Roy, he has looked contrite, passionate, hurt, wounded and defiant. People are swinging to his side of the argument in their droves.

Brendan comes back and says that Mick won't be coming down. We are angry now. Tired and angry. Paul Lennon of *The Star*, who represents us all at times like this, is allowed into the hotel and we see him negotiating. Maybe.

Soon Mick McCarthy can be seen in the common area downstairs in the hotel making phone calls and discussing matters with various staff members. He emerges onto the steps. We shuffle towards him and gather around like winos at a brazier.

Mick confirms that he is aware of various aspects of the Keane interview. Otherwise, it's a bad-tempered little session. It starts with the usual disdain for us. 'I haven't seen the interview, I've heard bits of it, of course I have. I've said along that I'm not going to conduct this affair through the media and that's how I stand still. I've not received any phone calls from Roy and the squad's not received any phone calls from Roy and I'm not really gonna conduct my affairs through the media. I know that's difficult for you fellas to understand, but that's the way it is. I know he's been on television and spoken to 3 million people, but he hasn't spoken to me.'

'If he speaks to you, might it change your position?'

'Well it's hypothetical. I can't answer that.'

'You're open to a phone call?'

'Well, I've not switched it off since I've been here. People know where I am. People can get in touch with me.'

'In the *Mail* yesterday, you said sorry would not be good enough?'

'The team is bigger than one person. I think that includes everybody, me as well. The team for me are paramount.'

'For three days you wouldn't speak about this and then it appears in a daily newspaper in England?'

I find myself shouting this at Mick McCarthy. It's been eating at me all night.

'Well it was all similar stuff,' he says. 'There was nothing more than I said already. I don't think it was. I haven't seen it. And if it was, then I certainly didn't intend it to be that way, a lot of it was done prior to it, or straight after it.'

I want to pursue this to the bitter end but there are other questions.

'What does he have to do to get back in the squad?'

'I've not heard from him. I've not heard a word. I know he's been on TV and spoken to 3 million people, there's not been a message to me, not been a call to me, to anyone here. I'm not going to say that . . .'

'Is a sincere apology enough?'

'Has there been one? It's hypothetical. The call needs to come.'

'Has Michael Kennedy spoken to you?'

'No, he hasn't.'

Frustrating?

'This is not what I wanted. There's a lot of talk . . . well I've always done my best, I've always wanted the best. Always, I've taken what I thought were the best decisions as a player and manager. I'm not going to conduct it further through you guys.'

And that's it. We are getting ready to dash back across Izumo when a taxi pulls up. Frasier from Sky emerges. Poor guy. He's shaking his head forlornly, 'I missed it, didn't I?'

And Tuesday morning grows on us.

Peace is just a phone call away. We file like the people who heard Neville Chamberlain must have filed.

We send our papers to bed with the cheering thought that perhaps it will all be over soon. The long, national nightmare is coming to an end. We can get back to living. Roy can get back to playing.

We adjourn for a little breakfast before heading to the Izumo Dome for training. It would be nice to sleep now, but the story is breaking. No sleep. Just coffee.

The team arrives an hour late for their scheduled morning training session and information comes into the press room via drip feed after that. Mick McCarthy won't be doing a post-session press conference as scheduled. Three players, as per the established rota, will give a press conference at 5.30 p.m. It's midmorning now. This is bad news and it's good news. The afternoon can be devoted to sleep.

People are beginning to drift back towards the hotel when word seeps out that the reason the players were late is because they met for forty minutes before coming to the training session. Now, we have to hang around. Now, we have to collar somebody who'll tell us what that was all about.

Seeing as how we are all going nowhere, Brendan McKenna tells us that there will be a statement issued by one of the players following the training session. It sounds as if the player might be wearing a Balaclava and styling himself a member of the Continuity Squad.

When training ends, we watch the players heading towards the bus. We assume that it will be Niall Quinn who will come in and read the statement. We see Niall heading for the bus.

What's going on?

Brendan McKenna, who hours previously had been so far outside the loop that he was unaware that Keane had even given a TV interview, takes the podium in the press room. Nobody can remember Brendan giving a major press conference before. We assume he is about to announce the postponement of the players' press conference that he promised us.

Instead, Brendan runs through the injury news from the squad, the nitty gritty of who trained and who didn't train. He gives the details as regards the timetable for press conferences, or the lack of them, for the remainder of the day. He announces that the team is due to visit a hospital this afternoon. Then he says, almost casually, that he has in his hand a statement from the players and staff following an earlier meeting.

He begins to read: 'Regrettably the manner of Roy's behaviour prior to his departure from Saipan and the comments attributed to him since, have left the staff and the players in no doubt that the interests of the squad are best served without Roy's presence. The players bear no malice towards Roy on a personal level and are looking forward to a successful World Cup campaign with the continued support of our loyal supporters, both home and abroad.'

The seventy-four-word statement is a goodbye note. It withdraws all the goodwill towards Roy Keane that had existed earlier. It's a sensation.

Just a few hours ago, Mick McCarthy had appeared to be making moves towards reconciling with Keane. Now the players have killed the process stone dead. What a U-turn. What does it say about Mick McCarthy's position now?

After the statement, there is a vacuum. No players or management to speak to. Somebody will come at 5 p.m. Has there been a coup? Why did the players not have the guts to come and speak for themselves?

Now the issue seems no longer to be about Roy Keane, but about the viability of Mick McCarthy's job. It's about player power. Mick McCarthy suggested that he was still waiting on a call from Keane, but the squad closed that door and are now deciding on their own composition.

For a few hours throughout Tuesday afternoon, that's how it hangs.

Then, at 5 p.m., Niall Quinn comes to the media centre. His performance is a little overwrought, but so is the day. He gives the best performance yet seen in this press centre. He brings a little dignity, sincerity and emotion to the party. Unfortunately, he can't offer clarity.

He promises that, once we hear Mick McCarthy's press conference later in the evening, when we hear the whole story, then the players' statement and the timing of it will become clear.

'It's best to explain the sequence of events to you to help you understand. At 7.30 this morning, word filtered around that Mick had offered an olive branch to Roy. By breakfast time, thoughts were racing . . .'

He details his own efforts to bring players around to the idea of

Roy coming back. He gives an account of what the team learned of Roy's interview. He speaks obliquely of the team meeting this morning.

'I think after you speak to Mick, you'll understand that we had no alternative,' Niall says with regard to the statement.

'Did he make it clear that it was either Roy Keane or himself?' we ask.

'I think it's really up to Mick to give you the details,' said Niall, 'but you wouldn't be too far away.'

Niall leaves by one entrance. I slip out another entrance hoping to nab him and find out what's going on. I see him hop, all alone, into a taxi and speed off.

At 8 p.m., Mick McCarthy comes to the press centre. There is a feeling among us now that he might resign. We'll be doing McCarthy Era pieces all night now. Mick's press conference, though, ended in just eleven minutes of farce.

'Is that right?' he says tersely when told of Niall's words about the meeting this morning and what the players perceived as a threat to resign. 'Well, I didn't give them an ultimatum, nor a recommendation. If the players wanted the situation reversed, I would go with them. I would back them.'

So a sharp difference in the players' version of events and the manager's.

But nothing seemed right with the manager. McCarthy is accompanied by Brendan Menton, General Secretary of the FAI. Brendan is a bright and peaceable man. He wants things here to be short and sweet. Mick McCarthy wants to explain a few things. As Mick makes to answer a question, Brendan cuts across him, 'We are not interested in exacerbating this situation.'

McCarthy: 'I think there's some issues to be answered, of course, Brendan.'

Menton: 'I think this is not the time.'

McCarthy: '*No*?'

Menton: 'I think the important thing is preparation for this game.'

The air in the room is thick with sour feelings and bad temper now.

'Mick, did you accuse Roy of feigning injury? Did that start it?'

'No. He lost his temper from the first second I spoke.'

'He lost his temper?'

Brendan Menton intervenes again, 'The association doesn't want to revisit this, the timing of it, resurrecting itself. I think Mick has said what he has to say.'

'I think the question was in terms of picking and choosing games actually,' continues Mick McCarthy frankly, 'but it was about friendly games and playing in friendlies. He said, "No I don't play in them anymore. They are for other people." Yes, the Iran game was mentioned in terms of picking and choosing games. I'm not going to go down that line.'

And Brendan Menton makes one final intervention. There is shouting now. I am aware of people shouting to my left but I can't make out what they are saying. That's because I'm shouting at Brendan. I'm on about the *Daily Mail* column again, how we respected the manager's wish not to talk about Roy Keane for days on end and he goes and flogs the story to the *Mail*.

Brendan closes the press conference down and virtually leads Mick by the ear away from the scene. We are left with a gaping disparity between the manager's version of events, as to what happened in the team hotel this morning, and the team's version of events. We have an admission that Keane's commitment had been questioned at one stage on that night in Saipan. We had no chance to ask Mick the vital question. Does *he*, in his heart of hearts, want Roy Keane back?

Conclusions? That what Mick McCarthy feels about Roy Keane will not be allowed by the FAI to interfere with attempts to get Roy back in harness. Conclusions? It's bigger than Mick or his job now. Conclusions? The FAI will have the smart-boy-wanted signs in the window by the end of July. People head back to the hotel for another marathon session of writing and telephone calling.

We are lost in words and tiredness when Roy Keane releases a statement at about 4.40 a.m. our time on Wednesday morning. Final efforts to retrieve something worthwhile from his relationship with the team and McCarthy have failed.

It's a short and dignified statement. 'No purpose served . . . wish the best . . . etc., etc.' Why he couldn't have sat on it for twelve hours is a mystery to me.

Now, everything has to be rewritten in this context. It's over. Rewrite with finality. At about 6 a.m., my eyes are saying goodbye to their sockets. I am cutting and pasting and rejigging and rewriting four pieces at once. I am falling asleep in the chair. Three thousand eight hundred words of cut and paste are ready to go. Then I can lie down. Fall asleep properly. I'm online. I go to transfer everything and send it.

But I lose the lot. Somehow I lose the whole fucking lot.

In a panic, I start pressing buttons. Worst thing I can do.

The phone is ringing now. There's a knock on the door too.

I pick up the phone.

It's Mary.

'Hi.'

I am about to cry.

'I've lost everything.'

'What?' she says, 'I can't hear you.'

'*I SAID THAT I HAVE FUCKING LOST EVERYFUCK-INGTHING.*' I am screaming down the phone.

'Oh,' she says, 'well, I'll talk to you later.'

Emmet has just come in the door. He retreats.

I ring *The Irish Times* systems people, although I know there is nothing they can do. I've screwed things up with my panicked button-pushing. We waste a few minutes jumping through the hoops and then they pronounce my pieces officially dead. I start again, suddenly wide awake, as if my veins had nothing but black coffee running in them.

Another dawn. The thrill is gone. Roy is gone. All hope of any enjoyment from this World Cup is gone too. From today we're just picking up the pieces.

Thursday, 30th May

This is epic day number what??? Where are we? What happened to the football?

Why do I feel so tired? Is this my life?

Mal said to Emmet on the phone some time last night that he thinks we've been missing the boat a bit on injury news from Izumo.

Injury news! Emmet and I are both pissed off for the day. Injury news!

Again, it's the old rule of bastardliness. The bastards in the office get more bastardly with every bastarding mile further away from them you get.

We decide to take some time off. If the team all break their legs this morning, so be it. We're in an injury-news blackout. We head up to Izumo's principal attraction, its Shinto shrine at Izumo Taisha.

In Japan, October is called *kannazuki*, or the 'month with no gods', because all the gods are said to gather here in Izumo Taisha until Hallowe'en when they get back to business. This being a place of dignity and almost perfect serenity, we have to almost whisper our own little Roy Keane jokes, when we learn this news. We are with a team who are without their god.

In the trees and along the walls and almost everywhere, there are little petitions written on white scraps of paper and posted to the gods. There is a ritual to each one. You post your note and with two bows, four claps and another bow, you can express your petitions to Okuni Nushi-no Mikoto, the principal god of the shrine. Luckily for us, Okuni Nushi is respected and loved as the god of good relationships. Maybe it's too little too late, but it might make Mal more sensitive in his criticism of our injury-news output.

It's beautiful here at Izumo Taisha. The solemn mountains behind the shrine stand guard over it and, in this little haven, the birds sing and the monks wander quietly and some of the 8,500,000 worshippers who come here every year pass through.

The team, tracksuited pearls before shrine, came here yesterday. Today, Emmet and I are sitting watching it all when we spot Mick McCarthy with a TV crew. He's writing a petition and hanging it on a tree. There would be an exclusive, 'Mick's Petition To The Gods'. We decide to leave it between Mick and the gods.

It's been a bad week for everyone. Not much glory or joy. The debacle of the final day of the controversy is becoming clear. The foolishness of Mick McCarthy just relying on extracts of the RTÉ interview; the black comedy of Brendan McKenna misunderstanding when the players asked him to make copies of their statement, which they intended issuing after Mick McCarthy's press conference as a gesture of support; the crossed lines between Mick McCarthy and Brendan Menton as Menton tried to prevent Mick from saying anything that would scupper late and renewed efforts at a deal; the fact that Mick McCarthy left that press conference with most of us writing him off, went home and sat up waiting for a few hours for Roy Keane to call him – and the call never came.

There's a realization now that, if an empty apology was all that was needed, well then, the whole thing was just silly anyway.

We sit for a long while looking at the scenery, soaking up the peace, and reflecting that, if this was Ireland, there'd be two eighteen-hole golf courses attached to the shrine. There is no piece of our culture that we won't hustle. If we had sacred cows, you'd be eating sacred burgers by now. Maybe that's part of the problem. We don't know what's important anymore.

For the English colleagues who are here with us, it's a different kind of story. Generally, they like Mick McCarthy and don't like Roy Keane. They feel Roy behaved badly and Mick didn't. I don't think they understand the fuss, the magnitude of what has gone on at home, the fact that nothing else, nothing else at all, has been spoken about for a week. How could they understand?

As a race, we Irish are as gullible as hillbillies really and, since the great gusher of wealth began eight or nine years ago, we've decided that it's unlucky for anyone in the tribe to ask questions of anything except the past. The present must be unmolested. We have a national consensus on that. We have money now, *ergo*, the present is good. This Keane thing, though, for all that his rant was shot through with meanness and hard words, it has shocked us.

The loveable Irish singalong thing isn't good enough for him. The half-arsed charm that we retail to the world has been questioned. The shamrockery and the blarney. This guy is demanding a higher standard. At football in recent years, we've drawn a large part of our national pride from the fact that we're not English, that we can hold our drink and have our singsongs and make friends everywhere we go, and that's just our team. Questioning that whole ethos, our own way of doing things, has made us uncomfortable. We've always loved the fact that we could substitute passion for professionalism and get away with it. Now what?

The last few days are just beginning to settle in our heads. So much weird stuff. Paul Kimmage has been on strike all week, refusing to work for the *Sunday Independent*. To us slaves, Paul is Spartacus.

Paul filed his Roy interview last Sunday and, as usual, it was excellent. In the course of the piece, he asked Roy about his tattoos. On Roy's upper-right arm, he has had the names of his four children inked into his skin. Paul asked, 'But not your wife?' and Roy laughed broadly and said that this issue has been raised at home and he likes to tease his wife by saying to her that they'll always be his kids, but she mightn't always be his wife. Paul has dutifully signposted this as a joke, yet somebody has taken it and run it in large print across the front of the paper, above the masthead. It deliberately gives the impression that Keane is talking coldly and disparagingly about his own wife, who it has been rumoured all week will be the subject of a tabloid stitch-up this morning.

Paul is disgusted and typically he is sticking to his guns. His paper have messed the wrong fella about this week. It may be the biggest story in quite a while, and it may be killing him not to be writing about it, but he has shut his laptop until he sees an apology on the front of the *Sunday Independent* this weekend.

And so much more is going on. So many vapid commentaries and pieces of idle speculation. Guesswork and hackwork all mixed in with better stuff. Niall Quinn told me this morning that he has already had a couple of notes of apology from various members of the media for things they got wrong this week. I decide not to tell him about the 'English Cunt' column.

It's been the oddest week of our professional lives. Or at least as odd as the week when Michelle Smith won all those swimming medals. The nation has been convulsed by this. It has overshadowed the formation of the government. Famously, the row has made the front page in India, which is currently contemplating nuclear fisticuffs with Pakistan.

It's only football and we shouldn't have got so overwrought, but it's in the blood. We Irish suffer tragedy, whereas the rest of the world suffers inconvenience. World War II was known to us as The Emergency. Call that a war? It didn't affect us. Sure Cromwell was worse, when you think about it.

Here was a story that was big by any standards. We were aware that the rest of the world was paying at least some attention. So we went crazy. It was like, validation.

The need for validation is a habit that dies hard with us. I remember as a tyro sportswriter covering an exhibition tennis match in Dublin in the early 1990s when Martina Navratilova was asked by an older journalist how the ovation she received compared with other ovations she had experienced.

'It was certainly a great ovation,' she said kindly.

'Was it better than other ovations?' he asked.

'It was certainly very good,' she said. 'I was very pleased.'

'Was it the best ovation you have ever received?'

Navratilova was looking worried now. Was this some sort of a trap?

'I don't know. It was certainly great to hear that applause.'

'But was it the best?'

'It was a fine ovation.'

'But you wouldn't say the best ever.'

Courageously, she took that avenue.

'One of the best certainly.'

Pause.

'Then what was the best?'

We don't know now if this is the best or biggest story we'll ever work on. Already we're hoping not, because, even forty-eight hours after it ended, it's beginning to look overplayed. We know though that in thirty years when we are old farts, or older farts than we are now, we'll be talking about this week, and the word Saipan will still mean only one thing to Irish people.

After lunch, the team do some more community service. While we've all been warring for this past week, the team have had the additional duty of smiling politely at our hosts here in Izumo. In exchange for the overwhelming hospitality of the people (they offer more cups of tea per day than Mrs Doyle from *Father Ted* manages in a series), the team have visited hospitals, attended ceremonies and coached kids.

(Today, by the way, the team will attend a farewell ceremony when they will be presented with something called a Lucky Hummer. Those of us familiar with American slang have noted that a hummer is a euphemism for the act of fellatio. There's great anticipation, therefore, as to who will accept the lucky hummer on behalf of the team and sincere and respectful hopes that it isn't presented by His Excellency Major Nishio of Izumo.)

In the soft diffuse sunlight that seeps into the splendid Izumo Dome in the afternoon, the team have a closed session and then split up to give coaching lessons to hundreds of the local kids. It's a quiet, ordered business. The players must have wondered as the children moved with such solemn and respectful purpose about the comparatively raucous and individualistic culture that we all come from. It's hard to imagine a Japanese Roy Keane.

The children received the coaching with such delightful enthusiasm that it put smiles back on the faces of the players. They're acting like stars again. In the Izumo Dome (48.9 metres in height folks, there'll be a test on this stuff later), there hung one of the many banners that the local people have erected as well-planned acts of spontaneous celebration. It said: 'Fight Irish!' and it was subjected to almost as much interpretative analysis as was the gnomic announcement of Mick McCarthy when he came on the PA to announce that there were two minutes of kiddie coaching left. 'Losers Go Home!' boomed Captain Barnsley, and as the echo bounced around the dome (1.43 metres in diameter!) people wondered if he was stating a fact of life for the benefit of Keano, or merely parroting Eric Cantona in the Nike ad.

Injury news for Mal. Jason McAteer is back kicking a ball – so two bows, four claps and one bow everyone.

Watching the players fighting their way to the team bus is a pleasure. Hundreds of Japanese teenagers, most of them wearing plaid school skirts, press forward and beg for autographs.

'Garybrin!'

'Garybrin!'

'Garybrin!'

They love Gary Breen.

On the bus, meanwhile, Damien Duff has the window open and is making to throw his shirt to the crowd in the manner of a newly wed bride tossing away her bouquet.

At the end of the day, Mick McCarthy gives a determinedly

upbeat press conference at which he announces he had just two hours sleep the night before. Those of us who haven't slept a wink since Tuesday, listen resentfully.

Friday, 31st May

Friday arrives. We leave for Niigata. At the Green Morris Hotel in Izumo, our pretty press translator for the week is giving hugs and kisses to everyone as they depart. I see some of the sadder bastards queuing two or three times. We've only been gone a couple of weeks.

Another day, another journey. After a while, the company of journalists begins to pall, even on each other. On these soccer trips, we have coagulated into cliques who sit together and talk together and travel together. Some of us plain don't like each other, and some of us, well me anyway, hold long-standing grudges, but mainly it's just that the work we do is seldom private. We see the worst of each other. We are answerable for each other. My dumb opinion gets printed along with your considered one. Your fatuous question precedes my shrewd one at a press conference. His paper's nasty headline causes her favourite source to shut up shop. And we resent the fact that athletes and players see us as one homogenous collection of sleazy doughballs when, in reality, we each regard ourselves as being the only one of the bunch who actually hungers and thirsts for righteousness' sake.

There's that and there's the sort of suspended adolescence that we are all stuck in. As Jimmy Cannon said, sportswriters are entombed in eternal boyhood. Every day a new beginning in the Toy Department. Slate wiped clean. New story. New game. Next interview. We move blithely on, skimming the surface of every-thing, hopping on the pond lilies above a deeper world. We're surprised when people remember some published slight from two years ago. We are shocked by the sheer intricacy of the real world. We're momentarily baffled when some old story resurfaces with more to it than we had ever allowed for. We write about people who live in another universe, but we exist in quite an odd place ourselves. There's a dimension missing.

So when we travel together, we don't bother with the superfi-cial niceties. We sit with who we like and step past the rows of empty seats near people we know, but don't like. We read each other's stuff and criticize in the safety of other right-thinking hacks. And, by and large, we avoid confrontation.

There's no Keano news today. No Keano news is good news. We're back on the treadmill of matches and previews, but, of course, Keano is like Banquo's ghost now. Many of the English journalists seem pleased that he's gone. The rest of us are fear-ful. I've still not quite worked out why he divides us in this way.

For instance, on a Sunday not long before the World Cup, the entire soccer staff of the *Observer* newspaper in London were asked to pick the ten best players in England. Keane didn't rank in the top ten. David Beckham came third. As an example of jour-nalistic subservience to hype, it seemed to be a classic. As an instance of how Keane divides opinions, it was perfect.

You want to argue over Roy Keane? In Ireland, the only argu-ment is why is their any argument left? You want to suggest that he is not the best footballer in the world? You want to put the case that a guy, who earns a reputed £100,000 a week for playing footie, is already overpaid. Bah! Don't be a fool man. By any measure, Keane is the one getting short-changed.

Any Saturday afternoon when Old Trafford is full of paying customers or any Sunday afternoon when the satellite subscribers burrow into their sofas and crack open the tinnies, the one thing they are sure of is that, if Roy Keane is playing, he will be giving 100 per cent. No tricks, no gimmicks, no frills. Is there any other player of whom that can be said week in and week out? And if he is playing, does that player have anything near the influence that Keane has?

From Barthez to Van Nistelrooy, with Beckham, Blanc, Scholes, Veron and all the others in between, Manchester United should be formidable without Roy Keane. Instead, time after time, in his absence they look no more imposing than well-paid men filling shirts. That's why Keane is the world's best player. He won't win any prizes for circus tricks and he won't win any Mr Congeniality baubles either, but what he brings to a team, beyond the ferocious ability to win the ball and distribute it, is character, the ability to lead by example, the fearlessness to lay it all on the line.

That's why I can't understand even his mortal enemies being glad that he's not here for tomorrow's match. The further we get from Saipan, the sillier the episode seems to get.

Anyway, we go straight to the Big Swan stadium to get accredited. Lovely stadium. Lovely, swift process. No freebie bags.

The team are training in the evening, but the last twenty minutes are the only ones that shall be open to us. We are inclined to make a fuss about this but, it transpires, the entire session is on closed-circuit TV in the media centre. So we fiddle around working out the phone system and keep on complaining about the facilities and keep an eye on the TV screens for broken legs or Roy Keane being parachuted in from the skies.

After France '98, the press centres are a severe disappointment.

No ATMs, which seems a small thing, but it is causing me a personal crisis as I had put all my advance money into my bank account, intending to make withdrawals as I went along. There is no proper travel centre or accommodation centre and a severe shortage of internet connections and IC phones over which we may file. We're not happy.

It occurs to me, as we head towards our hotel, that I have no idea where I am. One week in Izumo and I couldn't say whether it was in the north, west, east or south of Japan. Same with Niigata. Travel certainly broadens the mind.

Tomorrow is match day. Ireland vs Cameroon. Who knew there'd be football too?

Saturday, 1st June

Saturday games are a joy for us. No pressure. No deadlines. We have all day Sunday to choose our words and pare our thoughts. It's a virtual holiday, so.

Emmet and I arrange to meet friends in town before the game. We have lunch and a drink and a walk around and head to the stadium. The difficulty with this outburst of sociability is that it has taken us out of the system. Once out, it's hard to get in again. We spend at least half-an-hour wandering around outside the Big Swan Stadium looking for a way to get into the media area. We arrive hot, sweaty and cranky. I blame Emmet. He's way more sociable than I am. And it's led us to this.

At the game, Gerry Hand, who works for the *Star* or the *Sun*, I'm not sure which, is sitting behind us. Gerry is one of those people who likes to talk a team through a game. Very loudly. He calls every pass, bemoans every wide, questions every refereeing decision. After ten minutes I stand up, take a shotgun from my bag and blow him away.

Actually, I just look at Emmet and roll my eyes but . . .

The game finishes sometime near 6 p.m. One of those triumphant snatched draws that we Irish have always been good at.

We go down to the mixed zone to get the quotes. Ray Treacy greets us. He wants us all on the bus in a few minutes. He proposes that we let one press representative get the quotes from the players and that these quotes then be distributed. Ray is ignored.

With Mick McCarthy, we're all walking on eggshells now really. We go behind to Cameroon. Come back and get a draw. Who knows if this is good or bad? Mick comes into the mixed zone and he's decided it's good. We hacks, second that emotion. There's a hundred-quid sweetener for anyone who'll say, 'Do you think we'd have won if Roy was playing?'

It goes unclaimed.

We get to the airport herded impatiently on and off the bus by Ray, who is crankier than a newly neutered cat. And we end up sitting around at the airport for an hour, pissed off and moaning. When, finally, we get on the plane, we find the players are already aboard and have been for an hour. They are pissed off and moaning about us.

It's a sour moment in a good day.

We fly on to Tokyo and make another bus journey out to the town of Chiba. It's close to midnight when we arrive. The team are deposited in the New Otami Hotel, next door to ourselves in the Prince Makuhari. Unpromisingly, our hotel is reluctant to give us food but, finally, we are served Japanese pub snacks on the fiftieth floor overlooking Tokyo Bay. It costs about £15 just to breathe the air in there. The bills are astronomical. The clamour for receipts is deafening.

Receipts are a theme of our lives. A long trip like this will always end up costing you some of your own money. The fewer receipts you get, the more it will cost.

Last week, five of the English journalists went out for dinner in Izumo and ate well, nothing raw and nothing domesticated, being the gastronomic rule they live by when away. At the end of the meal, the bill came. Everyone threw in the right amount. The receipt came. Just one. Consternation.

'Five copies please.'

Shrug of shoulders. Baffled look. A linguist from the journalist group intervenes.

'*Five copies please!*'

Another blank, half-terrified look. How have I failed you as a waiter?

Another journalist tries. Steps forward. 'Let me through please, I am a master.'

'*FIVE*,' he shouts holding up all his fingers. '*COP-EES. PUH-LEASE*!'

'Ah, yes,' says the waiter 'five.' Everyone bows and the waiter beetles off to set about his task, which he completes in minutes and returns, drum roll please, with a tray of five coffees.

Beaten men, the journalists drink up and leave.

By 2 a.m. in Chiba, most people are living out of the vending machines in the lobby.

Sunday, 2nd June

Nothing Sunday. A lovely nothing day. Myself and Emmet work through most of it, sending stuff back for the Monday paper. It's harder to work when the immediacy is lost, and the Keane business followed by the match has left us stale and tired. My stuff at least seems flat and old. There's no real pressure though.

We are under orders to try to bring the story on a little, given that the nation watched the match early on Saturday morning and will be reading our reports and colour stuff early on Monday.

The team are lying in and lolling about and (lucky bastards) meeting their families. There isn't a lot of follow-on which can be done.

Frankly my dears, we don't give a damn.

Monday, 3rd June

Back to training. Today we begin a phase of the World Cup that will provide us with some much needed rhythm and routine. Training. Press conferences. Work.

Hurrah! We are like babies, we need our routine.

We investigate the facilities at the media centre, a big room that is based in an out-of-season Waterworld attraction right beside the team's (excellent) training pitch. Some sympathy for the FAI today. Even when they are doing us a favour, they seem to screw up. We get to the press centre, which is an odour-ridden room facing out onto the disused pools and waterslides. The desks are plentiful and laid out in neat classroom rows. The FAI were already out here in February on recon detail.

Ta-da, we are told. Surprise! ISDN lines for everybody!

The snappers are delighted. The rest of us roll our eyes. Our laptops can't work off ISDN lines. Plus, there are supposed to be four computers provided with proper internet access. Instead, there are just four laptops lying on a table connected to nothing except the electricity mains. We gather around Brendan Menton and whinge. Brendan is a nice man. He promises to get it fixed. And he does.

Tuesday, 4th June

We play Germany tomorrow. In Ibaraki. The *Herald* has run with a big story about the team not travelling to Ibaraki to train today. They are going to travel there tomorrow instead. Words like farce and shambles are taken out and used again.

Mick is pissed off. The FAI are pissed off. I, who was about to file a similar story for tomorrow morning, act as if I am pissed off too.

The FAI, it transpires, have scouted the route and given Mick the option of going or staying and he has decided to stay put. No drama. It's just that, if we had a proper communications service setup, somebody would have told us all this. Instead, we work in a vacuum most of the day. Except for the waste-of-time press conferences the team provides for the *Evening Herald*.

Wednesday, 5th June

Match day. And a hard-working day too.

A. J. Liebling used to say that he wrote faster than anyone who could write better than him and that he wrote better than anyone who could write faster than him. It was true for old Joe, but it's also every sports journalist's conceit. We judge each other by how good we are under the cosh, as we call it. Big days like these always have an edge of pressure to them. You hope you write faster than anyone here who can write better.

The coach journey to Ibaraki takes an hour. We note this down.

We will be working on the coach on the way back for as long as our batteries hold out.

The game is another snatched draw. A great drama though. Ireland equalize in injury time, which is good fun but a journalist's nightmare. All the clever notes you have made in your notebook and laptop as to why we lost this game are shredded. The mood of your piece was going to be a sombre post-mortem, now it has to be a hat tossed joyfully into the air.

Bizarrely, Mick is grumpy at his press conference afterwards. He's back! Old grumpy is back! He sits on a high stool in the media area with a microphone in his hand and he looks like a nightclub crooner.

He's washed out and worn and falling back on his native gruffness. This whole adventure has too much romance, too much swashbuckling, too much complication in it for him. By nature, he believes that every silver lining has a cloud, so he looks out on the sunny delirium, narrows his eyes and decides he'll bring his brolly, just in case.

'Well it's fine when you come like this and you have results like the two we've had,' he says. 'But I wonder what the reaction would be if we were beaten one nil in both games? I'm a bit perverse maybe but I wonder about what would be said about my players then. Thankfully we haven't lost. Changes are great, aren't they? If they work. I could be a complete flute sitting here if they'd gone wrong. You'd say, "Hey we were doing well at four-four-two you should have left it. You shouldn't have gone three-four-three." It's just the fickle nature of football. I said at half-time what I wanted to do and I had that plan in my head. Isn't it nice when it works? It's the difference between being a buffoon or a wonderful, tactically astute coach.'

In these delirious moments, we want to assure Mick that, no, we are the buffoons, we are the complete flutes, but the moment doesn't seem right. Something about his demeanour suggests he knows it already. We ask personnel questions, trying not to appear too flutey.

Any injuries?

Myself and Emmet do well with the nanny goats. Every player bagged except Gary Kelly. Still I have a moan. I want to be doing something apart from colour fluff and quotes and am promised that I can do an overview-type piece for the next game. Immediately, I want to moan that the workload is now too big.

Still the day was good. The old excitement is back. It's a walk on the wild side now, this tournament. In perfectly ordered Japan, our Irish World Cup adventure is a riot, a sun dance, an anarchic subversion of football logic. It defies analysis. Ninety-two minutes gone today and good old Niall Quinn shook off his decrepitude. Robbie Keane, that impertinent whippersnapper, did the rest, and suddenly the final whistle has gone and the Irish are doing the cancan in the Kashima stadium, when minutes previously they'd lain dead in a narrow grave. Daft.

And so it goes on, our tale of the unexpected. We get a sound draw with Cameroon. Germany slaughtered one apiece. On to Yokohama next Tuesday, with only the inept Saudis in our way. And, after that, on to who knows where? The busier the better. The more we work, the less we miss home.

When we got back tonight, the hotel staff applauded us all into the hotel. We lapped it up and went to our rooms to work.

Thursday, 6th June

All my enthusiasm has gone again. I have to do follow-up stuff from yesterday. This is a horror show. This is writing in a vacuum again. I hate doing follow-ups. I have heard the players are going golfing. It's true, the team hotel is deserted, like a ghost town in fact, and I have to provide 1,000 words of follow-up.

I go into every permutation and eventuality I can think of regarding our last game. From us winning it, to rain stopping play, or an act of God intervening. It fills about 400 words. I go back over all our previous World Cups and other key games. God, I don't know how this nonsense is going to read, but I'm falling asleep just writing it.

Eventually I file. I learn later that the team has been to Disneyland, not golfing. 'Where would you golf in Tokyo?' says John Brennan of the *Sunday World* to me incredulously. So, a huge howler in the intro, everything else dull, dull, dull.

Knackered.

Wish I was dead.

And I get paid for this.

Before I go to bed, I toss in a preview of tomorrow's Argentina vs England game. Confidently, I predict that England will get hammered. Everyone says their preparation has been terrible. I decide that time must be called on Sven Goran Eriksson, 'A Swedish snakeoil salesman,' say I.

Feels good.

Friday, 7th June

I am off to Sapporro for England vs Argentina.

I meet a man, who transpires to be Jason McAteer's dad, as I am waiting for the bus to take me from Chiba to the airport. I've just seen himself and Jason in the lobby of the team hotel and said a quick hello. Now, he wanders up as I am waiting for the bus. He is waiting for Jason's brother Sam. Mr McAteer thinks I am a punter, a pal of Jason's.

'Jason's well pissed off,' he tells me, 'he's not in the team for next Wednesday. He's had all sorts with McCarthy. McCarthy says he's not fit, but Jason says he'd tackle a wall. Lad's gutted. He loves the jersey, loves it.'

I am mortified. This is all good stuff but, if Mr Mac knew I was a journalist, he'd be telling me none of it. I should put my hands to my ears. I should identify myself. I should vow never to repeat it. Instead, I change the subject to sightseeing. As soon as I get on the bus, I ring Emmet with the team news. I'm not sure why. I issue so many injunctions to him about sources and not betraying Mr Mac, that it's all but useless to him.

The office has reserved a ticket for me on All Nippon Air. Japan, though, is a cash society. They are not used to this sort of behaviour. It takes an hour, and a committee of seven, to liberate the ticket. Finally, a manager emerges and announces that they have kept a ticket for me. They all bow deeply. I bow back. Just a form to fill out and I can have the ticket.

Time is short by the time I get to Sapporo. I'm supposed to be meeting a couple of friends, but I head straight to the stadium instead. It's a hideous indoor dome. Outside, I bump into David Walsh, an old friend who is here working for the *Sunday Times*. We are wending our way around the stadium when we are passed by the Argentinian team bus behind a blaring convoy of police out-riders.

What a sight! The bus is stuffed with people. Almost everyone is on their feet or hanging out of a window. They are singing and stamping their feet. Pressed up against a window, but singing his head off, we see Gabriel Batistuta. David and I are sure that this is a sign that Argentina will win convincingly.

Inside, I am seated in the middle of the English media contingent. They are an unfriendly bunch at the best of times, and they haven't even been getting on well together during this trip. Rumours of big fallouts and betrayals abound.

One hack has attempted to kick another's hotel door down. One group got leaked the English line-up for their first game and made a big show of high-fiving each other in the stands when the team-list confirmed the leak. The English contingent have no trouble in ignoring me completely.

I make contact on the mobile with Dave and Jim, my friends. Dave is from Kildare. Jim is from Sheffield. They live in New York and have a long-standing friendship that is cemented through football. Jim has come to many Irish games over the years and has always been good and gracious about our success. Tonight, Jim has scored really good tickets through work, and I can see the pair of them down below me just a few rows from the front.

This, by the way, is another dodgy accommodation trip and I warn Jim and Dave that I may have to sleep on their floor. As of kick-off time, I have nowhere to stay.

When we get to half-time, I call Mal. He's cock-a-hoop. We got you a room! By now, I'm too pissed off to be happy. Just before half-time, David Beckham slipped home a penalty for England. Instinctively, as the ball hit the net, I looked down at Jim and Dave. I could see Jim uncoiling with joy and Dave, ever the Irishman, sort of slumping.

It's worse. England are playing well. Not beautifully or excitingly. Just well.

They win. Dave and I have recovered our spirits by the time we all meet for a drink in downtown Sapporo. There's a slight edge of menace in the town tonight, but nothing truly ugly, which is a relief. I'm on alert to write about baton charges and arrests, should any occur.

It costs about ¥110 to get to the Mitsui Urban Hotel in the middle of the night. There are English football fans strewn like war dead all over the third-floor lobby. I get to my room and collapse. Three hours later, it's time to go. I walk, naked, to the window to see where I am. Outside the window, literally close enough to touch, is the nose cone of a jumbo with pilots and staff wandering around inside adjusting their instruments. They are close enough to adjust my instrument had they a mind to.

I tell you, there are airport hotels and there is the Mitsui Urban. I check out. It's pay as you leave here, no credit cards here. Down the escalator from the third floor and the doors open straight into the departure hall.

I meet Russell Kempson of the London *Times* at the airport. Russell usually covers the Irish trips, but not this time. He's here on a freebie. Two days. Straight out. Straight back. He's doing colour stuff. He looks like death. I suppose I do too.

We have a slightly disjointed conversation and toddle off in opposite directions. Around the world on a freebie and then filing copy and flying straight back? Journalists are too weird.

Saturday, 8th June

Back in Chiba, Sapporo feels like it never happened. Emmet and I are going to buy an Ixy. Each!

Yes. The sensation in Chiba is the deal that Eoin Hand has struck in the local supermarket for the purchase of Canon Ixy digital cameras. Hacks who don't know how to switch on their laptops are milling about trying to buy one of the things. The manager has sold about twenty in the week and stocks are low. That's what happens when you get so many rugged individualists gathered in one place.

All over Chiba, there are men with sunburned faces walking around with these shining little pieces of metal wondering how they'll explain the purchase of same at home. Most have manuals that are written in Japanese. Those who were twentieth and twenty-first in the queue (Emmet and myself) have been bitterly disappointed to find all the Ixys gone. Those who hesitate are lost.

We have been promised that by this afternoon re-stocking will have taken place.

I don't know the first thing about digital photography. I know this though. When you are a male of a certain age, Japanese technology stores become the new sexual-fantasy retailers. The Canon Ixy feels so much like the perfect gadget. When Emmet and I point them at each other in the shop, we can press a button and freeze our photos in the button in the back. It's fun, fun, fun. And the snappers say that the retail price here is half what it is at home. That's good enough for us. It's not spending ¥350, it's saving it.

When we get to the shop, though, they still have only one Canon Ixy left. Our enthusiasm drains. This is the sort of frivolous item of major expenditure best made in groups.

A little later, I run into Niall Quinn and his family. They are heading to lunch. Kindly, he invites me along, but I pretend I've eaten. Watching him dangle his little girl on his knee will make me too homesick. I watch them disappear off into the mall in Chiba, happy and content in the sunshine. It must be nice to have reached the age as a footballer when you can sit back and take stock and actually enjoy the experience of a World Cup. So many guys on the team seem bowed down by it.

We have been joined in Chiba, I notice today, by the great Malcolm Brody. Malcolm is seventy-seven and is covering his thirteenth World Cup.

Opinion on this feat is divided. To some he is a great, great man. To the majority of us, one question about Malcolm remains unanswered. Thirteen World Cups – why would you be arsed?

We all hope fervently that, when we are seventy-seven, we will have better things to be doing than dragging our old bones around from the media shuttle to the media centre and back again.

Still Malcolm is at the centre of the best filing story I know of. He was in Moscow once, and trying to get through to the copy-taker in Belfast to file his story. Moscow, in the old days, was a tough place to file from, but Malcolm was a resourceful reporter and got patched through to Leningrad where his plight was explained to the operator, who patched him through to Talinn, from where he was patched through to Paris and so on via a series of tortuous multilingual explanations and begging noises till he got through to the London operator and finally to the front desk of the *Belfast Telegraph* back home. It's close to deadline and he knows they've been waiting for his call.

'Malcolm Brody,' he announces triumphantly.

'Ach, Malcolm Brody is away off in Moscow.'

And the line goes dead.

Sunday, 9th June

Paul Kimmage is in the wars again. He has been running an entertaining weekly column with Jason McAteer. This week, the key part of the column is the news that Jason was on the verge of going home during the week.

He played in the Cameroon game when he declared himself to be fit. It transpired that he wasn't fully fit, and this has been a little talking point among the players, but, not surprisingly, we in the media are all concentrating on Ian Harte's apparent lack of form. Yet, as Jason's dad disclosed to me exclusively the other day, Jason 'has had all sorts with McCarthy'.

This revelation and the story of Jason dispiritedly packing his bags to go home has somehow got onto the front pages of two other Sunday papers this morning. Paul is furious. He reckons the story is a lift. I mention my conversation with his father to Jason just to let him know that a version of the story was out and about anyway.

Nobody is very interested.

Chiba is beginning to eat at our souls. It's a concrete city. Unbroken, charmless concrete. The place has been reclaimed from the sea, and if the sea had any decency at all, it would claim it back. It's a soulless wasteland and, what's more, a plate of 'mixed sausages' (very mixed) in the hotel requires a second mortgage to be arranged. To the disgust of the management, who shut the hotel down at nine sharp every night, the Irish, ever adaptable, have begun to treat the vending machines in the lobby as a twenty-four-hour pub, and at any hour of the night or day, you can catch friends lolling around the place with tinnies in hand.

The team and their retinue of fond journalists have settled into life without Keano. His name has become a bad word, and we hacks never use it in the presence of players or management. His image has been removed from the back of the team bus here in a gesture that reminds you of those empty plinths you see in places like Bucharest.

A few of us have had the seriously discomfiting experience of sitting at training sessions in front of a man who is a brother or a close friend of Mick McCarthy's. Mick is on the pitch but his brother/friend speaks with precisely the same voice and intonation and gruffness. It's stereo Mick and we spend the day wondering what Christmas Day with the McCarthys must be like.

'Hey I'll tell you what. Them socks will do for me. Aye, and there's a pair of them an' all.'

'Well, if they don't match, I'll tell you what, I'll put me backside in Burtons window, over a bacon slicer.'

'You lot'll probably twist that someway to suit yourselves.'

'Who're you talking to Mick? You hearing them press voices again?'

Today Mal mentions to me that he needs a player interview piece for tomorrow. Players, needless to say, are queuing outside my door day and night hoping to secure some good interview time with me. Since doing Roy in Saipan, I have had a small success in getting a short exclusive and guarded interview with Steve Staunton.

Nothing else.

Which isn't surprising. We haven't paid into their players' pool, we've been implicated in getting their captain sent home, and things aren't good here.

Still. It's a challenge. I wander across to the lobby of the New Otami Hotel and decide to corner the first viable interview subject I see. An hour passes and not a single player wanders through the lobby.

Change of plan. Call Gary Kelly. Funny and friendly. No answer.

Plan C. Gary Breen. Pay dirt. He'll do it.

2.30 p.m., wait at the lifts on the second floor.

I wait and wait. Uncomfortably, David Connolly and his parents are hanging around the lifts as well. Apart from noting that he's been in a bad mood for six or seven years, I have never written a kind word about David Connolly. In fact, I often like to use Mick McCarthy's line about David having a face like a 'slapped arse'. I resolve to be more sensitive about the terminal ennui of David Connolly. Meanwhile, time passes slowly as we all pretend not to be noticing each other.

At 3.05 p.m., Gary strolls out with a million apologies. He's been having a haircut. I quite like Gary Breen and am certainly not going to quibble over punctuality. I start setting up.

'Ah yes,' he says as if he has just remembered, 'about the interview. Stan has said we can't do any one-on-ones.'

'Why?'

'Other journalists are complaining,' he says.

I'm taken aback. If some people are being refused interviews and others are getting them, surely nobody would be crass enough to lodge a complaint with the team. Of course they would.

'Who complained?' I bark.

'Dunno,' shrugs Gary, not at all intimidated by my stern tone.

I change tack quickly. Better rescue the current situation first. Media warfare is no concern of Gary Breen's.

I tell him that Stan himself did a one-on-one with me a couple of days ago. Breeny weighs this up. He has a reputation for spiky independence off the field and attention deficiency disorder while on it. It's mid-afternoon. He's bored anyway.

'Fuck it then,' he says.

I pronounce him a prince. We cobble together a half-decent little piece.

As I am leaving, I see Niall on the balcony doing an interview with a TV crew. I wave breezily. Yet another day gone past without us doing any work on his book.

The snappers are on form tonight. It's about 1.30 a.m. and a few of us have finished work and are sitting around the lobby milking the vending machines when a gang of them arrive in. Buzzing as usual.

They have fireworks. Photographers and fireworks. Surely there's a bylaw? There is some bright talk about releasing them here and now in the tall lobby of the Prince Makatui. The snappers, apparently, feel they should do this in celebration of tonight's Japanese victory over Russia. They feel the hotel would appreciate it.

It is noted that the famous win has made zero impact in life here in Chiba. The town is still dull and listless. As a kindness to the populace, the lads decide that they will release the fireworks outside. All the better to share the joy.

We all shift outside for the display. The boys don't have a lot of fireworks, but they are good ones, not the little squibs we get back home. These things can really light a town up. Swoosh! Fizz! Bang! The rockets are off into the night sky over Chiba. The snappers are like kids lighting the blue touch paper and running away before they get burned. (Rightly so. They have a bad record with fire. At Italia '90, it was an Irish photographer who courageously stuck his penis into a flaming glass of Sambuca and had to be hospitalized.)

Suddenly all hell breaks loose. Two dark-suited managers emerge in a panic from the hotel. In Laurel and Hardy fashion they begin chasing the snappers around the forecourt of the hotel. Those of us who have emerged from the lobby as spectators double up in appreciative laughter. Strangely, the simple act of laughter makes the spectacle even better. The two managers are so polite to their guests that they join in our laughter every time they run past us, affecting to be creased up by the hilarity of it all.

'Please stop, Sirs,' they call after the photographers who are lighting fireworks as they run around in merry circles.

At one point, it seems as if the junior manager is being encouraged by his senior to throw himself on top of a lighted firework before it explodes into the night. His alarmed face causes the laughter to rise to near fatal levels. The senior manager notices this and pretends to be laughing at the good of it too. He even slaps his thigh and mimes a firework shooting off and a young hotel manager diving on it. Then he says, 'Please, please stop!'

We are just coming to our senses and remembering our manners when, next thing, all attention is diverted to the roadway. From nowhere, a long convoy of Japanese Hell's Angels has appeared. Being Japanese Hell's Angels, they are stopped at a red light at two in the morning. No regrets for the wild bunch.

The snappers are drawn to this spectacle like kids to an ice-cream van. They go flitting off down the road after the choppers and the Harleys. This is a lucky break because, now, the local police have arrived.

The snappers spot that the constabulary are here and they begin fleeing the scene in mock panic. They run in all directions, hiding behind bushes and popping up their heads here and there while we point at them and shout.

'Over there, Officer.'

'There's another one over there, Officer.'

'Arrest that man!'

'Use your weapon, Officer.'

Conscious that they are becoming central to the entertainment, the police make a few dutiful attempts to round up the lads. At one point, they make a half-hearted effort to take control of the pedestrian overpass that arches over the road, but the snappers give them the slip and emerge from the undergrowth shouting slogans about the Chiba Six.

They slip back into the hotel and off to bed. Bad-ass fugitives.

Monday, 10th June

Mick is cranky as a weasel at this morning's press conference. He passes close to me on the way out and gives me an annoyed snort. Whatever friendship was once between us seems to have become a casualty of the trip. My name is somewhere in there, whirling around in the list of resentments he feels over the Keane affair. I know too that haranguing him over the *Mail on Sunday* column didn't sit well either.

Over the years, I've always been a supporter of Mick's. Any friendship had to be incidental to that though. The job has to come first. That's how he'd see it from his side anyway. His great weakness, however, is that he can never understand that we aren't here to cheerlead. Not always anyway. We have to be allowed to call things as we see them. Mick has high standards of loyalty when it comes to friendship. Calling things as we see them isn't good enough. He sees me as a traitor.

The four players brought to the media centre today are Gary Kelly, Alan Kelly, Jason McAteer and Robbie Keane. This is as good as it gets in rota terms, which isn't very good.

True story. The other day after a press conference, Emmet and I walked the couple of miles back to the media hotel. Nearing said hotel, we met Neil Silver of the Press Association (who, because we are the wittiest folk in the world we all call Hi-Ho) and Hi-Ho had just finished filing all the press conference stuff for the PA who were at that moment bouncing it out to outlets all around the world. The radio and TV guys were doing likewise. The old *Irish Times*, with its version of events, wouldn't be hitting the streets for almost another twenty-four hours. And the players are the ones who are narky!

Much of the press conference is spent on the Jason story. Jason is unsure where he's going with this one. Outside in the corridor, before he came into the press conference, I chatted with him and he said that it had all gotten out of hand, that he's a man who compulsively likes to tidy when he is annoyed and he had been in the process of tidying everything into a suitcase when Mick Byrne had come to his room and asked, not unreasonably, if Jason was going home.

Jason says that he replied 'yeah', but in a sarcastic tone. He supplies a sample of his sarcastic 'yeah', which precludes me from asking if tidying when you are annoyed is not the gayest thing a footballer has ever confessed to.

In the press conference, though, Jason adjusts his stance and says that he and Mick Byrne discussed the idea of Jason going home on medical grounds. I don't know if this is true, but it makes a better story than the compulsive tidying version. Apart from that, the press conference is a severe anti-climax.

The team have been getting bored with these daily affairs and getting slightly cranky too. Access to them is increasingly limited, which is a small mercy because decent questions are running out.

Today, though, there had been a quiver of excitement in our ranks. The big hitter from the news pages of the *Sun* had called and asked for directions to the daily press conference. He would be coming out from Tokyo. He would have a question he wanted to ask. There is widespread anticipation about this. This question, whatever it is, could potentially unleash a seismic controversy at least the size of the 'Goodbye Mr Keano' affair.

The regular sports snappers from the *Sun* are a little nervy lest they be mowed down in an indiscriminate backlash from the players.

The press conference draws record numbers. The big hitter is standing over by the wall. Throughout the proceedings, he looks primed. The usual questions are lobbed in. 'What do ye think of the match balls?' 'Have ye been into town?'

It's all just foreplay, though, as we wait for our man to toss his grenade. Like a good pro, he doesn't just arrive in and step on everybody's lines by throwing his question in first, he waits till we have all had our fill of banalities. He waits till we can stand the tension no more.

'Final question,' says Trevor O'Rourke, the PR guy who is running the show today.

'Yes,' booms the big hitter, 'over here. This is for all four of you players.'

We pause. All four of them! Mercy, but this is going to be big. More sleepless nights beckon. This could derail the whole delicate media–team relationship again. It'll be raining seven types of shit by lunchtime, boys.

'What,' says the big hitter, 'do each of ye think . . .'

Yes. Yes. Yes. What do they think of these allegations of bestiality? He's going to make them deny that they mess around with farm animals. What do they think of Osama bin Laden being invited to play centre midfield? What do they think of the news that they have each been filmed snorting cocaine out of the bellybutton of Mick Byrne? Yes. What do they think of the Third Secret of Fatima being specifically about Richard Dunne?

'What do each of ye think,' says he and he pauses again for effect, 'of the fans?'

Of the fans! For crying out loud. He's doing a fans' story. Our backsides are off and heading for the door before the players can reply.

'Smelly, fickle and tedious,' say the players. Of course.

Tuesday, 11th June

Match day.

If the team progress, we leave Chiba at 9 a.m. tomorrow. We will be headed for Seoul. Ray says the hotel there is 'genuinely five star'.

'Literally five star, Ray?' we ask.

'Genuinely,' he says.

Well then. C'mon ye boys in green.

We may be getting out just in time. There's a storm heading our way. A typhoon to be precise. The typhoon is called Noguri, which apparently means 'cunning animal'. We Noguris of the press box have been wringing the typhoon thing dry in our intros. We have all recommended that the team plays with the typhoon in the first half at Yokohama.

The game is a squib. Saudi Arabia–0, Ireland–3. Noguri doesn't show.

Duffer scores and he does a restrained little celebration during which he must have burned at least three calories. The best moment is when he is asked about it afterwards and says, 'You just go mad, don't you?'

Robbie Keane does a little bow-and-arrow number at the end of his post-goal somersaulting. Soon they'll need time added on at the end of games to enable Robbie to get through his celebration routines.

Gary Breen scores the best Irish goal of the tournament and, being a defender, doesn't really know how to celebrate. He just puts his hand in the air as if he is looking for an offside decision. In the press box, many and lame are the little jokes about the unemployed footballer (Gary is between clubs right now).

We inject a little excitement into our copy. We are looking forward to Seoul tomorrow. Emmet and I send over a great mountain of stuff from 'under the cosh'.

Chiba has grown stale and boring. The second round of the tournament means escape. We are excited. In the copy, you can almost discern our little tails wagging.

Wednesday, 12th June – Seoul

We are staying downtown. We hardly see the players anymore. Of course, that hurts the players' feelings but we have to be firm. After a month, we feel entitled to our privacy. No more interviews lads, we're sorry, no more photo opportunities. We've co-operated enough for one tournament.

We had a memorable morning on the way here. Every sort of foul-up. The plane, when it arrived (a couple of hours late) was too small so, when we got to South Korea, Ray told us that, surprise, he'd left all the journalists' gear behind. It would be along presently.

The flight was bumpy in the extreme but, fortunately, we were fed just enough breakfast to give us heartburn. Nobody had digested enough to actually puke.

We arrived at Gimpo Airport in Seoul, to be told that the official welcome committee had gone to meet us at Incheon Airport, an hour out on the other side of the city.

Consolations abound though. We come straight into Seoul on a belching little bus and the city is beautiful and epic. Ray was right, the hotel is five star. We want to loll in its luxurious confines, but nothing will suit the team but to go training tomorrow. Bah!

Thursday, 13th June

Ah, the things we've seen and the places we've been. This is day whatever of the endless journey, and we are in a cab to Soojong Gu Sanggok-dong Military Sports Facility. Out along the Olympic Expressway, the high rises of Seoul on one side, the broad majestic Hangang river on the other and the taxi driver barking merrily all the way, although we can't grasp a word.

When we get to the gate, the soldier, young Private Jumpy with the authoritative Kalashnikov, wants to know what exactly we think we are doing here. Given that the Irish team and the elite forces, the crack troops of the Irish press corps, are 300 yards up the road, it seems like a silly question, but he's the one with the gun, so he doesn't get a silly answer.

We show him our beautiful laminated accreditation dangler, which identifies us as part of the World Cup family or a distant ne'er-do-well cousin thereof. He is not impressed. He wants the letter. No letter. No go. So we fish out the letter. It is a photocopy of a letter actually, and it is on FAI notepaper with the FAI logo attached. Not exactly a symbol that prompts the response 'that'll do nicely thank you', everywhere you travel. The letter is short and is written in Korean script. We have no idea what it says. It may say, 'I am an Irish journalist. Shoot me.'

Whatever. It works. We are ushered through.

The Irish team's presence here on the Soojong Gu Sanggok-dong Military Sports Facility needs a little explaining, apparently. It was one of those things that grew into a brush fire of controversy when nobody in the FAI even knew that matches were being played with. Apparently, there were three training facilities on offer and the Turks, who were here before us, took one. Of the other two, both equidistant from the team hotel, Mick McCarthy liked the military setup best because A) it suited Ian Evans's parade-sergeant manner on the training field; and B) the pitch wasn't bumpy and, having lost a man already to a bumpy pitch, it behoves us all to be careful.

This all got passed down the information superhighway of rumours and Chinese whispers that links the team hotel to the media hotel 200 yards away. Mick had been asked to train the team in a disused quarry!

The most frayed, overused words of the trip were pressed into action again. Farce! Fiasco! We lit the blue paper and waited to use the big one: 'Training Ground Bust Up!' Alas, the FAI have intervened with the truth and those of us who would have missed the story altogether in the first place nodded our heads in disgust at the impetuousness of our colleagues. Not that Mick McCarthy would thank us for it later.

At the Military Facility (which is what we old Korean hands call it for short), the training is overlooked by a man who we shall refer to simply as the Brigadier General. He has a long surname attached to his rank and we wrote down that surname on a scrap of paper when we heard it but we have since lost the scrap of paper. There are good security reasons for handling it this way.

Anyway, the Brigadier General watches the Irish team train with a look of curious disdain on his face. Perhaps he has a private combat course he'd like to push Richard Dunne through, perhaps he fancies Ian Evans as professor of square bashing, either way, you suspect he'll be betting his hard-earned won on Spain. (The won is the currency of Korea. Those of us who have tried to tip these proud people have been told, 'No. You can keep your oul won.')

Various supplicants are taken to meet the Brigadier General as the training unfolds. Brendan Menton of the FAI is ushered forward and, in fairness, if you thought the Pope looked overawed to meet Paul McGrath back in 1990, you should have seen Brendan Menton turning on the reverence with the Brig. General. It worked a treat, and soon a large icebox of soft drinks was produced for the press. We all reached for the cans of Pocari Sweat, diet of champions.

Duff (knee), Keane (groin), Staunton (thigh), Quinn (agedness) and Kilbane (ankle) sat out the training, and it occurs to many of us that we would prefer that those five play and the rest be injured if it were to come to the crunch against Spain this Saturday.

The Brigadier General doesn't share our concerns. He sits and watches it all as his translator/flunky de camp comes and goes with mysterious titbits of information, 'The Great Lee Carsley, Sir. They call him Geezer, Sir.'

When the training session finishes, the squad race towards the air conditioning of the bus. They lose anything up to half-a-stone training hard in these conditions, mostly from running towards the cool of the bus at the end. Mick McCarthy waits on the pitch and the Brigadier General rises from his seat and walks down the steps towards him. The mountain coming towards Mohammed. This is a moment that will have the North Koreans eating their hearts out. Stiffly (well Mick McCarthy), they pose for a photograph, shaking hands. On and on, the handshake goes as the cameras click and whirr. Both men smile tightly and gaze into the middle distance. By nightfall, we speculate, thousands and thousands of copies of this photo will be dropped on North Korean villages just to demoralize them.

We get another taxi back to Seoul. The driver is eating garlic-scented chewing gum and his armpits also appear to be issuing the scent of garlic. He keeps to a steady thirty miles an hour in the chaotic traffic and the only sounds out of him are the occasional parping of his horn and the burping of his garlicky breath.

Afterwards, back in the team hotel, there are two press conferences, one with Mick McCarthy and one with the players.

The press conferences have been deteriorating as the time goes on. Mick is pretty certain now that we hacks are the spawn of Beelzebub. He rejects us and all our deeds. At every opportunity, he makes it clear that there is only one way to look at journalists. Down.

'What was the problem with the training facility?' asks some suicidal maniac straight off the bat. This is how cabin crazy we have become. You never ask the hard questions at the beginning.

'I had a choice of three,' begins Mick and goes on to explain the whole thing. 'The training facility is fine.'

'There was a suggestion that there was a complaint to FIFA?' asks somebody else. We're pushing the envelope here now. It's not very big either.

'Well,' says Mick loudly in a voice dripping with bitter sarcasm, 'we had a great result the other day and we qualified for the last sixteen of the World Cup finals and I'm here talking about bull. Again. I've not made any complaints to FIFA . . . Any football questions?'

Yikes! Somebody makes with a footie question. 'What did he think of the Spaniards?'

'We couldn't see any weaknesses, so we've decided we'll have to hide the ball!' says Mick, but it's the sort of joke Hannibal Lecter might make while taking the fava beans and a nice chianti out of the fridge. Nobody laughs, except Brendan McKenna the press officer.

We have thirty minutes of very strained questioning in which the Spanish journalists present try to make useful contributions and we all hope one of them will ask about Ian Harte and whether or not he'll play. Hartie is having the sort of crisis of confidence that a cow gets just outside an abattoir. We are all reluctant to ask about this right now.

The Spanish ask if Mick can remember playing against José Camacho in Cork in 1985. He can't. 'I'm sure he's got a big dossier though on my days at Barnsley,' he says sarcastically.

It gets worse and worse.

Any changes imminent?

'I've told you for the last two weeks our strength is in the way we play, why the hell anybody should want me to change now is beyond me . . . If I had to rely on people in here to give the team confidence we'd be knackered! . . . I will not sit here and criticize my players. Never have, never will!'

It's all so childish and unnecessary. We know that, if we ask about Ian Harte, Mick will carry on like a baby and make a big deal about it when all he has to do is kill the matter by saying that he has every confidence in Ian Harte.

The players are ushered in for some light relief. Shay Given has a calming effect everywhere he goes. Collectively, we have a premonition about penalty kicks.

'Packie mentioned to me that, after the game, the next step is penalty kicks, if it goes that far. I said I'd fancy taking one myself. He said, "You just worry about saving one", with his grumpy head on!'

That's the way. We just need the odd good-humoured line, a touch of the anecdotes to keep us happy. It's not hard. We talk penalties for a while. And then we throw a few questions at Richard Dunne and Steve Finnan just to keep them happy.

Then it's off into the Seoul evening, making bad jokes about dog stew. Nearly a month together.

To be honest, the end can't come quick enough.

Seoul

The week leading to the Spanish game limps by pleasantly. Seoul is a nice city to wander in, and after Chiba's antiseptic dullness, it's good to be somewhere that is just teeming with life and character.

Mick McCarthy continues to look worse every time we see him. I think maybe he is in a state of shock, seeing trouble hiding behind each tree. I imagine that when he surveys the national delirium concerning the team's arrival in the second round, he knows that the flip side is a hysterical sense of national expectation.

Which could lead to disappointment. Somewhere down the road, Mick is probably going to get rained on. A win against Spain will hold the storm clouds off for a while longer though.

The game looms at the end of the week. The team is decidedly bored by now. So bored that Robbie Keane gives me a nice long one-on-one interview for Saturday's paper, confirming me as a new member of his fan club.

At home, Ireland is jubilant and raucously expectant. When Roy Keane skipped out, we expected the team wouldn't be long about coming home after him. The second round is a bonus. Playing a flakey Spanish team is even better.

McCarthy is suspicious of all these happy vibes. This whole

business has been too much of a roller coaster for a man who doesn't like change. He looks washed out and worn away and he has been falling back on his native gruffness for defence. In the course of a single press conference this week, he could be heard lambasting us for writing his team off and then laughing at us for assuming Spain were favourites.

On the second night here, the Koreans played and the streets had to be closed down to traffic for half a day before the game. In a remarkable coincidence, everyone came to town wearing the same type of red T-shirt. The Koreans gathered like a huge blob of ketchup and went mad in a quiet, Dufferlike way. You haven't seen crowds till you've seen Korean crowds. They gathered. They cheered in unison. They clapped and exuberated.

Then they tidied up after themselves and went home.

If you ever have to have half-a-million people in your house for a function, make sure they are Koreans.

The photographers have found a club called the Woodstock, which is contained in a building that is a shopping mall for all of life's bigger experiences, comprising, as it does, a church, a brothel and a rock 'n' roll stage. It's like the old Emo Phillips joke concerning the kid who prayed to God every night for a bike till he finally realized that God didn't operate that way, so the kid just went and stole one and asked for forgiveness. The Woodstock offers the devil's own music, original sin and the chance for patrons to walk home every morning with a soul as fresh and new as the dawn.

Many of us hacks have taken the opportunity to head an hour north of Seoul to see the demilitarized zone, or DMZ, between the north and south of the country. It's a fascinating trip.

There is a tunnel here that the tour guides bring tourists down. It is called the Third Tunnel of Aggression, and the South Koreans discovered their North Korean brothers building it a few years back with a view to invading the South. Having seen Korean football crowds, we are ready to believe that the South could well have been invaded via this tunnel, and the whole country could have been annexed without upset or littering.

In the tunnel, we wear hard hats and bend our heads and trudge along through the subterranean hole in the granite, bemoaning the fact that we aren't allowed to take photos of each other. 'It's not like the North Koreans don't know the tunnel is here,' we argue. The Third Tunnel of Sarcasm, they call it now.

On Sunday, we travel to the southern gateway of Seoul, to Suwon. For our Suwon Song.

All week we have worked ourselves into a fever telling each other that we quietly fancy that we'll get a result here. There is consternation in the press box when the crafty Spaniards drop Nadal. We'd planned on them playing Nadal. They can't drop Nadal. He's older than Niall Quinn. We need him to play. Somebody complain to FIFA.

After that, there is a forlorn inevitability about the night. There are moments of pure excitement, of course, not least Ian Harte's penalty miss, Kevin Kilbane's failure to put the rebound into a gaping net and Robbie Keane's injury-time penalty, which takes the game into sudden-death territory. Here, we fail to notice that the Spaniards have only ten men.

The penalty shootout has a curiously fatalistic feel about it. There's no way Robbie Keane can take them all, so there's no way we can win. We watch the Irish spray the ball about creatively from the penalty spot and then go down to gather the losing quotes.

All Irish adventures end up in these circumstances, players being hounded by hacks for sad, sum-it-all-up quotes. In fairness, the boys are good. There's a weight gone from their shoulders. They'd talk all night now, if they didn't plan to drink all night.

Their reaction is not untypical. For players, the World Cup is a long tournament, a long time to be together. By necessity and inclination, they aren't great travellers. There is disappointment at being beaten but going home and getting a holiday sounds good.

Next day, Monday, we have our final press conference with Mick McCarthy. As a surreal touch, it is held in a huge boardroom containing a massive oval table with a microphone drooping towards every seat. Every hack who comes in has a joke about it.

'This is Captain Picard of the Starship *Enterprise*.'

'On behalf of da five families I'da jus like to say that no way can we take this matta of the shooting of Johnny Big Guts lying down.'

'The Greens' committee has decided . . .'

'I'm sorry counsel, but my client wishes to assert his right not to answer that question on the grounds that it may incriminate him.'

Best joke belongs to Liam Mackey from *The Examiner* who pretends we are the board of Pfizer and begins pointing all the microphones straight at the ceiling. By the time Mick comes in we are all giggly and restless, which is unfortunate because we fully expect that he is going to resign, that he will say that he has had enough over the past month and wants to get on with real life.

The odd thing about how it all ended up on that last night in Suwon is the way in which our exit from the tournament crystallized the arguments between Keane and McCarthy.

We went out with bravery and passion. We lost a game we should have won. We went out because we couldn't score penalties, missing four out of seven.

So, Ireland's World Cup ended in one of those evenings that

Roy Keane despises. It ended with the classic Irish moral victory. Which isn't to say that McCarthy didn't hate losing to Spain. Just to recognize that the game threw up fodder for argument. The game threw up different reactions. Mick argues that it be seen as a glorious failure. Most people, still caught in the passion of the match, would agree. Keane's argument is that there is nothing glorious about failure.

Mick seems slightly offended that we should seek to examine the anatomy of a second-round game that we lost, but, by common consent, should have won. Forensic analysis centred on the penalty shootout and the half hour of football before it.

'Practising penalties is garbage', is Mick's opinion, which is frank and trenchant enough surely to admit some argument and questioning.

Indeed, the comment seems to articulate the essential difference between the competing philosophies – Keane's 'fail to prepare/ prepare to fail' view and McCarthy's more intuitive approach.

On the pitch in Suwon, Mick asked for volunteers to take the penalties. Some good kickers kept their hands down. There is a school of thought that argues that practising penalties can't be garbage though. Practising anything till it becomes a mechanical reflex has to be useful, that's why golfers practise three-foot putts till they are blue in the face. Most of us have no idea what it is like to take a penalty in front of 40,000 people but highly paid foot-ballers do. They play in front of that sort of crowd every week. Does the notion of asking for volunteers not create a psychological barrier, while, at the same time, opening the back door for an excuse? Well done for being so brave anyway.

Would there not be more sense in appointing penalty takers number one to eleven at the start of a tournament, letting everyone take care of their own practice at the end of training and letting individual players visualize the moment and the atmosphere in anticipation? Too many games these days are decided by penalties.

Of forty-eight knockout games in the last three World Cups, ten have ended in penalty shootouts. That's a better than 20 per cent of a game going to penalties. Is the notion of volunteers the best way?

It's not a personal thing. It should be possible to argue the point in the abstract with Mick. We all accept that he has done superbly to get us here, that he has put a broken team back together while he's been here. He often berates us for not asking enough about football itself but, when we do, he's never happy.

In the end, our departure was decorated with all the great Irish traits. Passion, hunger, drama and honour. It was a better way to leave than the way we exited from USA '94, when we went home after a whipping.

McCarthy brings that passion and all that unique ability to motivate players to the table. He can play that hand in any argument over technique. I'd love to lock us all into this boardroom though. I reckon that, after a short while, the honesty would begin to seep out.

I don't believe there's a person in this room who 100 per cent believes that Ireland could have won this World Cup. We've all settled for the glorious exit. Probably the only man in the world who believes we could have gone the whole way is sitting at home in Manchester, fuming.

We ask the usual follow-up stuff. Mick says early in the conference that he'll stay. Roy Keane's name gets mentioned for the first time in weeks. Mick's happy enough to leave that alone with a quick, 'No comment.'

Mick rises and leaves. As he does so, for some reason the room bursts into applause. Why? Because he's a good fellow who despises us? Because we are big fans? Do we think it will make Mick like us a little when the European Championships start? Just to be safe, we begin making up a list of those who refrained from the clapping and send it to Roy. Who knows?

It's an odd way to finish what has, basically, been weeks of hostilities since Roy Keane went home. The trouble between media and manager is nobody's fault in particular. Mick needs somebody with him just to whisper in his ear occasionally that the best way forward sometimes is to be loose and open. It doesn't have to be nose-to-nose, in-your-face stuff all the time.

Most of the time, there hasn't been enough basic information available. The media access to the team was grudging and badly organized. The demands from home for copy were immense. That's what World Cups are about. Everybody seemed to realize this except the Irish.

Most of the journalists are going home with the team tomorrow. A few, including Emmet and myself, are staying on in Asia till the end of the tournament.

We've got stuff to do now. We have to make our own arrangements from here on in. At least we don't have to go to the Phoenix Park to see Joe Duffy in one of those ghastly welcome home ceremonies that the country has become so good at.

Nobody deserves that.

III

Time Added On

'There are two kinds of sportswriter: those with good sense and the ability to go on to other things and those with neither.'

Leonard Schecter

Tuesday, 18th June to Monday, 1st July – Asia

A small Irish contingent remain on in Seoul. We are forgotten, but not gone. The World Cup is ours to step through now, cherry-picking the games, getting back to the more familiar business of previews, profiles and quotes. We go to press conferences where no tension accrues. We write a fraction of the number of words per day that we are used to.

We miss the madness though. We miss the support network and the gossip and the bitching. And, after weeks of responding sullenly about being told where to go and who we can speak to and when we can get the bus, well, it's odd and a little exhilarating to be free to make our own way around Asia.

The paper is cock-a-hoop. They have mined more words out of myself and Emmet than anybody thought possible. We are to keep going till we make little stubs of our typing fingers. On the Tuesday after the team leaves Seoul, the two of us fly back to Japan to cover England's game against Brazil.

There is a plan and there is a contingency plan. The plan is that we will both base ourselves in Tokyo and split up the games that take place on Japanese soil. The contingency plan, only to be opened in case of dire emergency, is for me to return to South Korea if the South Koreans continue their improbable progress through the tournament.

On our way from Incheon to Tokyo, we are adopted by a very

large German who introduces himself as a former football hooligan. He is a well-travelled chap and lists a large number of countries he has been to, and an almost equally lengthy list of places he has been banned from. He says that he has reformed now, although he also says that he has been doing a lot of TV here in South Korea, using his expertise in hooliganism to alarm the locals. His current hobby is travelling to places once occupied by Germany and seeing what influence is left. He can tell that Emmet is more sociable than I am. Emmet gets the phone number to file under the 'hooligan' section in his address book.

When we get to Tokyo, after a series of delays, it's dark and it's raining and we seem to have more baggage than the average rock band takes on tour. Emmet has a hotel booked already. I go to the accommodation desk at the airport where they offer a good deal if you pay cash in advance for two weeks at the Inter-Continental. I weigh up the chances of South Korea progressing. Zero. Two weeks please!

Our first mission, should we choose to accept it (instead of accepting redundancy), is England's big game with Brazil. The paper has decided to give this the full works in terms of coverage. We are the full works.

We travel down from Tokyo to Shizuoka, a small rural town which has had an international football stadium grafted onto its meagre infrastructure. Or near its infrastructure. The stadium is miles away from the town. It brings a whole new meaning to green-field site. It is green fields, then some fields in which they appear to be growing tea, then some forest, and then a mountain on the bottom of which is the stadium. Even the road up to the stadium is brand new, two lanes of fresh, sticky blacktop.

Halfway through the preparations for this competition, the Japanese had begun to feel the unpleasant sensation of recession and had second thoughts about building all these new stadiums. They called up the South Koreans and wondered aloud if it wouldn't be more sensible to desist from the pissing contest both nations were engaged in, and just build fewer stadiums. The South Koreans politely said that Japan could do as it wished, but that South Korea would be building ten lovely stadiums for its visitors to marvel at.

The Japanese shrugged and got back to work on these edifices that they'll have no real use for when this month is over. We imagine them just letting the forest re-grow around the stadium when the World Cup is over, until, finally, it disappears from view and from civic memory, only to be discovered by some dazzled archaeologist in the next millennium.

We spend an afternoon in a Japanese rail office buying rail passes and booking tickets for various trips between now and the end of the World Cup. As it turns out, England vs Brazil is scarcely justified in the end.

England exit the tournament with such timidity that even we Irish feel let down. How could such a placid bunch have oppressed us for 800 years? Makes us look bad.

Since before the World Cup, I've been touting my opinion that England's adventure would end in tears. Nothing personal. I think of this as the Eamon Dunphy technique. In a thirty-two-team tournament, which can have only one winner, you look smartest by writing off every team's chances. Thirty-one times you'll get to remind people, that as you predicted, this team had a flaw right at the heart of it.

Anyway what about these English losers? They don't get bounced out of the tournament, they put on their coats and show themselves the door. Just when the mean boys had become jaded with taunting David Seaman about his mid-life crisis hairdo, old

David gives them fresh material for mockery. Poor Seaman came, saw and swished like a pony beset by midgets at a second-half free kick of Ronaldinho's. Next thing, he was picking it from the net. In the press conference afterwards, Ronaldinho lets it be known that, not only did he intend to score, but his good mate Cafu can confirm this. Damning! The goal will be one of the lasting images of this World Cup. The highlight reel of these sorts of howlers that Seaman has put together will be shown on telly when ever he pops his clogs.

It reminds me of the fate of one Fred Snodgrass who, having left baseball to enjoy a career which earned him millions as a businessman as well as the mayorship of his home town, died at a most-advanced age only to have his obituary begin with the words: 'The death has occurred of Mr Fred Snodgrass, who dropped a fly ball while playing for the New York Yankees in the World series of . . .'

In the mixed zone afterwards, we wait interminably. The Brazilians come through in high spirits and we gather around Ronaldo just to share a little part of his goofy world. We notice that for Brazilian journalists there is no such thing as objectivity. They are hugging the players, singing to them, cheering them. The English contingent are so cold with each other now that you could catch frostbite just being around them.

A group of the team's black players emerge, keeping themselves to themselves and provoking some quiet comment. David Seaman comes through the media area shedding tears and needless apologies. 'I just want to say sorry to the people I've let down badly,' he says and breaks down.

This causes an outbreak of bad temper amidst the hackery, who are already irked enough at the Japanese stewards who have been bothering everyone with their insistence that nobody can use their mobile phones in the mixed zone.

When Seaman gets all weepy, there is pushing and shoving to the front so that everyone may witness it first hand. The handlers move Seaman on before he falls to the floor and starts shouting, 'Why? Oh, why?'

Then the recriminations begin. Those close enough to the tears to be able to reach out and dab the keeper's face haven't asked any questions. They say they felt sorry for the bloke. Those at the back pose the counter-argument that states that for a month Seaman has been the surliest bastard in the Orient. He hasn't spoken a word to the press. Coming out and blubbering like a baby is his way of making sure he doesn't get clubbed to death in the morning papers.

It's getting nasty when David Beckham, the scapegoat deluxe of England's last World Cup exit of France '98, emerges. There is a deathly crush of journalists. We move towards him and the tanned vacancy of his face. We gaze up. He's wearing his socks and carrying boots in his hand. He makes a sweet, inarticulate speech from the heart.

'If anyone tries to make a scapegoat out of David Seaman, I think it would be an absolute disgrace. I think he's been the best goalkeeper in this tournament. It wasn't his fault, the goal. I think it's been a fluke goal.'

Becks has been there, say the hacks afterwards. If it is in permissible taste to mention crosses, well Becks has been crucified on that very cross. The way the boys talk you would think that the process has nothing to do with them. And in a way it doesn't. Everyone here needs to be allowed use their mobile so they can ring their offices and find out what sort of line the paper is going with.

In a way, it's a shame to see an England team look so wan and insipid. Most of us, who couldn't bear to see them win the thing, prefer it when their exits are plucky but brave. The Japanese aren't with us on this one. The Japanese love the English. Beckham is a god here. Bizarrely, even the English fans will be missed.

This is another sign that the world is ending. Most of us who covered France '98 come out in rashes when forced to recall being anywhere near English fans, especially that phase of the tournament when they began picking on journalists. In Japan, though, the English have been loved and, in their turn, they have been good-humoured.

On the train to Shizuoka today, they sang and sang. Just the same tuneful little ditty over and over for an hour, 'We're on the train! We're on the train! We're on the train!' It might have been tedious, but when you've heard their brothers-in-arms chanting, 'You're going to get your fucking heads kicked in,' it has a certain innocent charm.

They came and they went, and they left not an ounce of menace anywhere in the air.

Leaving Shizuoka today, almost three hours after the game ended, the locals were still lined along the road back into town, just standing there to applaud the English. The majority of them are wearing English jerseys with David Beckham's name on them.

Beckham must be in more than his customary state of benign bewilderment. Four years ago in France, he couldn't catch a break. This time, weakened by injury, he has genuinely had a poor World Cup, but there's scarcely a journalist working in England who'll come out and say it.

It's late on Friday night when we get back to Tokyo, but Emmet and I have had a brainwave regarding the weekend. Turkey and Senegal are playing a quarterfinal on Saturday night in Osaka, not far from Kyoto, a town that is allegedly worth seeing. We will trip down to Kyoto tomorrow afternoon, have dinner, go to Osaka for the game, and sightsee in Kyoto on Sunday.

The only fly that can possibly enter this ointment is if South Korea beat Spain in Gwangju a little earlier on tomorrow. In that case, I am under instructions to fly straight back to Seoul for the semi-final.

Of course it happens. We take the Shinkansen, or bullet train, from Tokyo. Three hundred miles in three hours really pegs your ears back. One moment we are in Tokyo, the next we are wandering around Kyoto on Saturday afternoon, unable to find a single place showing the Korea vs Spain game.

Kyoto is steadfastly ignoring the World Cup. We try bars, hotels, restaurants. Nothing. Finally, we come upon a garage in a back street where the mechanic is sitting on an overturned oil drum watching a little portable with bunny ears (on the telly, that is). He moves to switch the telly off when I stick my head in. I feel like George Orwell's creation, Winston Smith, quietly making contact with a like-minded soul, but fearing that Big Brother is watching. I point to the TV and make a silent, enquiring gesture. He makes zeros with his oily thumbs and forefingers and puts them up to his eyes like spectacles. No goals in Gwangju. I bow. He bows.

The Koreans go on to win on penalties. The weekend of tourism and culture is ruined. I'd read somewhere that, at one stage in Japan's rather cussed relationship with Korea, Japanese soldiers would be rewarded for the number of Koreans they could dispatch. The method of proving just how many Koreans you had killed was to cut off the noses of the deceased. You got paid by the nose. Apparently, and one would imagine much to the disgust of Koreans, the noses are all buried in a mound somewhere in Kyoto. Ghoulish though it sounds, I was keen to see this. A mound of noses is not something you get to see very often.

Instead, the morning after the Turkey vs Senegal match, I get up early and trek back to South Korea. I'm on the bus to the airport when I read in my Kyoto guidebook that the Shinkansen train from Tokyo to Kyoto deposits you in the ugliest part of town. Ah. That's why we managed to see just one of Kyoto's 1,600 Buddhist monasteries and none of it's 400 Shinto shrines, and no Korean noses.

Sunday, 23rd June

The Koreans play Germany in the semi-final on Tuesday. I've just a quick column to write today. Some Sundays, the business of the column can really weigh on you. You spend the weekend worrying that recent columns have been miserable, poor, unloved little orphans sent out into the world to fend for themselves without an ounce of intellectual nourishment but, this week, you are going to beef it up with big thoughts. So you do, and nothing happens. No reaction. Nothing. The following Sunday, you toss out some dross and slag off Manchester United and get forty letters. There's something shallow about columns. Eventually, I send some dross down the phoneline to D'Olier Street. Will try very hard next week.

Seoul again. Will call home later. Travel drains you but there's a self-important thrill to be had when you call somebody up and when they say, 'How is Tokyo?', you just say, 'Nah, I'm back in Seoul.'

I note that, on Tuesday, it will be six weeks exactly since I've seen Mary, the kids and the cat. The cat could be a world leader now for all I know.

Still, could be worse. For a few brief shining days in this year of financial disaster for my poor old paper, I am retaining hotel rooms in two Asian capitals. If I am to single-handedly bring down the paper this year, I will do so in style. I call room service. It's nice to be back in Seoul.

There has been much debate in the press corps over the last few weeks as to which is preferable: Japan or Korea. The majority has plumped for Japan, resisting those of us who insist that the stifling code of Japanese manners really masks, not just a distrust of foreigners, but a disdain for them too.

I haven't been treated with any disdain in Japan, of course. None of us have. But I have a distant cousin who lived there for ten years and, the more she got to know about the language and the people and the inflections of conversation, the more she came to realize that she was considered inferior. That may be just the Japanese attitude to my extended family, of course, but for argument's sake, I have elected to enlarge and transpose it so that the Japanese are complete xenophobes. I don't know why, I just like the garrulous Koreans a little better.

Japan and Korea are knotted together for the purposes of this World Cup, but they are as different from each other as England and Ireland – as different and as rivalrous. They are only co-hosting because neither country could stand to lose to the other in the bidding process. They have outdone each other like *nouveau riche* neighbours in the preparations for the World Cup.

I like Japan, and Tokyo has something different and interesting to offer every day, but I prefer the easy-going life of the Koreans. I love the broad rivers and the interesting smells and the fact that the people laugh easily and long. There's a hustle and bustle about the place that seems homely in a way.

And then there's that small, unforgiven matter of Japan having occupied Korea for thirty-five years, not so long ago. There's an inclination to root for the underdog.

The surface of Japanese life is a comedy of manners, an endless cavalcade of formalities and customs that charm the newcomer and conceal what people (OK my distant cousin), who have lived here a long time, say is a deep-rooted dislike of foreigners.

There are moments, of course, when the manners thing just bowls you over. In Sapporo, early in the morning after the England vs Argentina game, I was at the airport surrounded by a sea of departing English fans, when we all enjoyed the heart-warming sight of a uniformed young woman running through the airport terminal late for work. She was so embarrassed by her wanton lack of decorum that she bowed at everybody she passed as she sprinted past. She looked like a water hen on speed.

The Koreans are a different kettle of fish – cooked fish for a start. They enjoy a more informal, philosophical existence than their neighbours. In Japan, one risks losing the elevator altogether as all parties gathered at its gaping doors bow and beckon to each other to step aboard first. In Korea, you'd be trampled to death and the last thing you'd hear was hearty laughter. They enjoy a belly laugh do the Koreans.

And they've been laughing all month. From the time the World Cup was granted to these countries, the unannounced competition within a competition was to see who could stay in the longest: Japan or South Korea. Both nations appointed foreign coaches, but the Japanese got a jump on the Koreans and got their man first.

Phillipe Troussier, who looks more like the actor Rick Moranis, arrived in Japan in 1998 and launched his reign with a friendly against Egypt. The following year, the Japanese side finished second at the World Under-20 Championships, becoming the first Asian side to reach the final of a FIFA-sanctioned event. The Japanese were too stifled by politeness to sing it but, in private moments, they hummed their tune, 'Are You Watching South Korea?'

The following summer, Troussier took an under-23 squad to the Sydney Olympics and steered them to the quarterfinals, Japan's best performance in the competition for thirty-two years. A month later, the full Japanese squad won the Asian Cup. The following summer, the only goal they conceded in the Confederations Cup was to France in the final. The French had already toasted the South Koreans 5–0 in the first round. Many thin smiles in Japan.

The Koreans tried to secure the services of Aimé Jacquet, the former French manager. Their failure to do so disappointed those of us working on Jacket vs Trousers subplots to describe the Asian competition within a competition. Instead they employed a Dutchman. In newspapers, of course, this means just two things for headline writers: 'Koreans Go Dutch' and 'Koreans Buy Dutch Master'.

Guus Hiddink had only eighteen months to create a squad for the World Cup. By the time he took over, the South Koreans had enjoyed a gutful of their perfect neighbours and he must have been able to sense the quiet desperation of his new employers.

It would be typical Korean luck for them to be overshadowed by their old enemies. The Koreans, after all, nurtured the first pro-league in Asia, the still extant K-League (founded 1983), only to see it eclipsed by the vulgarity and imported stars of the unimaginatively titled J-League. They plugged away anyway.

They completed an airport the size of a city in Incheon and built a Bertiesque stadium nearby, even though the city has no team. The city itself has its history, though. English sailors from a ship called the *Flying Fish* landed here in 1880 and introduced soccer to the local populace. They'd had to wait a long, long time and when, a month before the World Cup, Hiddink announced that the World Cup had probably come a year too early for his team, a nation wept. We always told you, Guus. World Cup 2002. 'Remember that date, Guus,' we said, '2002. What's happening in 2002, Guus? Don't make with the big shrugs. World Cup, Guus.'

The signs weren't promising, but now it turns out that Guus was just pulling the nation's leg. He was making the joke. When you look at his squad, you realize he must have been. Some of his squad are playing in their fourth World Cup. Sure the Korean record in five previous appearances in the finals is 'played fourteen, lost ten, drawn four' and that includes a 9–0 hammering from Hungary and a 7–0 wipeout against, erm, Turkey, yes that Turkish team of all the talents.

In fact, the greatest Korean memory of World Cup play belonged to their dour neighbours to the north, just across the DMZ. In 1966, at Goodison Park, North Korea led a legendary Portuguese team 3–0 after twenty-five minutes of a World Cup semi-final.

Then Eusebio clicked into gear and scored four goals, and the heroic North Koreans wound up losing 5–3.

The North Koreans had already beaten Italy up at Ayresome Park, Middlesborough, however. I love the story of Italian hubris. Famously, the Italians had gone to see the them play before the tournament and pronounced the experience to be like watching *una comedia di Ridolini* (Signor Ridolini being a Chaplinesque Italian film star of the 1920s). Italy lost 1–0 and went home in shame, the manager sacked instantly. The goal scorer, Park Doo-Ik, went on to become a dentist. You can read that fact once a day if you keep up with English-language papers here.

It has played like a nagging cavity on Korean minds all year that their team might exit before the Japanese. So, when Japan were eliminated against Turkey early in the same day, and South Korea beat Italy, it was as if the World Cup was over and had been awarded, in perpetuity, to the Koreans.

Hiddink had built his team in a style that, funnily enough, the Italians should have understood. From the defence upwards. In a rematch against France a couple of months ago, Korea closed the margin to a single goal and played with different central defenders in either half. They set up training camp in Europe in March and went five games (Tunisia, Finland, Turkey, Costa Rica and China) without conceding a goal.

Smart boy Guus. Now the South Koreans are the story. The crowds. The influence this is having on the culture of a nation. Chris Davis from the *Telegraph* has been covering the Koreans as a sideline since we first got here. He stayed on when some of us went back for England and Brazil. I think Chris is about to turn native. He's fallen a little in love with the place. The fact that the hotel lost his software when they were fixing his computer for him and gave him a room upgrade to compensate, has helped the process, but he's certainly smitten.

Now South Korea has just got the toothless Germans to get past and they are in a World Cup final. There's some optimism about that. I haven't been able to book a flight back to Tokyo anytime before Sunday. I'm flying to Osaka and getting the train instead. Travelling back and forth from Japan to Korea the long way has been a drag, but this is a little piece of history you wouldn't want to miss.

Yet if you're looking for Germans to collude with in creating romance, you're barking up the wrong tree. They're not sentimental really. Word among the German hacks is that this team was sent off to the World Cup, unloved and unwanted, and their ugly battling has earned them a loyal following. 'They are more loved than more efficient teams,' say the German boys laughing hugely at the daffy, madcap German humour of it all.

Tuesday, 25th June

In Tokyo, I purchased a video camera. I spent most of the train journey to Kyoto filming Emmet for my first feature, to be called *Man on the Train in Japan*. Finally, he lost his temper and I told him the film would now be distributed with the new title *Red Faced Man on the Train in Japan*. He stared, unhelpfully, out the window while I fiddled with the camera, checking the daily rushes. I then realized that I hadn't been filming him at all, just making his face appear on the little monitor screen. I told him I had left the rushes on the cutting-room floor, that he'd never work in this town again.

This morning, I get up early and begin filming what people will see as my actual first film, a short, but absorbing, feature called *World Cup Semi-Final Day in Seoul*. Print media are forbidden from filming anything inside the stadium, so there'll be no actual World Cup semi-final in the film but that, in itself, is a caustic comment on the interplay between a people, their passion and their media.

I film a nice sunrise from the hotel-room window, but when I play it back, I can mainly see my reflection standing naked in a hotel room filming the sky. The people cleaning the office building across the street can see the same thing. Art!

There's a lovely, slow, building sense of anticipation to the day. I wander around and film anything I'm not too shy to point the camera at. Mainly buildings and monuments. By the time I should be leaving for the stadium, Seoul is a long, swaying field of red poppies.

This is a nice image but a tragic one also. The hotel desk informs me that it is a land swaying with so many red poppies that there are no shuttle buses going to the stadium. To get there, they would have to mow down other red poppies. It's late when I take to the underground. I really need Emmet with me when I go on the underground. Although Emmet and I are very entertained by another member of the press corps who, apparently, collects airline refresher towels as a hobby, Emmet himself is a few evolutionary steps down from the common-or-garden trainspotter. He used to work in the London Underground and now likes visiting undergrounds. I am entertained by this until now, when I am stuck in a major underground station in Seoul and the usual rule for getting to a match (follow the crowd) doesn't apply because virtually all of Korea is coming into the centre of town to watch the match together in a big square. Help!

I get to my seat in the stadium about fifteen seconds before kick off. I sit sweating, and possibly having a mild coronary. Two hotel rooms in two different Asian capitals might be unavoidable and unforgivable. Missing the match?

The love story ends.

The Koreans almost turn the semi-final into another night of wonder. They bow out, though, without tears or self-pity. They raise the roof with gracious applause for their conquerors. They release their firecrackers into the sky anyway, and they linger long on the stands and in the streets singing their songs and chanting in unison. Something sweet and fundamental seems to have happened to Korean life these past few weeks, something that will last longer than a World Cup.

On the pitch, it was all cut and dried once Michael Ballack scored for the Germans. The ball crossed the line and flipped a switch somewhere in Korea, momentarily silencing the delirious home crowd. The giant screens at either end of the stadium had been cleverly tricked out with coloured lines to monitor the decibels below. Green for mere din. Yellow for riotous cacophony. Pink for the neighbours in Japan to start complaining about the racket and apologizing for the business with the noses.

Ah well. This was a sort of arrival for Korea. Hosting and being successful, they proved something to themselves. When the dawn arrives tomorrow, the land of morning calm will have been returned to its customary state of quiet repose, but people's hearts will be beating a little bit faster. The Koreans have been the best thing about this World Cup.

Meanwhile Germany, the most seasoned and uncurious of travellers, move back to Japan. I go with them.

Sunday night/Monday morning, 30th June to 1st July

For us, the World Cup ends in the rain. Not just any old rain but an epic deluge of it on Monday morning, July 1st.

We covered the World Cup final last night with a sort of beaten weariness. It's a strange event for sportswriters. As a kid, the World Cup final is bigger than you could ever imagine. One match every four years. Great landmarks in the sport.

For a journalist, though, by the time you get through the great banquet of football that precedes a World Cup final, you've had quite enough thank you. Enough of the teams, the travel, the game, the writing, the whole package. And Yokohama, the venue for this World Cup final, is distinctly unimpressive. The stadium is old and there is no elevator to the cliff top where we media sit. Getting there is a slow drudge up about fourteen flights of stairs, symbolic, perhaps, of how we all got to the World Cup in the first place. We suspect, too, that the match will be a crock, that the Germans will be found out at last. Such a novel World Cup doesn't deserve an all-blueblood final, but it has one.

Yet it's a World Cup final! You have to pinch yourself. I'm here! This is dream stuff. I'm here and paid to be here. In some way, through some dumb luck, I must have made progress in my profession. Ten years ago, I would have killed for this privilege. It's a long night nevertheless.

We get back to Tokyo from Yokohama at about 4.30 a.m. and pack our gear. By dawn, it is time to head to the airport. The interval between the end of gear packing and the arrival of dawn was about twelve minutes. Outside, the rain is coming down in great sheets. There's nowhere to have breakfast.

Clive White of the *Independent* makes an alarm-call request for fifteen minutes later. He so badly needs to close his eyes. I would like to do the same, but I know I wouldn't get up again. I like Clive's style this morning. Like many of us, he has hired a mobile phone for the duration of the trip. We are supposed to post these back by registered post or drop them into an office at the airport. Clive runs through the hotel lobby towards the airport shuttle bus and with a neat hand-off pass, deposits his mobile into the arms of a bellboy who instinctively says, 'Thank you, Sir.'

The last shuttle-bus journey! We are bored and sour on each other's company by now. Dying to be home, sick of football, sick of writing. How many ways are there to describe the choreography of a goal being scored?

We have spent seven weeks in this sensory deprivation chamber, an unreal world where football is all that matters. Dimensions and perspective are the first things to go.

There is a prolonged row at the airport as KLM look to charge us each about $1,600 for excess baggage. Poor KLM. They are messing with the wrong bunch of hombres this morning. Dion Fanning of the *Sunday Independent* makes a desultory attempt to lighten his personal load by removing a pair of chopsticks and placing them carefully in his carry-on luggage. The machine isn't sufficiently calibrated to calculate the precise saving involved here. So we argue bitterly. They relent.

Seven weeks of football, of egos, of travel, of each other. Ten different hotel rooms. Sixteen flights. Countless shuttle buses. Press conferences. Stress. A catastrophe of battered metaphors and simple-minded clichés, of 100,000 words written. There should have been health warnings.

Yet we'll miss it and we'll begin to sentimentalize it shortly. The lads will be playing some dreary qualifier, a goal will arrive and we'll be in the stands with our arms raised like the fans we try not to be. We'll be there, quietly yearning for the next time.

Wednesday, 3rd July

For a week after the World Cup, I am wiped out. Everywhere people are still talking about Roy Keane. The abiding Irish memory of the World Cup seems to be Roy Keane walking his dog.

I haven't thought about Roy since Mick and the team went home from Korea. I am surprised the nation is still obsessing. Surprised by how much World Cup stuff we missed just by being at the World Cup.

At the end of a week at home, I call Niall Quinn. Mischievously, Niall has told his publishers that we got 'tons of work' done at the World Cup. They have sent me an e-mail to tell me they are very excited about this news.

In fact, we have two short tapes, yet to be transcribed. I arrange to come over to visit Niall the next week. I'll have my sirens flashing.

I have an irritating tendency to beat my breast piously when it comes to journalistic ethics. And then I wait for my own hypocrisy to be pointed out. The fact is, we all have our price. I hate freebie trips. I rail against them, arguing that, if somebody takes one, if somebody absolutely must take a freebie, well then, the fact should be advertized all over any piece they may write.

Then again, I have a room full of complimentary bags from events. It may be just that my price is lower than everyone else. I operate at the bottom end of the market. A free bag and I'm anyone's.

I think also that it's a bad idea to write a book with, or enter into a commercial deal with, any player or athlete about whom you are going to have to write or commentate objectively in the future. However, I know that, if Roy Keane had asked me to write his book, I would have said yessir and become his personal mind-slave for a year. Characters as interesting as Roy Keane come along once or twice a millennium.

I would have fancied the challenge, and the pay cheque.

As for Niall? I made a few attempts last year to persuade him to write a book of his own. I gave him a copy of my own favourite sports book, *The Game* by Ken Dryden, a former Montreal Canadiens ice-hockey keeper who captured the essence of a whole sport and the essence of Canada, in his account of his final year playing. I love that book. I see its influence on so much that has been written since.

Niall didn't take to it. Only afterwards did I begin to hope that he didn't think I was trying to muscle in and force him to do a book with me. If a player can write, and Niall can, well I'm convinced they should write.

Then a few weeks before the World Cup, Niall called me and asked would I help him with his own book. He put it more tenderly than that, in fact. He said, 'Listen, will you help me out with this fucking book?'

He'd done a deal, was in trouble and needed a hand. Flattered? I was bowled sideways! I would have said no except that, in ten years of covering sport, I haven't met a better, more decent person than Niall Quinn. So, naturally, I was keen to get closer to see if he might be a crack cocaine addict or a loan shark. Something, anything. There has to be a dark side.

That was late April. Now it's getting towards the middle of July. I have done nothing for Niall, except talk a good game.

I sense disillusion, which could be interesting. Perhaps Niall will have a homicidal temper. Maybe, if I continue to do nothing, Niall, in a radical departure from his Mother Teresa image, will have my legs broken, my kids abducted, the head of one of his horses left in my bed.

It's an unworthy thought, of course, considering he's just finishing off the process of giving away his testimonial money, has spent half the World Cup trying to make peace between the warring factions, and, anyway, from what I saw in Saipan, can hold his drink like a man with hollow legs. If that's not the stuff of national heroes, I don't know what is.

Still, in standard sportswriter fashion, I am on the lookout for something to bitch about when I pull up to Niall's house in Sedgefield, just outside Durham, in yet another in the series of tiny rental cars I have managed to hire this year.

During our last conversation at the World Cup, on the night the team lost, Niall had reminded me once more of his most urgent desire to retire from the game at the earliest chance. Then he and the lads had disappeared on a drinking spree for a couple of days and I haven't seen him since. However, instead of sipping the last of the summer wine, Niall has just begun work as a player/coach with Sunderland. I say he's a pathological liar. He says he couldn't turn down Peter Reid. Reid's theory is that he will bring some spirit back into a troubled dressing room.

Niall's new job is our only difficulty in fact. Niall has to get up early these days and work till early afternoon. He's not saying it's coalmining, but it's a change of gear. We start our sessions of unravelling his life in the mid-afternoons in a room of his house.

Niall, like myself, isn't genetically programmed for dealing with early mornings, and soon he is stretched out on the sofa yawning and I'm lounging in the big chair just asking questions on autopilot. I'm suffering from sympathetic tiredness, or else, having fallen asleep during our first interview, my body has come to associate Niall's stories with sleep. This can't be good.

For a few days, I think we both just doze off. It doesn't augur well for the book. It really doesn't. The publishers want to call the book *The Mighty Quinn*. Niall and I are resisting heroically, but can't come up with anything we like, *Rumpelstiltskin, A Life in Football*.

A couple of times, I suggest to Niall that we change venue for our chats, but we can never decide on anywhere. A series of pubs are suggested, but we know that a switch to any licensed premises would be fatal. We continue with the sleepy afternoon sessions.

Not that it makes a whole lot of difference. The convenient thing about working with Niall is that he has a fine memory for detail. During the first week, we talk for hours in the afternoon and I spend the evenings, or the following morning, checking facts. But he never gets anything wrong. If he says that X played in a game, well then, X played in it.

We're both still a little obsessive about Roy Keane, of course.

Roy's book is coming out in early August. I spoke to Eamon Dunphy on the phone the other night, and he told me that the thing is finished. He's shown it all to Roy and Roy likes it. Certainly paid off for Roy then, this business of going home before the World Cup to walk the dog and make a start on the book.

'It's hard putting words into somebody else's mouth, isn't it?' I said to Eamon.

'Ah I dunno, is it?' he said mischievously, knowing that I'd written about ninety such words at that stage.

The two weeks with Niall are easy though. When he's wide awake, he's the best of company. When he's dozing, he slips into an odd mode of speaking that is amusing to listen back to on the tapes. He starts speaking in the way that sportswriters write. I think, subconsciously, he is doing this as a convenience for me, so I won't have to translate the quotes. Jaded, Niall says things like, 'And then I met my great old pal, the Arsenal and Scotland legend, Charlie Nicholas', or 'It quickly developed into an evening which none of us would forget in a hurry', or 'Don't get me wrong, I respect your continental players, it's just that . . .'

We skip through the thirty-five years of his life at a good old lick and, towards the end, there are long minutes when we look at each like an old couple and wonder what's next.

'What will we talk about today?'

'Whatever. Anything you want.'

'Well is there anything we haven't spoken about?'

'Dunno, is there anything else we need to speak about?'

'Dunno. It seems grand.'

'Should be enough, shouldn't it?'

'I'd say so.'

'Can you think of anything else?'

'Not really.'

'Will we go for a drink in a little while?'

'OK then, we'll try that.'

It's enjoyable, but I'm glad when our time together is over. Mary is working on a Masters thesis, we've been trying to sell our house, the kids have been off school and I've only been home for about five days since the middle of May.

And I often have the gall to write that footballers and athletes are selfish.

Sunday, 14th July

Weekend home from Niall and Sedgefield. Pleasant duty today, it's the Leinster Football final. Dublin vs Kildare.

And it turns out to be the first day of summer, the first immersion back in the real world. Truly, it has that sense of beginning or renewal about it. Dublin and Kildare conjure up what is, by consent, the best match of the season so far and gift it to the biggest GAA crowd to have gathered anywhere since back before The Beatles' first LP.

The sun shines down on the perfect green nap of Croke Park. The place tingles with electricity all afternoon long. The stadium, full and dancing with colour, is a wonderful spectacle in its own right now. And, today, Dublin bring a panache to the proceedings, a flair that seems just right for Bastille Day. The style and the swagger of it – brings me back to when I was a kid. For years I didn't even suspect that Dublin had a team. Then, in 1974, when I was eleven, they sprung out of nowhere and won the whole thing. Ever since then, nothing can make me tremble quite like a sky-blue jersey against a sunlit Croke Park sod.

I've always had a sneaking fondness for Kildare though. My grandfather was a big fan of the Flour Bags for some reason, which I can't explain, but it has to do with Larry Stanley, who he met once or twice. Because of all those sessions listening to stories about how sublime Kildare once were, how they can never be written off, etc., etc., I always fear them irrationally.

Today, though, Dublin are like a city team again. They have a way about them, a style exemplified in the two goals they score in front of the teeming Hill 16 end. Both goals are cheeky, skilful throwbacks to the great days when Dublin teams surveyed opposition team sheets like fat men study menus and, when they score, they spark off delirious celebrations on and off the field. It should be the distinguishing mark of Dublin teams that, not only do they score goals, but they take an evident delight in them.

I notice that less than a handful of the Dublin players were even born when the county made its modern breakthrough back in 1974. Perhaps it is as well that tradition doesn't burden them. By being so free of that weight, they serve tradition all the better.

It's all set then for a glorious, blue summer. A new manager, a young side, a simple game plan. You can see the blue flags hanging from houses and trailing from cars, you can feel the anticipation jangling throughout the city. In a World Cup year, a year in which we have sent the national team to represent us, the arrival of this team represents a triumph of timing for the GAA.

Our soccer achievements in Asia already have a sort of 'so what?' feel about them. Keane is the sole lingering fascination for most people. Dublin are the coming story of the sporting season.

When it's over, we go bounding down towards the dressing-room area. Since it was rebuilt, Croke Park offers media facilities that are as good as anything anywhere in the world. We have a fine media working area, nice workrooms, a wonderful press box with monitors and elevators to cart us up and down (are you listening to this in Yokohama, those fourteen flights of stairs were no joke).

And yet, somebody always spoils it. Something in the heart of the GAA regards the 'meejah' as inherently evil. Funny business. Up to no good.

There's always some resentment. Every Sunday, Gerry Grogan, who looks after us in the press box, leads us down to the dressing-room area. Every Sunday when we get there, we start to meet the resistance. We meet a couple of men in blazers who think we are schoolkids. Some Sundays, it has come close to fistfights. There's been pushing and shoving, curses and threats.

The irony is that, in a world where the competition (in the form of the Premiership) gets the sort of publicity that is overcooked and virtually inescapable, the GAA needs to have its players speaking to people, it needs to create heroes and storylines and to generate interest.

So, today, on the day when Croke Park has been rocked and shaken, when Gaelic football has gotten its sexy groove back, the GAA decides to introduce a new method of dealing with the press after matches.

There's a dozen good stories to be told. At least a dozen. We'd love to be down here recording the words and thoughts of new heroes like Alan Brogan, whose father graced this place so many times, or Ray Cosgrove, discarded on the scrapheap of Dublin football until this summer, which he has made his own. We'd love to speak to Johnny McNally about what it's like to be made redundant from your job on a Friday evening and to win your first Leinster medal on Sunday afternoon. We'd love to spread Paddy Christie across a headline or two, but all these conversations are closed off to us. We are corralled into a room and told to wait. We will be given what the GAA thinks we should be given. When? Whenever.

Nevermind. Tommy Lyons, the energetically talkative Dublin manager, finally bounds in. At the worst of times, there is good fun in Tommy Lyons, and sheer exuberance in him at the best. Right now, he is exuberant.

'We'll talk all night lads,' he whoops, catching our mood as he hops in. Hard to tell if he's joking or not.

He looks at me.

'And I owe you an interview T,' he says. He always calls me T. Tom is too much of a mouthful when you have as much to say as Tommy does. It's true, he does owe me an interview. In a shock decision, he turned me down for one in the spring. I don't think Tommy had ever turned down an interview before. My guess is that he was just saying no to see what it sounded like.

Still it hurt.

I argued with him and he promised that, the week after the team won the Leinster final, he'd do one. Good enough.

Right now, we set our tape machines to the long-play setting, just in case he's not joking about talking all night.

Sunday, 4th and Monday, 5th August

Between working on Niall's book and writing the Monday column and taking holidays that I'm due from seven weeks of World Cup duty, Dublin's summer adventure has become sort of a leisure-time activity for me. I wander out to watch the team train a couple of times with no intention of working, just watching.

I battle into Arnotts one day, and almost get killed in the war zone that is the queue to buy sky-blue replica shirts for the kids. Even in the summer of Keano, Dublin jerseys are outselling Manchester United ones by seven to one in the capital.

It's a movement! I wonder will the GAA be smart enough to tap into it. Seven years ago, when Dublin last won an All Ireland, they threw up a superstar called Jason Sherlock who could have sold the game for a decade. He was the player of the season and the story of the season. But, he was resented.

The players who were selecting the annual end of season All Stars back then snubbed him. The new Dublin management let it be known that it wasn't impressed by him. He was spat at by a county-board official. People had a go because he was too good, too fond of soccer, too flash, too ubiquitous, too popular, too brown.

And the GAA wasted the best thing to ever happen to Dublin GAA.

It's a people thing. That's the best and the worst of this crazy organization. It's what makes the GAA different to cover than any other sport anywhere. When we get to Croke Park today, word is out all over the place that Tommy Lyons isn't here, he's in the Blackrock Clinic. Sick. The level of detail that the average GAA fan has at his or her grasp is astonishing. A sparrow doesn't fall without news of its demise spreading through a hundred GAA clubhouses before it hits the ground. People in Croke Park are saying it's a heart problem, but that the official version will be that it's stomach trouble with Tommy.

Everyone has a version.

It's a big story, of course. Dublin (and we in the media) is without the totem, the boss, the quotes machine.

Paul 'Pillar' Caffrey, one of the vice-presidents in the Lyons administration, has been selected to assume executive control. He doesn't have access to Tommy's speechwriter though, and we miss the old Lyons touch. Last time out, he created a new word for the lexicon. Arseboxing. He is against arseboxing and several times urged that there be no more arseboxing over various issues.

Pillar is a good story though. He's about what is different here. He's a community police officer in the inner city. He was on duty in uniform here in Croke Park yesterday. Today, he's the boss; today, he walks the sideline and calls the shots in front of almost 80,000 people.

Dublin and Donegal draw. Cute Donegal men. The trapdoor opens, but they refuse to fall through. They wear the seen-it-all faces of the men they couldn't hang. Dublin have a bad record against Donegal in modern times. Donegal's refusal to lose sends a shiver through the city.

Pillar is the only unbeaten Dublin manager in history, but down in the catacombs under the main stand, he has problems of his own.

'We're meant to be flying to Spain in the morning for our holidays,' he says waving a hand at his wife and children who are standing nearby wearing sombreros and carrying buckets and spades. 'So there's a few not happy.'

And you know that, however much a policeman in the inner city may need a holiday, there is no way that Pillar is stepping down off this carnival ride right now.

Replay looks set for two weeks. Pillar will be there. We all will.

Saturday, 17th and Sunday, 18th August

For better or worse, Niall's book is finished.

·I'm still exhausted. At the very last minute, I have cried off going to Munich to cover the European Athletic Championships.

I'm glad too.

The great Roy Keane summer extravaganza reopened this week. Roy's book is ready for the shops, which means that, in order to justify its juicy advance, it must first suffer the indignity of tabloid serialization.

This serialization brings out the worst in the media. All the world knows that scarcely anybody has read the book. All the world knows that, for the huge fee paid to be justified, the serialized extract must be sexy enough to cause a storm and sell papers. That, in turn, will sell books. That's the game. That's a fact of life.

Logically, all other media should ignore the serialization, review the book on its merits when it arrives, and thus put an end to the whole crazy process. Instead, the coop is suddenly filled with headless chickens. Squawking madly.

Roy's book has been bought by the *News of the World*. The extracts have been suitably toxic, the sort of stuff you'd only pick up with a pair of tongs. How Roy reached down Alf Inge Haaland's throat and removed his beating heart as the prawn sandwich brigade cheered on.

We knew this would be the case. Yet the judgements have been swift and loud and predictable.

Across the news and sports pages of England, Keane ranged in caricature form from being a foaming-at-the-mouth psychotic to being a man who, it was confidently asserted, 'doesn't give the impression of having a well-thumbed library'.

Ostensibly, much of the outrage centres on the business of Keane's tackle on the rather self-pitying Haaland. The incident, a moment of crunching violence, has been shown in slow motion more times by now than JFK's last drive along Dealey Plaza in Dallas. It was Keane's vigilante-style retribution for a perceived slight on the day eighteen months earlier, when he snapped his cruciate ligament. Roy uses some graphic language to describe his intent and motivation as he went in to hurt Haaland.

I don't think he has ever pretended the tackle was anything but deliberate. He stood over Haaland abusing him after he made the tackle. He didn't argue one word when he was sent off. However, it suits everybody to throw their hands up in the air in shock.

'Cripes! So it was deliberate? Why you swine! We shall have satisfaction, Sir. Send the ladies to the drawing room if you please.'

The English papers are eager to hang and flog Keane. Someday, somebody should anthologize some of the more hysterical pieces being written across the water. Keane is a stain on the English game. A terror from which the eyes of young children should properly be averted.

Of course, the tackle is no more excusable or no worse now than it was when it was committed eighteen months ago. It's still horrible. Nobody who saw it doubted the intention. Keane's foot drawn magnetically to Haaland's knee. Crunch! Then Keane standing over the victim spitting molten fury at him. If there was moral outrage, then was the time to express it. Nobody who saw the tackle was in any doubt that there was a history of animosity between the two men. Did anyone in the world think it was all an accident back then when Keane was given a three-match ban?

None of this makes what happened right. It just makes the current fuss a little hard to take. It just means that Keane is the story of the summer and that his apparent dementia will run and run on the back pages.

We are going through a summer of media craziness. Keane is the rod upon which all lightning must strike right now. If Roy Keane is to receive additional punishment now through the courts (as is ludicrously threatened) or through the FA, it is for candour.

Naturally, Alf Inge Haaland is no more seriously injured now than he was ten days ago before we had sampled a word of the Keane book. And, anyway, with regard to putative litigation it's his other knee that aches.

Apparently though, we'd all sleep easier in our beds if Roy Keane would just deny intent or pretend to be sorry. Not for the first time this year, the Keane case reminds me of the old story about Brendan Behan appearing before the district justice and asking him, 'Which would be the least offensive to his Lordship, if I made an insincere apology or if I didn't apologize at all?'

There is no winning this argument for Roy Keane. And perhaps that's the price you pay for moving in a world policed by tabloid newspapers. A passage of mellow thoughtfulness was never likely to get picked out and serialized. We were never going to get Roy crippled by terminal ennui. Roy has the cardboard cutout image of himself to live with, horns and all. It's that version of him that we all want to write about this week.

Better news at home.

Tommy Lyons is no longer unwell.

He and I spend a pleasant afternoon in his office somewhere in the deep southside, yarning about football and media and anything that enters his rummage-sale mind. Tommy likes talking. The tape recorder likes recording.

And today, a Saturday, his Dublin team respond to him. Another win necklaced onto this string of summer pearls. He's back. And the fun begins. It's the big time. Limited amount of shows now available. Welcome to the cabaret.

Tommy props himself on a table in the Dublin medical room and the place fills with media and the merely curious. The lame and the halt have to form a disgruntled queue outside.

'Well, is Goggins a defender lads?' asks Tommy. Coman

Goggins has just proved emphatically that he is, having hinted otherwise two weeks ago.

'Ye're poor judges lads,' continues Tommy.

We are, but he's going to rub it in anyway.

'Ye give him an All Star one year, then ye write him off the next.'

True. All true. This is the way to handle media relations. The Lyons method. If you have something to say just say it. No point sitting there seething or being resentful or paranoid or fearful. We're not worth taking that seriously. Throw it all out on the table. Throw so much out that people can't be bothered sifting through it. Talk so much that nothing you say is a sensation any longer. Talk till our ears bleed.

The GAA could learn so much. Roy Keane in his remoteness is chopped liver in the media right now. He's fair game. Tommy Lyons? You can't give Tommy Lyons stories away now. We know all there is to know. No big deal left.

Next summer, I'm asking Tommy Lyons if he won't give media summer schools to those who are communicatively challenged.

Sunday, 18th August

Sunday comes around and a classic hurling game between Tipperary and Kilkenny in Croke Park comes with it. Again, we head down to the catacombs. Again there's pushing and shoving. Next week, I'm bringing a gun and taking somebody hostage.

Today, though, we find the normally reticent Kilkenny manager, Brian Cody, leaning against a wall. He's a big, tall guy with a countryman's red face, all his capillaries broken by freshening winds. He knows the game too. The fickle nature of it. He was once booed by his own county people and never forgot it.

So he seems to live for the game now and not the trappings.

This has been a great volcano of a game. The beauty and the passion of it has sucked the reserve out of Brian Cody. He is illuminated with excitement. It dances in his eyes. You can see why guys like him do this job for so many hours, and for free. You see why other guys follow him wherever he leads.

'I'd no idea what to do lads, to be honest,' he says to us and describes the heat of the game, the fury of it and himself just letting it wash over him.

This is one of the moments of the summer. As good and as interesting as some of the scores we have seen today. As riveting as Saipan. A quiet man just thinking aloud for a change. When Brian Cody speaks this afternoon, there is a whole new insight; you can see why the people in the dressing room next door care for him and want to play for him.

Today he stuck D. J. Carey back into the team even though D. J. came back out of retirement just a few weeks ago. There wasn't a murmur of dissent. Tribute to the genius of D. J. certainly, but tribute also to the wisdom of Brian Cody. He understands enough to know, and to transmit the thought, that not all players are equal, that some are special.

I look at him and try to judge him like I judge all managers these days.

Can I imagine him calling a team meeting to berate Roy Keane? Or D. J. Carey?

Tuesday, 20th August

Together again. We are in a big room in a hotel down by the docks in Helsinki.

Mick McCarthy, Jason McAteer and Kenny Cunningham, are having turns at the top table. All the usual suspects are sitting across the table staring back.

It's only weeks since Mick was applauded out of that boardroom of the Westin Chosin Hotel in Seoul. The applause doesn't appear to have changed his opinion of the general hackery. We are still *personae non gratae*.

He will be offering no review or critique of the Keane book thank you. Mick's own version will be hitting the shops in due course. Until then, he's saying nowt.

We always have Kenny Cunningham though. Jason McAteer, who is playing the role of Captain Fantastic this week, has already offered the opinion that he would rather spend the price of a Roy Keane book on buying a Bob the Builder tape for his son. This is brave talk considering that Sunderland play Manchester United in a couple of weeks. Perhaps players should give marks out of ten for each other's books. It might make them a little more philosophical about being given marks out of ten for their performances.

Anyway to Kenny Cunningham. Other players say there is more to Kenny than meets the eye, that the cheeky-chappie image he brings into press conferences is a veneer for a guy who is often thoughtful to the point of being morose.

I'm glad to hear this. Sometimes Cunningham is so self-deprecating that you wonder how he survives at all in professional sport. I remember once a group of us surrounding him in a hotel in Dublin and asking him about newspaper reports linking him with a transfer deal to Celtic. Kenny earnestly argued for ten minutes that a great club like Celtic wouldn't want to be having anything to do with a player like him. Things couldn't be that bad at Celtic.

Apparently though, he was up at Sunderland a few weeks ago discussing a transfer and Sunderland found him to be an altogether flintier character, well capable of addressing and articulating his own interests. Which goes some way to explaining why he commands so much respect around the place and makes it somewhat less of a surprise when he sits down and discusses the Roy Keane issue in a more mature and considered fashion than anyone in the panel has felt able to.

'I won't be pitching a tent outside WH Smith's, roasting me marshmallows,' he says when asked will he be buying a copy, 'but maybe Roy might send a few to the lads.'

We love this. Not just an answer, but a joke too.

'Are you surprised by the fuss Kenny?'

'I'm not surprised by it, absolutely not. Roy is such a high-profile individual, and he has been such a key component for the Irish side over the past number of years, it is no surprise that the story has run over the summer and until now. It's an obvious footballing story. I'm sure it will run and run over the next couple of months. We have some important games coming up and it's a situation we can't really affect. We have to remain focused.'

'Interested in the book?'

'I'm not one for picking up football biographies, but I wouldn't like to dismiss it and say I'm not interested in what Roy has got to say. You have to pay him a certain amount of respect because of his stature in the game, not only at club level, but also at international level to this point. I think it shows a lack of respect to say I'm not interested. By virtue of the fact he has led Manchester United, the most successful club side of the last couple of years and he has led his country in the manner that he has, I wouldn't say I have no interest.'

'Oh.'

'He has his own reasons for writing the book. In some respects I find him a fascinating character. We've all spent time with him in the last couple of years, he's an intelligent young man to be honest with you. It's always interesting to spend time around those people, especially with the amount of success he's had on the football pitch. I spent some time with him, lunches, dinners, times around the hotel. It's always interesting to hear what people like that have to say.

'Sum Roy up,' we ask.

'I couldn't consider myself a close confidant. I wouldn't sit here and tell you what kind of an individual he is. That's down to the people who know him best, his family and his close friends. They'd tell you. It's obvious the attributes he has. Ball winner, demands high standards, demands them of those around him and of himself. He's intelligent, private, good sense of humour, good wit, he can be interesting company, but he has a private side and he doesn't open himself up. It's probably better to comment when we've all read the book.'

You know what Kenny, you'll never make it as a sports journalist. Too reasonable. Listen has he got cloven feet? A little tail? 'Do you miss having him around?'

'Certainly as a footballer he was world class. I couldn't make an argument that we are stronger without him. As a team we would be stronger but it's not football reasons why Roy is not in the squad. It's more complex.'

'Is the team spirit stronger?'

'That's a very difficult question. It's not an area where players should get involved. We can talk about it but we can't affect it. It has to be resolved between Roy, the manager and possibly the FAI. Those are the channels.'

Wow! If we could all get that much intelligence and balance into our acres of Roy Keane coverage.

We wait around to the end of the session to see if a bolt of lightning will smite Kenny Cunningham for having the temerity to speak like a grown-up at a press conference.

Nothing happens. And the tabloids don't turn him over the next day either.

Strange.

Wednesday, 21st August

We are sitting in this lovely little stadium. We have what is called the Perfect Stadium Conversation.

'Why can't the FAI build something like this?'

'It would be perfect.'

'Or even that place we were in last night [for the under-21 friendly].'

'Perfect.'

'Look at this. Perfect.'

'I know.'

I have had this conversation in practically every city in Europe. Tonight, Mick McCarthy lays a few things to rest. Not Roy Keane but a few other things. His team win 3–0. And it truly is his team. A bunch of kids and some old Mick loyalists just ran through Finland with a sense of confident disdain. It's too much to be calling this little friendly the dawn of a new era, but it looks like the beginning of a distinct new phase in Irish football history.

Emmet and I go out to dinner later. We argue bitterly over Roy Keane.

Hey Roy! It's brother against brother, father against son, hack against hack in this never-ending war you started.

Thursday, 29th August – Manchester

Big day.

I arrive early. Book a room for few hours. I'm an hour-and-a-half early in fact. Time for a short nap and a shower. The phone rings. Mr Keane is at reception.

I don't know why Roy Keane does this. Or even if it is something he does with everyone. He's always early. For someone like me, who is always late, it's disarming.

I am in Manchester to speak to him about his book, his life, the fallout from Saipan, etc. I don't know why, but apparently *The Irish Times* is the only Irish paper he will be speaking to. Well I partly know why, we sold Penguin the rights to use the Saipan interview in full.

There was even a little spat over it. I told Eamon Dunphy I was happy for him to use it for free. The paper, whose straits were still dire, looked for a few grand and got three in the end. Penguin demurred initially. Now the Keane book looks like it will outsell the Bible. We should have got a percentage on the back end with optional movie rights.

Anyway, it helped nail down this interview.

I dash up to reception to meet Keane. He's all smiles and good humour. When we get back to the room, the keycard won't work in the door, of course. He enjoys this comedy for a moment or two, asking me if I've got the right room, musing over what it will do to his reputation if he is caught breaking into somebody's room in a Manchester hotel. With a journalist.

Finally, he spots a chambermaid. He summons her. Tells her the door won't open. Her eyes are as big as saucers. Wordlessly, she opens the door for him. For all she knows, he could actually be about to rob the room of its contents. But it's Roy Keane and this is the epicentre of his fame. She looks like she'd willingly take the rap for him. That's something I've noticed actually, I haven't yet met a woman (who doesn't live with Mick McCarthy that is) who doesn't support Keane in this thing. Women love him. Good luck to him. It's just another element in the mix.

You notice it everywhere here. When he walked through the lobby here a minute or two ago, he sent a wave of slackjawed silence before him. Every head just follows him, gazing at him. It's little wonder his book is a phenomenon. People are truly fascinated by the man.

In the room, he takes a seat, puts his feet up and asks if there's been any news since I last spoke to him. Well, where to begin . . .?

He asks about Niall and the book. I tell him that we are trudging through about 250 legal queries at the moment. 'Anything to do with me?' he asks, delighted.

Off the record, he seems quite chatty about Niall and Steve Staunton, etc. On the record, he wants them to know that he's still hurting, still hanging tough. He considers their participation in that Saipan press conference by Mick's side to have been a betrayal. He points out that even when Phil Babb and Mark Kennedy were done for jumping on a policewoman's car in Dublin one night, he stuck by them because they were players.

What seldom comes across in Roy Keane articles, and there are many of them appearing at the moment, is his genuine likeability. The market demands Roy the monster. The market usually gets what it demands. the *Observer* has photographed him recently holding the head of a dead bird. He didn't demur. He's like this occasionally, almost existentialist in his passivity. In his off-field life, he reminds me a little of Mersault in Camus' *The Outsider*. Sometimes Roy stops railing and allows things happen to him, just to see where they will take him. An odd quirk.

In interviews, he never rules any subject out, never arrives with an agent or a PR flack, never dodges anything and never denies anything afterwards. He just lets it unfold. I think he gets taken out of context. There is a widely circulating quote at the moment wherein Roy says that he hopes he doesn't sound bitter, but, as far as he's concerned, Mick McCarthy can rot in hell. Maybe he said it, and maybe he meant it. From what little I know of Keane, though, I can't imagine him saying that without at least a little smile to himself.

It is on my mind today to ask Roy Keane if he is an alcoholic.

This is a tabloid thing to do. What he drinks or if he drinks isn't my business, or anyone else's, really. Yet it would explain a lot about the man and his struggles. One theory about Saipan is that Roy had a drink or two on the plane on the way over and he was in the process of punishing himself hard when things fell apart on the island. This behaviour would sit with a certain pattern. In his book, Roy has made allusions to struggles with drink.

Perhaps, today, he'd like to talk about that part of his life. Perhaps he feels that in drink there could be an explanation. Perhaps he'd like to tell me to fuck off.

After about three quarters of an hour, I broach the subject, more obliquely than I had intended. Instead of asking straight out, 'Are you an alcoholic? Or is that something you would ever speak about, either way?' I ask him about 'the rumours of alcoholism'. I screw it up.

I often do this in interviews, especially when I'm conscious of wandering offside. Once interviewing the Offaly hurler, Johnny Pilkington (undoubtedly one of the great interview subjects of all time), I got it into my head that I wanted Johnny to talk about drink. He did, but it wasn't enough. I pushed and pushed till he stubbed out his cigarette and said tersely, 'Is this not more about your attitude to drink than mine?'

Roy hardly draws breath. He says he's heard it said, he's heard all sorts, he then lists a few of the better rumours he has heard and waves the subject away so thoroughly that I have no way of getting back to it and asking him if he wants to explore it properly.

Perhaps, if drink is an ongoing problem, explaining the dimensions of the problem would help explain Roy Keane. That was my theory. Otherwise the interview is fine but, when it finishes, I have that one big regret. The tape goes off and Roy lolls back in his seat.

'All your fault of course,' he grins, 'yours and Paul's.'

I laugh. This is a common theme in a good number of letters I've received. People think the paper should never have printed the interview, despite the fact that Roy has reproduced it in his book to illustrate how straightforward and harmless it was. He said much worse about his club colleagues the previous year when Bayern Munich knocked Manchester United out of the European Cup.

With regard to Saipan, there are things, as I have discovered in the previous ninety minutes, that he is still angry about. Mainly, what he perceives as betrayals. By and large, he seems on the way to putting the summer into some sort of perspective. He can make jokes, good ones about the whole thing, he can relate the experience and the essential hard loneliness of it better and more vividly than his book suggests.

His book is sitting on the table between us. When we've chatted for a while about the fallout from the last interview we did, I decide to break one of the rules of the game. I shove the book across to him.

'Seeing as you're sitting here and I helped ruin your life, can you sign that for me?'

He laughs, but immediately I regret asking. The key with interviewing big names is never to behave as if the person you are speaking to is any better known than somebody you might sit beside in a bar. If they are boring you, you have to let them know. If they make good conversation, your body language tells them.

Going to interview Keane in the past, I have turned down dozens of requests to get him to sign this, that and the other. The key always is never to act like a fan. With Roy Keane, getting him to sign things seems even less professional than with other players. Now, on impulse, I've asked him to sign a book.

Quickly, he scribbles the words 'Best Wishes, Roy Keane' and shoves the book back. Immediately, he gets up to go.

'I wonder, can I get out this way?' he asks and slips out through the curtains into the hotel gardens beyond.

I sit there cursing myself for being a halfwit. I decide not to send him a copy of Niall's book.

Friday, 30th August

This morning, I am in the car driving the kids when the mobile rings.

'It's Roy. Roy Keane here.'

I almost hit a ditch.

He has made a relatively harmless comment about Denis Irwin in the previous day's chat and he wants to retract it. He's a little annoyed with Denis for having something loose to say about the summer's troubles, but he doesn't want to attack him or denigrate him. Can I understand that?

No problem. It wasn't a very good line anyway and, as of last night, had no chance of making the piece, which had plenty of better lines and bigger targets.

On the phone, Roy goes back over the Haaland business again. His theme is that he certainly meant to hurt Haaland, but never to finish his career. Players tackle each other to hurt each other all the time he says.

'So that's it,' he concludes, 'good luck.'

'Who was that?' ask the kids.

'Roy Keane,' I say.

'Wow. Cool. If it rings again, can I answer?'

Tuesday, 3rd September

'Jaysus,' says the man in the other line. 'I thought *The Irish Times* would have somebody to do this for you.'

By 'this' he means standing in queues outside the Russian Embassy. I become all red and flustered. The rare excitement of being recognized has come hand in hand with my exposure as a low-level operative in my low-level field.

Not only am I queuing here, but it's not the first time. I'm a great queuer.

I should explain to the man in the other line that we've just laid off one third of our staff under grim and demoralizing circumstances and that all the queuing specialists that we used to employ have gone. We're learning the true price of things now, us toffs.

Instead, because I've been recognized and because I know that none of the other 100 or so people here have any idea who the hell I am, I just blush and mumble.

'Nah, too cheap,' I say.

I can tell by the man's expression that this has come out as, 'Nah, duh eep.'

He looks at me and nods his head politely.

The Russian Embassy on Orwell Road is an intriguing place. I came here one afternoon a year ago to get a visa in order to travel to Moscow the following day. I had the wrong idea about *glasnost*. As I came upon the embassy gates, a car happened to be passing in, so I turned in too and followed the car a little way up the drive. I had no sooner got the front tyres onto the embassy drive when all hell broke loose. Men, who mightn't have been called Boris but who looked as if they should have been, came running from all directions.

Much shouting.

Squirrels dropping from trees and assuming sniper positions on the lawn.

Me rolling down window to say, 'Oh sorry.'

Me reversing all too hastily onto Orwell Road.

Me waving apologetically at everyone who is forced to brake hard following my reverse manoeuvre.

Not good.

I got out of the car and walked up. The Russian Embassy doesn't let you go near the embassy itself, it invites you into a little hut at the gate where it processes various visa requests. I was under the impression that Russia would be just panting to get a piece of my *Irish Times* expenses action.

Russia couldn't care less. 'The embassy only opens in the mornings for visa applications.'

'But the flight is in the morning.'

'Too bad.'

'Can't you do something? I have to do work over there.'

Finally, I was sent off to get a sum of money in cash (€130 I think) and a passport photo of myself. I returned and handed both over. A visa was issued in about twenty minutes, with a growl.

So here I am again. An old Russian Embassy hand. Cunningly, I have absorbed none of the lessons of last year. I am here the day before. Queuing and desperate. Ireland are playing in Moscow at the weekend, these lines outside the embassy are like something you'd see in, well, Russia. To their credit, the embassy staff handle it all with their customary lightheartedness. We queue. We pay up. We get told to come back tomorrow and queue again.

Saturday, 7th September – Moscow

We've just been beaten. Well beaten. Everything came home to roost tonight in the Lokomotiv Stadium. All the things that this Irish team have been getting away with, well we're no longer getting away with them. The rules have changed.

After the World Cup, and after Finland last month, there was giddy talk of a serious assault on the European Championships. Now we're going to struggle even to qualify. First game of the campaign. We've just conceded four. I've never watched us concede four goals.

The press conference afterwards descends into farce as

quickly as the Irish performance that preceded it. The managers are expected to sit and give their views at a table at the end of a long narrow room. The setup gives the impression that the managers are being backed up against a wall. There are some press seats in front of the managers and then a bank of cameras, then a great crush of drinkers who have been supping at the bar just behind us.

Mick McCarthy wears his tight-lipped smile and his stern, blue suit to this shindig. His Russian hosts don their party clothes. This is never going to be a happy time. The Russians are giggly and delighted with themselves.

'Please comment to this game,' asks the Russian translator. Sternly like an interrogator in old Ljubjanka jail.

'It's been a bad day at the office for us in terms of defending,' says Mick. 'I think we came here certainly trying to win the game and I believed we could. We've conceded goals, it's the first time we've conceded four goals, we've conceded goals which we wouldn't normally concede and we've been disappointed.'

He rambles on.

A translation follows. While it is unfolding, in fine throaty Russian, the bar just behind us in the press area is filled to overflowing now, with a great swell of ruddy-faced merrymakers. And the PA begins blasting out a happy tune. Of all things, 'Will Ye Come, Will Ye Come, Will Ye Come To The Bower'.

So, any questions?

Irish journalist: 'The early mistakes, did they affect confidence?'

Mick McCarthy: 'Perhaps, they set the tone for it.'

Translator: 'Excuse me, I must translate this question.'

PA system: 'Will ye come, will ye com . . .'

Russian journalist: 'Translate please this.'

Translator: 'Repeat the question.'

PA system: 'To the bower . . .'

Irish journalist: 'Did the early mistakes affect confidence in defence?'

Translator: 'Excuse me. Again.'

PA system: 'Will ye come, will ye . . .'

Irish journalist: (slowly) '*Damage* Confidence. Did they damage confidence?'

Russian translation follows as continued questioning about accompanying certain parties to the bower plays over the PA.

Mick McCarthy: 'Can I speak now?'

Translator: 'Yes.'

Mick McCarthy: 'I don't think the start to the game helped, well that's not us, we usually play it forward and pen them in and play at a high tempo. Giving them an early chance didn't do us any favours of course. Whether it had an affect on the long-term game? I can't put that defending down to that early start. We got out of that lethargy.'

By now the noise level is becoming an issue. The folk at the bar are whooping it up. The journalists are talking among themselves. The translator and the chair of the press conference are having a little sidebar chat.

One more question. The translator moves in. All business.

While the words are being recast in Russian, the Irish questions continue. It's dog eat dog now, there having been a breach of protocol earlier when the Russians didn't bother to translate any of their own manager's questions.

McCarthy speaks of Robbie Keane, of the gambles he took in the second half. So on. The Russians growl among themselves.

The translator has had enough. One senses the gulag beckoning for Mick McCarthy. He makes a request, sublimely oblivious to newspaper deadlines and stuff like that.

'Could somebody who understands Russian please take my answers down and after I've gone give them to the Russian journalists. It would make life a lot easier for all of us and I would appreciate it.'

The request is ignored totally. As it is translated, it provokes hoots of Russian laughter. There is some Russian spoken at the table. More laughter. Mick McCarthy's face is like thunder now. Four goals conceded and then a nightmare with the press goons.

'Was it a fair result?' asks a Russian journalist. You can tell it's his favourite question, the one he always asks in order to demonstrate his keen insight.

'Could have been more goals,' begins Mick McCarthy, when swoosh! Sliding tackle from the same source.

'Would the presence of Roy Keane, in football terms, have made a difference?'

The name of Roy has now been uttered. We await thunder and lightning in the sky.

'Perhaps,' says Mick. 'I've said all along I'm not going to hide from this . . .'

We all think, have you?

'. . . Not if he's recovering from a bad hip it wouldn't have tonight. He may well not have played anyway. That's something I can't do anything about. It's not going to make any odds if, after every game, it's going to be dragged up as to whether we can play better with him. We're always a better side with him, he's a world-class player. I can't deny that. That's as plain as the nose on my face. But he ain't here, he's not going to be here. I can't affect that.'

Another question. More Russian laughter. The translator and

the chairman are in comedic cahoots. We are dying to hear what the question is.

McCarthy has had enough though.

'It started as a farce and it's descending below that,' he says. He gets up and he leaves quickly.

Sunday, 8th September

Scene: We are checking out of our nice media hotel not far from Red Square. Usual gouging on phone bills. Hacks are gathering around the reception desk to query call charges in bewildered voices.

One hack approaches.

'What's this?'

'Room service, Sir.'

'When?'

'Last night, Sir.'

'Look. The match was on last night. I came back and worked. No room service, do you understand?'

'Sir?'

'Yes.'

'It is not really room service.'

'Well, what is it?'

'We put that name and that amount when it is pornography on television, Sir. It is pornography.'

'Oh, well thanks.'

We get to Sheremetievo Airport, Moscow. This afternoon, many of us are working at the All-Ireland hurling final. We are in a hurry to get there. It is proposed, however, that Mick McCarthy will not do a press conference till we get back to Dublin.

A delegation goes and persuades him to speak to us here. We feel that, on the morning after the team concedes four, the balance of power has shifted ever so slightly.

Mick walks into a little glass-walled cubicle in the departures area. We follow him in. The Sunday papers have savaged him this morning. When he gets on the plane, he will see one headline that says 'Mick Moscow'.

He doesn't know it yet, but he must expect it.

In the press conference, which takes place with us all standing up, Mick is coming to terms with the night before. He's trying to put answers to his own questions. He has his own inquest to perform first. The wheels have come off for some reason that he'll have to work out next week.

Meanwhile, with his backside offering the first parma-thin slice of Barnsley to the infamous bacon slicer, well, he needs to see us media like he needs a 4–2 spanking.

'I don't think we were over confident. You don't suddenly get over confident and arrogant coming to Russia for a game. I knew they had good players. No surprises either. The tempo of the game was very high from the start. If we beat them in Dublin that result is finished with. We have to beat them in Dublin now.'

We dance awhile. Talk about the positives. Eliminate the negatives. Discuss how we've become a scalp to be hung on other belts. Quinn missing? Very bad. Stan missing? Yeah, too bad.

One question left to be asked. That other guy who has been missing. Mick McCarthy won't accept it, but it has to be asked. I ask it. Purple heart for valour and all that.

'Roy Keane. Any change in the weather there?'

'It's something we—' he breaks off. Starts again. 'He got a hip injury, he's out with that. He said he's not going to play. It's not going to change, that situation. You know better than I.'

But Mick's face has turned hard now. He stares at me, 'You speak to him on a more regular basis. Why don't you go chat to Roy? That's not for me. I think that situation is far beyond repair. I think you'll find that the guy has told everybody that. It's not going to make it any different. I'm getting on with the team I've got. These are the lads I'm concerned about.'

'Could it be worth one final try?' Paul Hyland asks.

'I'm not going to go down that road.'

'No?'

'I'm done guys. Thanks for your time.'

His face is black with temper. He exits abruptly for the second time in twelve hours, his wounds still fresh.

Monday, 9th September – afternoon, Croke Park

The sour taste of Moscow is gone by tea-time. Kilkenny win a decent All-Ireland hurling final. The story of their own excellence, their pursuit of perfection this season, that has been the narrative.

In the Kilkenny dressing room, with the Liam McCarthy Cup lying on his kitbag, Andy Comerford stands on the bench and speaks to the players he has captained all year. This is the soul of the GAA. We are prying on those moments when an ordinary man expands his horizons and seizes the respect of others. He speaks passionately, with a mix of authority and humility.

'You can all hold your heads high lads. Thirty men got us there and every one of them was needed. I'll say one thing lads, respect yourselves and respect your families. Celebrate for sure, but

Kilkenny were always men that were humble. Always remember that you're Kilkenny hurlers. Whatever way you celebrate, do it with dignity and do it with pride. Be proud of what you achieved. Respect the jersey. Always remember that you are Kilkenny hurlers.'

He stands down with the roar of applause coming towards him. Kilkenny hurlers. All-Ireland champions. The jersey. The dignity. The pride. That's the story of the season for me. That's the narrative of one team's excellence.

Standing here among the hurlers seems like the perfect antidote to the misery of Moscow. Those three days with the unhappy, miserable professionals were morale sapping. That sense that sport isn't just sport anymore, is pervasive. It's hard to think that once the players we were with in Moscow used to say that they would give anything to wear a national jersey and they actually meant it. Now, they mean it some of the time. Now, it's a corny thing to say. It's possible to come away and play for your country and be miserable about it. Standing in this dressing room in Croke Park, it strikes me that, whether Mick was right or Roy was right, the legacy of Saipan is this infection. It won't be right till both Mick and Roy are gone and the passion is again more valued than personal pride.

I gaze at Andy Comerford and wonder what his life would have been like without hurling. Without sport, what vent, if any, would these extraordinary qualities of his have had. He's had to make accommodations in his life that Roy and Mick could never dream of. He's had to grow his skill while making a living for himself and doing all the things that people do in the real world. And here he is lifting a cup with 80,000 people cheering and it's a journey that hasn't been confettied with money or contracts or agents. Just a journey worth making.

There are guys earning many thousands a week from sport who could have learned something by being here today and listening to Andy Comerford.

Saturday, 14th September

When you are away a lot in the course of a sporting year, you tend to sentimentalize and idealize what goes on at home. That's the only explanation I can give for a fatal lack of judgement in early September. I forgot myself and went to a press day for the Kerry football team. Forgive me.

Perhaps, I have been deranged by Dublin's exit from the championship. Perhaps, I just hungered for the mileage.

Some things in sport are given. Mike Tyson doesn't get to date your daughter. Mick McCarthy doesn't have a sense of humour about Roy Keane. Kerry press days are not for the benefit of the press. Nope.

Kerry press days are all foreplay and no consummation. Four-and-a-half hours of anticipatory journey and then a rebuff, a slap on the cheek.

Not today. I have a headache. I've never done anything like that before. No means no. Just what sort of a man do you think I am? Kerry press days are an elaborate form of tease. Only fools and young fellas go to Kerry press days.

I'm not the brightest fish in the pond, however. When Mal says, 'Hey, why don't you do a big Páidí Ó Sé piece for the All-Ireland final weekend?' I bite down hard on the hook.

One definitive Páidí interview coming right up.

I call Páidí. Tell him that I am coming down (again) and this time it's the definitive interview. 'Got that Páidí?'

'Sure,' he says. 'You won't do a Keane job on me?'

'See you Saturday.'

Páidí is unconquerable though. He will let you squeeze his knee, but will go no further. He'll pass the time but he's not loose as a goose. He's a tease. 'Sure,' he says, 'I'll see you on Saturday.' When Saturday comes, he's buttoned up like the most devout girl in the Amish community.

I hit Killarney around lunchtime and head straight up to beautiful Fitzgerald Stadium where the press day is unfolding. The sun is shining, there are kids everywhere and lots of Kerry friends scattered about to detain me in conversation. It looks like a happy scene and it takes me a few minutes to find an actual journalist.

'How's it going?'

'Usual waste of bleeding time.'

I find Páidí. He's talking to a group of reporters. I wave at him and indicate that I'll be waiting for him. He gives me the big nod.

Finally he comes over.

'Where will we go?' I ask.

'Sure we'll do it here,' he says.

I'm a bit nervous about having such a long conversation standing on a football field, but it's a beginning.

'We'll walk and talk,' I say, intending to steer Páidí over towards the dressing-room area.

He folds his arms and shuts his eyes and waits for the first question. Okay. We're hardly walking or talking now.

Two questions into the big interview, he opens his eyes enough to make little slits of them and asks suspiciously, 'When is this for?'

He uses that tone of voice that old movie actors deployed when they'd say a line like, 'Hey, just whaddaya tryin' to pull here, Mister?'

News that the interview piece is to run the day before the All-Ireland final and not in some special to celebrate the winter solstice hits Páidí hard. He winces. He'd never thought that this might be an All-Ireland final piece.

What small piece of enthusiasm he once had for the project drains out of him.

If we were playing chess, which in a way we are, you might say that he switches to the classic Yerra defence.

In the Yerra defence, the answer to every question is preposi-tioned by a sucking in of breath, a slight grimace and the soft exhalation of the word 'yerra'.

The ensuing answer is purified and distilled through the yerra. All controversial impurities are removed.

'What makes you a good manager?'

'Yerra, I don't know.'

'What have you changed about the way you handle players and people over the last few years?'

'Yerra, that's not something I'd like to be talking about the week before an All-Ireland final.'

'Has this been a hard summer for you personally?'

'Yerra, it has and it hasn't. I wouldn't be one to talk about that now.'

'Was the loss of your brother a hard blow for you?'

'Yerra.' Pause. 'That's private.'

Páidí deflects every question. One suspects he has a capsule of cyanide secreted in his mouth ready to chomp down on if he thinks you are getting anything out of him. There are a limited number of things that he feels comfortable speaking about.

How terrific Armagh are.

How Kerry can't be sure of their own form.

How anything can happen on the big day.

After just a few minutes, I am ready to just give up. It's not going to happen for me today. Páidí remains as difficult as the north face of Everest. Yet he is a challenge just because he is there.

Pity. The job has changed him. Diminished him in some ways. Expanded him in others. Getting this job, keeping it, winning All Irelands, it has been his greatest achievement. Yet he acts smaller because of it.

He's less of a legend now, more of a worried man. You can't walk into any football bar in Kerry and not hear half-a-dozen wild Páidí stories. But you can walk into Páidí's bar and watch him clam up, see him apply the lessons he has learned the hard way. Everyone is waiting for Páidí to screw up. So he rolls himself into a ball like a hedgehog.

You can see him, year in and year out, coping with the doubts that people have had about him. The tragedy is that his paranoia about the media has shrunk him and tended to deflect the light away from the achievements of his team. Kerry has been at the top for some years now, yet they have no profile, they leave no footprints.

Oddly, this is the one area he will speak to the media about. The whole business of not speaking to the media. The whole business of growing stronger out of failure and criticism and pure silence.

'I suppose I knew it, but I was a bit surprised that when I got the job, the image was that I was a wild man from West Kerry and shouldn't be let loose. But I had things to change and things to learn. It's not all about football.'

He came into the job with a reputation, which wasn't warranted, as a table-banging, cup-throwing, eyes-bulging type of manager who sent players out onto the field knowing it was easier to die out there than come back in and face him.

'I'm not the same person I was when I took the job, I suppose, and I'm not the same manager. You get knocks and disappointments along the way that change you. In this job, you get plenty of things to think about. In the winters, I go back to West Kerry and I think about them. I lie low and have a good think. Sure you'd have to learn something.'

Sadly, he's learned that, in Kerry, where even the stones on the road have hard opinions about football, it's wisest to keep his mouth shut most of the time. A word out of place will be parsed and analyzed and deconstructed for ever. Especially, if it is followed by defeat.

And defeat itself? In Kerry, it must always be a prelude to some bigger victory. The audience at La Scala would endure the braying of a donkey more graciously than Kerry people deal with defeat.

Eleven minutes into the interview, Páidí asks if we shouldn't wrap it up here. His face is a picture of discomfort. He looks as if his appendix has burst or as if he is willing it to burst just so he can have an excuse to get away.

He's cagey, not just about handing Armagh any cuttings to pin on their dressing-room wall, but about giving critics within Kerry anything to whip him with. He's cagey. Full stop.

He takes a little break from talking to sign autographs and pose for photos. He's a different man when he relaxes for these few moments. A little redhead proffers a programme to be signed.

'And where are you from?' says Páidí.

'Tralee,' says the kid.

'Tralee,' says Páidí, mock alarmed. 'Stacks is it? Wisha, would you not get out to the Gaeltacht and play some proper football.'

The little fella is delighted and a chat ensues, but Páidí glances up a couple of times. You can see he's desperately worried that the exchange will get into print, that people in the Austin Stacks Club mightn't understand that he's having the *craic* with a young lad, pulling a few townie tails. He's enjoying the kid, but he's fretting at the same time. This summer, there's an edge with Stacks.

'I suppose,' he says when he rejoins the adult world, 'that, over the years, I have let criticism get to me. As a player, I never really had it or, if I had, I knew it was coming because you know when you've played badly.'

That's as frank as Páidí gets in September with an All Ireland looming.

We talk a little more. Useless. There are 6 million anecdotes held against their will in Páidí Ó Sé's grey head. Never again, I say, as I head down the hill towards McSweeney's Hotel and the consolation of a good lunch.

The story has the oddest ending. A few days later, a series of photographs come across the wires and into the office. They are taken by Ray McManus, the great GAA photographer, and all depict Páidí in various heroic, man-of-destiny poses at spots around Ventry in West Kerry.

Clearly some trouble has been gone to. Sadly, we don't have a decent interview to run the pics with. A little while later, I run into Ray and ask him about the shots. 'Páidí,' he says, 'had invited him back to West Kerry to take them.'

'But why?' I ask.

It has to do with Páidí's legendary *piseogs* or superstitions. *Piseogs* rule Páidí's life and that of his team. They have to stay in the same places, do the same things. On an All-Ireland final day, they have to go to early Mass, not just for the religion, but because Páidí has a *piseog* that the team must see two red-headed women on All-Ireland day, and there's a better chance if they are up early. He has lucky journalists and lucky routines.

One such routine, from the old days as a player, is to have the legendary photographer Colman Doyle come down to Kerry to take photographs of Páidí before an All-Ireland final. It began as a routine gig for Colman and then became something that Páidí requested again and again, not from vanity, but from fear of breaking the *piseog*. For years, during Páidí's life as a player, it went on and on. Then, in the years between Páidí's playing and management career, Colman retired. So Páidí drafted Ray in as a replacement, hoping that the gods of the *piseogs* wouldn't notice. You have to have a little time for a man like that.

Wednesday, 18th September – Mount Juliet

Absorb this scene. I can't. It doesn't fit with my experiences of the world.

The eighth best golfer in the world takes his top off and stretches his arms above his head. He has the familiar mark of Irishness on him, a coppery-brown neck and a milky-white body that the sun never kisses. He folds his black polo neck with characteristic care and looks you in the eye before he begins unbuckling his trousers.

His trousers hit the ground with a soft swooshing noise. Padraig Harrington stands with the evening sunlight slanting through the window, stands wearing just his socks and his black Calvin Kleins. Boxers, not jockeys, if you're wondering.

'I need this,' he says.

It's been a long, long day here in Mount Juliet. But he promised. When I called him early in the week he promised, said listen, no problem, don't worry, we'll get it done. That's the mark of him. You call him the week before Ryder Cup week and he says, 'Don't worry.'

It's Wednesday. The twenty-four hours before a tournament begins are always the most high-pressured time in Padraig Harrington's week. His perfectionism drives him and torments him and every week time runs out before he has pared his game to the state he'd like it to be in.

And this week, of course, it has to be Mount Juliet. Being the resident pro, the golfer laureate, brings 2 million fresh demands a day. But he tells you not to worry.

I ask him what he has done today, as Dale his chiropractor starts to knead him, taking the long day out of his beaten muscles.

The timetable is all written in his head.

With the tournament so near he could smell it, he rises at 8.30 a.m. and eats breakfast. Hits the course at 9.30 a.m. and has physio for forty-five minutes. Then he hurries off to work on some putting before hitting shots for an hour. All of which brings him, neatly, to 11.30 a.m., when he sets out on a practice round with Paul Lawrie and Colin Montgomerie.

That finishes at 4.30 p.m., and he sits in the trailer car to be hauled back to the clubhouse until this form of locomotion proves unpopular with the public, so he climbs off again and spends half-an-hour ambling up through Mount Juliet signing programmes, hats and proffered limbs, having his photo taken – arms draped around people he's never met before, smiling on the great Irish public.

He grabs a bite and is at the range again not long after 5 p.m., working on one or two things he feels he needs to work on. Then he irons out a couple of worries about his bunker shots and his putts, and arrives, late again, for treatment on the physio table, where he will be doing this interview.

Ask anyone on the tour and they will say that this fella lying on Dale Richardson's bench, is the hardest working of them all.

He lies there, head facing the ground as Dale works away. My tape recorder is on the ground, beside his mobile phone. At one stage in the interview, Padraig's wife Caroline calls him. He explains that he is still at work.

He's a good earner, but it's work. He'd never complain about it, but he puts in the hours.

It's quite dusky when we finish. He curses the approaching darkness. He'd love to spend another hour on his putting before he clocks off work, but his body is out of whack since he did his ankle in July. Because he wouldn't stop practising, other bits and pieces went out of alignment in sympathy.

Harrington is the golfer who always thinks he's left the gas on, who's always going back to check. He doesn't mind the journey. He really doesn't.

We've all skulked around the clubhouse and the driving range sifting for the bad news on Padraig Harrington. In this Babel of bitchiness, there isn't anything bad to say. Nice guy. Works hard. Works real hard in fact. Harder than anyone out there. It spooks people a bit but, hey, for Harrington, golf is a manual, labouring job. Grind and graft. Gifts aren't given, they are hewn out of resistant rock.

And even this, squeezing an interview in at the end of a long, long day. It's taking care of business. Even still, I don't believe there is another player in the Top 100 in the world who gives his time like Harrington does, who provides the access he does.

If you wanted to provide a role model for kids going into sport, well this is the guy. He's the one you'd like your kids to model themselves on. No matter what they did.

We part at the door. It's the Ryder Cup next week, that's the point of the interview. I tell him dolefully that I don't get the Ryder Cup. I just don't enjoy it or understand it.

And he gives me a five-minute spiel on the joys of it, the genuine pleasure he gets in the team ethic, in the subtle change of pressure and expectation. It doesn't quite explain the Ryder Cup to me, but it tells me more about Padraig Harrington. He's had to bury a gregarious side to get on in this furrowed world.

Teams are what he was born for.

Tuesday, 24th September

Live long enough and you'll see everything. Armagh won the All-Ireland football championship this afternoon. I'm still not over the shock of it. There's a rule of thumb in the GAA – the team that always wins, wins. Tradition is everything.

Armagh don't beat teams like Dublin and Kerry. It's not part of the tradition. They can't think their way around that. They can't play their way around that.

But they have. They've beaten Dublin. They've beaten Kerry. The game's two greatest franchises. They've won their first All Ireland.

Today, they were four points down at half-time and the Kerrymen were coming out to play with a strong second-half breeze. John O'Shea in the press box said to me that he feared for Armagh. This might be a hiding they'd never recover from.

At the end, they covered Croke Park in a sea of orange. It has been one of those days when you can understand quite plainly what sport can mean, what it can do for people. People cried. People prayed.

One mystery about this for me. How little interest it all attracts outside the island of Ireland. No English newspapers send reporters or even carry reports, despite the huge Irish population there. A massive spectacle, an amateur final played in front of 80,000 people in a world-class stadium built by amateurs. This is a story in any language. It's something that runs against the entire grain of modern sport. It's about people, place and pride. It's about all the things that people lament having disappeared from other sports. Yet not one English paper is interested in a weekend in Dublin. For us it's a private function.

Armagh came to Croke Park this weekend, timidly fancied in some quarters, dismissed in most others. By half-time they had squandered the benefits of a good wind and a cheap penalty and we wondered if they were lingering in the dressing room so long because they were looking for a pulse. Nothing but the same old story we said. Pity the oul' Dubs aren't here we said. Then Armagh came out and told us that everything we knew about football was wrong.

At the end, there's only one man most of us want to speak with as we take the lift down from the press area – Kieran McGeeney.

McGeeney is an awesome character. I've watched him for some years now and never interviewed him, always a little shy of his intensity, a little baffled by what makes him tick. I've always suspected, too, that he has no time for journalists. Yet, after games, he is approachable and highly articulate. He speaks about excellence as if it is a place and he is making the journey there.

He wouldn't agree but, to me, he's one of the reasons why the GAA must always stay amateur. The purity of McGeeney's passion is unpolluted by money or agents or all the considerations of a professional life. He has the broad perspective of an ordinary man, yet he has set aside a part of his life, not just because he loves football, but because he wants to see how far he can travel, how good he can be. He is a latter-day puritan.

There's beauty in what he has achieved today, this season. He has dragged this team up a hill. He has been Keane-like in his influence. He has written another line in the poem of his career.

Looking at him makes me regret that I was never a better player. It's not just a regret that I never had the talent or the will, but a sense of loss that I never got to be good enough to sit in a dressing room with somebody like Kieran McGeeney, or Roy Keane, and to draw inspiration from their excellence. I was with the lads who flicked towels, talked about pints and hid each other's shampoos. We missed out on something.

'Kieran McGeeney doesn't talk,' says Benny Tierney the goalie, who grew up with him in Mullaghbawn, 'he does.' He said at half-time that he wasn't producing. That he could talk the talk, but he wasn't walking the walk. It started with him. He trains harder, he drives more miles. He's just a leader. We follow him.'

We glance across at McGeeney. He's drinking water. He's an island of calm satisfaction in a hooting, whooping world.

He hasn't the words to describe this day. He said that from the Hogan Stand, as he grasped the great, gleaming canister in his hand. He said it again in the tunnel outside the dressing rooms as we swamped him, and he said it quietly again now in his own dressing room, leaning thoughtfully with his back to the wall.

He has a notion though.

The world goes around and all the particles gather themselves and come around again and again. When Kieran McGeeney was walking behind the Artane Boys' Band today, in the pre-match parade, he did something he doesn't usually do, he looked up into the stands at the fields of swaying orange there and his gaze fell upon the face of an old friend and mentor, Charlie Grant.

When Kieran McGeeney first started kicking a football in the flatlands of Mullaghbawn, it was Charlie Grant who had charge of the team.

'He introduced me to football. He had a great love for it. He used to say, "Go out and play Kieran." He never tried to mould us at under-10 and under-12. Amazing how the full circles come. It's men like him and Joe McNulty, Justin and Enda's father who took me at minor, men like Peter McDonald and Pillar Caffrey in Na Fianna, all the people who shape you. It all comes out there today. Other players. Neil Smyth and John Rafferty and Kieran McGurk, fellas who show you wee things along the way. It all comes out on days like today, when you throw every single thing in. A wee piece of all those people was playing today in everyone of us.'

Kieran McGeeney started by saying that he wished he had the words to describe the day. He had. This was a day when his performance lacked nothing, least of all the right words.

Wednesday, 25th to Monday, 30th September

Back to The Belfry. Ryder Cup weekend. We stay across the street from The Rocket, Birmingham's 'Premier Lap Dancing Club'. I wonder if they haven't put the media in here because they think we like that sort of thing. How depressing. One look at The Rocket makes you realize that, if this is premier, it would be a dangerous mistake to go down the divisions looking for value.

Birmingham is full for the weekend, but the city isn't exactly *en fête*. To the man in the street, the Ryder Cup means as little as news of good crops in North Korea.

You should see the Ryder Cup media show. You really should. Objectivity is practically a dirty word this week. I think this is part of the media hard sell on the thing. Guys and gals who cover the golf tours sit in practically the same seats all week every week.

They deal with a series of individuals who come to the press tent to do their professional business in the form of press conferences and then disappear.

It's a good game to write about, but there's nobody to root for, nothing visceral about it. Nothing that gets your backside out of your seat or that makes you lean forward roaring. Everything is controlled. Everything builds towards Sunday evening. The eighteenth green. Presentation. Press conference. Add the top to your story.

But the Ryder Cup is a different side to the players. You see spiky individualists interact and respond to each other. You hear a word used that you don't hear during the rest of the year – 'we'. Journalists get carried away and charmed by this. They are fascinated by it. They like being part of the 'we'.

The Ryder Cup is what happens when a quintessentially individual sport gets processed into a team sport. For me, it doesn't work.

This weekend, I took Saturday off and wandered around Birmingham. Ninety-nine per cent of your Brummies couldn't give a toss what was happening out at The Belfry. The indifference was refreshing. I have a constituency out there somewhere.

On Friday, when I got on the media bus at Broad Street, four preppie Americans tried to follow me on board. Now the media bus was empty, bar me and the driver, and really he could have brought the preppie types to the gates of The Belfry where he was going to dump me. The regular shuttle services had stopped an hour ago.

'No,' he said.

'Well what's the nearest town to The Belfry, can you tell us Sir?'

'Yer standing in it. Ser.'

I could tell the driver didn't like the Ryder Cup. I wanted to reach out to him, explain that I too am a Ryder Cup agnostic. I wanted to place a hand on his shoulder and tell him that, like him, I don't feel European. Never have. Is there somewhere we could go? Some treatment we could get? Essence of Garret FitzGerald maybe. I know that from the Carpaccians to the Sugarloaf, the bunting is supposed to be out, but two of us, he and me, could be the start of a movement.

It's worse for me than it is for him though. He can drive people to the Ryder Cup and still be a non-believer. I'm under pressure. I need to get my head straight or I need to find a constituency.

The Sports Editor will be demanding the same in a terse phone call any day soon. Twice now, Mal has filled out accreditation forms for me to go to Ryder Cups and said to me sternly that there's no point in going if I'm going to, well, if I'm going to urinate all over the Ryder Cup.

'Don't piss on the thing,' he says, shaking his head and wincing.

I disagree. We are talking here about what I do best. Damping down by natural means. I think a large part of sports journalism should be the extinguishing of flammable hype by whatever means come to hand. That hurts his feelings though. Mal is a Sports Editor and, like all Sports Editors, Mal loves golf.

I can get into the idea of golf, but I can't get into this gung-ho European thing. Vulgar, post-Tiger economy Ireland is hard enough to love on its own. But do we have to love the guys who gave us that bland, middle-European, pedestrianized-zone look to install in our cities?

Really, I like the idea of a big, European, economic trough that we Irish people can keep our snouts into, I am an idealist after all and I don't want to have to listen to Irish farmers whining about their EU grants being taken away. No Sir. Also, I'm in favour of letting anyone else who wants to stick their snout in that trough and have unimpeded access, both in terms of immigrants and expansion. Yet, I'm not in favour of war in Iraq or Tony Blair or strudel.

And I absolutely draw the line at being asked to cheer for Colin Montgomerie.

It's taken The Belfry to restore my faith in this. Monty is a flinty individualist. That's his thing. He thrives on it.

It's an individualistic game processed for commercial/television reasons into a team sport every two years or so. For economic reasons, this sport for loners got inextricably wrapped up in the gossamer-thin bonhomie of the middle classes. The great heroes have virtually all been prickly misfits. Hagen, Hogan, Nicklaus, Player, Faldo, Duval, Woods, etc. They're not team players. That's the whole point about them.

Even this weekend, it comes down to Paul McGinley and a horrible putt. No team, no continent. Just one man and his nerve.

I don't believe that those guys up at the snow-fringed summit of the game genuinely feel they need the career move either. When Tiger Woods makes yet another 'gaffe' about the million reasons why he'd rather do well at Mount Juliet last week than The Belfry this week, it's worth examining. I believe that Tiger and Duval, and a good many other golfers, share my view of the Ryder Cup. It's a crock, but dropping out would cause too much PR damage.

I don't believe either that the Ryder Cup 'transcends the majors' (Sam Torrance) or that it is 'golf's showpiece' (Tony Jacklin). Any tournament that, by its nature, has excluded Bobby Locke, Gary Player, Nick Price, David Frost, Retief Goosen, Vijay Singh, Adam Scott and Greg Norman, to name a few, cannot be anything but a sideshow organized to cater for old-world snobberies.

I've been asking journalists here what makes them happy about

Europe beating America and they all say things like 'kicking American butt' or 'giving the Yanks a good thrashing'.

I don't believe that any event, the beauty of which is, as Garcia declared the other day, 'that the best player in the world can play well and lose,' can transcend in a sport that measures excellence as perfectly as golf does. I don't believe either that when Sergio kicked his bag and stamped his foot at the sight of Westwood's soft-putting miss on the eighteenth on Saturday, that he was filled with the spirit of Team Europe.

So there. It's all out and on the table again. Every time I write about not understanding the Ryder Cup, I feel I have to explain myself.

Generally this week, I've chilled in my little puddle of disenchantment as the high fives went down in the press tent. Some press tents have a smokers' room where people with similar lungs can go. This one should have a sceptic tank where fellow travellers of mine could drop in.

For periods, I've sat and tried to learn. I sat through yesterday afternoon, soaking in the Ryder Cup happiness, knowing that Mal would be distraught if I didn't get my head straight, that the paper would feel let down, that I hadn't become a good European or a good golf person.

And, of course, the Ryder Cup turned out the worst possible way for a man of my beliefs. Europe won. Not just that. The thoroughly likeable Paul McGinley scored the winning putt. My hero Harrington did his bit.

I am duty bound to keep telling people that it's a crock. I know that Paul McGinley is now the de facto king of the entire continent. It's me that's wrong. I know that neither McGinley nor Harrington will ever speak to me again. I know it's professional hara-kiri. I can't help myself.

Let me offer some more justification. There are twelve singles games on the final day. Singles games in golf? Doesn't that sound daft for a start?

Anyway, I'm never going to be rooting for Monty or Lee Westwood. Just can't. Won't. If they are playing poker with the devil for my soul, I'm cheering for the guy with the cloven feet. I like big Hal Sutton's drawl and I don't like stars who can't keep their religion in their pockets, so Hal gets the nod against Langer. Already it's USA 3, Europe 0.

I love David Duval, the quintessential golfer/nerd/loner, the definition of why this will never be a team sport. Darren Clarke? Too many stogies and Bentleys and moody press conferences for me. So that's 4–0.

On we go. Phil the Thrill or Phillip Price? No arguments. I stand for nothing if not for thrills. I stand for nothing if not flopping on the big occasion.

Björn versus Cink? Halved by virtue of my inability to recognize either of them. Fulke and Davis Love III go the same way. If he were plain old Davis Love, I think it would be an American win though. Europe wins the rest of the match-ups.

So that's it. 6–6. Europe tie by virtue only of the frivolous affectation on the end of David Love's name. Six all.

How can I get all hot and bothered about this when I like the Americans just as much? Hot and bothered I must get, however.

There are quotes to be got and matches to be followed. The Ryder Cup has less golf played in it than any regular tournament, but the media tent gets itself into such a frenzy that everyone does three times the work. Our little *Irish Times* contingent is in a state of perpetual motion.

Add to that the fact that everyone else is excited about who is winning. Really, I'm the sinner in the big revivalist tent.

See. There is room for heroism in the sportswriting game. I am a lonely voice, but I will not be silenced. I have my principles.

And by the way, the complimentary Ryder Cup bags were very disappointing this year. Brookline was much better in that regard.

Wednesday, 16th October

Death by football.

Here was a night of sounds, not sights. Thump! A Swiss man called Fabio Celestini curled a ball beyond the claw of Shay Given. You could hear the shocked whickering of the net. You could hear Fabio's jaw drop.

Some other things you could hear.

A pin dropping far away on the north terrace.

Introductory paragraphs being deleted in the press box.

An oath. 'Holy Shit.'

'Ssshh!' Then the rumble begins, passing up from the gut and around the ground, 'Keano! Keano! Keano!'

The belched chant of dissent. It dies. Three minutes later, a little more perhaps, the final whistle shrills, a mournful sound that, in another key, could be a bell tolling. Then silence briefly reigns before the booing breaks out, a Doppler effect running around the ground and into the distance like a plane circling and then passing.

Irish fans booing their team and their manager. A 2–1 loss to Switzerland. Just months after the World Cup.

Mick McCarthy has lost the war.

A tape recording of this game would be enough to tell the whole story. Just the sounds leading up to that final, visceral chant, 'Keano! Keano! Keano!'

And Mick thinks that those of us who scribble with pencils are hard bastards?

We make our way down to the band room for the post-match press conference. This has been a sucker punch. Nobody expected this. Losing at home to the Swiss.

Since the Moscow debacle, I have written a stern column rebuking Mick for his behaviour towards the media, for his cranky abandonment of the Moscow Airport press conference, his refusal to speak about the Keane issue, his insistence on always making it personal.

There have been phone calls from various people close to the manager. There is belated alarm that support is slipping away. Even I, who have stuck with Mick through so many bad times over the last six years, reckon there is an accounting to be done.

Now, just this very afternoon, I had been promised a one-on-one interview tomorrow morning or afternoon. I realize now that that's not going to happen.

Even if Mick decided, here and now, that he would do it, what has to be written in the next hour would be read by him in the morning. Hard words to take with your breakfast, especially for a man with a delicate digestive system.

The facts are stark. No points. No resignation yet. Hot words to be spoken. The wall against which Mick McCarthy's back is pressed right now is cold and unforgiving. He comes into the band room to see us though, with his chin jutting and his chest puffed. He breathes defiance.

There's nothing we can do for him.

He's a grown man. He's always said it's about the football. Not the off-the-field stuff. Not the media. He needs right now to speak about football in a cool, adult way.

But the football has gone. His greatest player won't play. He has lost his two opening qualifying games. The game is no longer pliable to his will. So forget everything else. That's trouble.

Here's how this press conference went. The most tense of Mick's six-and-a-half years in this job.

'Mick, was this the worst performance of your six-and-a-half years?'

'Good question Bob. Do you think it was the worst performance?'

This is an old technique of Mick's. Deflect the question back with sarcasm added. Demand to know where it is coming from. The days when it worked are past, however.

'No worse tonight than they were in Moscow, Mick.'

'Fair enough. Fair play to you. I don't want to go through that. It's possibly the worst I feel because of circumstances. In terms of effort and commitment of players, I've always got everything from them. I feel sorry for them. My situation has affected everyone. Affected them and team spirit and team morale. They want to come here and play well. They've always given their lot. I'm not going to sit here and criticize.'

The mood in here? We're used to gauging it and this time it's easy. Hurt. Disappointed. An edge of anger, but refusing to give anyone the satisfaction. For blame, there are the usual suspects. Always the same suspects.

'There has been the worm of doubt sown,' he says. 'It does affect players. It was a nervy performance in the first half. They worked hard to stop us playing. I had a go, made changes at the end. I take responsibility for that. I wanted to win it by playing three at the back.'

Do you know the rules of these press conferences? When the big question has to be asked, when the 'will you stay or will you go' moment arrives, the rule is that you get ten minutes of usable quotes before risking a walk out. Everyone has copy to fill. We do the mambo. We dance around it. Let it build. Will he fight on? We know the answer because we heard him breathe it on the TV.

'I'll keep fighting on unless someone tells me any different. I've a contract to 2004. Unless someone tells me different, I'll keep fighting on.'

'The atmosphere tonight. Did it disappoint you? What with the memory of the Phoenix Park so fresh?'

'It does disappoint me, but that's been driven from certain quarters. It was going to happen if we got the wrong result. What I can't get my head around is that we've gone from up there in standard of performance to down there. I think circumstances have affected players. They've entertained and thrilled people. They've enjoyed it. I've enjoyed being sat here and being a winner. I'm not enjoying being sat here being a loser.'

The question is coming, of course. Everyone is trigger happy. 'The future Mick?'

'The future,' he says. 'If the manager's circumstances are inhibiting the team should the manager walk away from the team?'

Steady now. Steady.

'Do you regret the timing of your book?'

'Not at all, read it. Stands on its own two feet.'

Here goes. It's been coming down the line anyway. Mick's been waiting. We've all been waiting. It's a radio guy with no half page to fill who asks it. Still it was time, it was time.

'You've mentioned that your circumstances may be influencing things. Would one solution be to walk away?'

All eyes lock onto Mick McCarthy's face. Question deflected with question routine? Even money bet.

'Why?'

'Because the fans turned on the players tonight as a result, maybe, of your circumstances.'

'Maybe so,' Mick McCarthy says sadly. 'Myself and the players have always given everything to this. No, I don't think I should change. I'm not going to walk away from it. If somebody else wants to make that decision, then fine. I'm going to walk away from here with my head held high and chin out and chest out because I always do my best. Nothing and nobody will change that. Well done, at least you were brave enough to ask the question. Congratulations.'

That's about it. He speaks about how these times aren't easy. About the months ahead. About doing the best he can. About Damien Duff's hamstring. And he walks out the door. Chest puffed. Chin high. Only his eyes betray his torment as he heads for his long winter of discontent. A dead man walking.

Occasionally, when we are working, we are accompanied by secondary-school students on work experience. The idea is to give them a glimpse of the special hell that awaits those who don't study, won't study. Generally, they go off vowing to become accountants.

I have two transition-year students with me tonight. Eanna and Stephen. They have come to the match and come with me down to Mick's press conference. The lads are fans rather than journalists and I'm keen to know their verdict on these scenes. After six years of Mick's press conferences, I'm a poor judge but I have a sense that to an outsider these are ugly, sour affairs.

'Thought he was really rude,' says Eanna.

'Is he always like that?' asks Stephen.

He's not always rude and he's not always like that. I don't think his family would recognize the person he becomes when the strain is on and he has to come into the band room to talk to us. I don't think anyone who hasn't been in there can imagine the tension that sucks the air out of the room on nights like this.

I think the two lads will be enquiring about accountancy careers tomorrow.

Wednesday, 30th October – New York City

Three of us in a taxi. Patrick Bolger, the photographer, Sonia O'Sullivan, the legendary runner, and me.

We are headed out from Manhattan for Brooklyn Heights on the far side of the Brooklyn Bridge. I love this journey. Bridges are a hobby of mine. It's been a long while since I was on this one, my favourite. I bore Patrick and Sonia with tales of its construction.

Sonia is here for the New York marathon, which takes place on Sunday. She's run in one marathon before, in Dublin, on a whim. She won comfortably. She's excited about this one, this big city, the fuss, the new phase of her career.

She's changed too. A few years ago, getting her to take a morning off to do photos and an interview in the week of a big race would have been impossible. She's up for this though, relaxed and chatty.

When we get across to the plaza at Brooklyn Heights, we can look back at Manhattan. It's cold and wintry and the sky is chalky. The view is disappointing. Robbed of the Twin Towers, Manhattan doesn't look like itself anymore. The place is disfigured now.

In the distance, though, the mustard yellow cabs ply the canyons of Manhattan and right behind where Sonia is standing and stretching, doughty tugboats with funnels painted candy-apple red haul long, flat dredges along the broad, brown Hudson. As Patrick clicks away, she stretches an elegant limb towards the sweep of the Brooklyn Bridge and notes that right now, right here is where she wants to be. Forget the past. Forget the future. This is the spot. This is the town.

It's extraordinary. She has always liked a big stage and this place seems to fit. On Thursday, there was a press conference for the leading athletes in the Tavern on the Green in Central Park. Sonia drew the biggest crowd. She sat at the podium with the other athletes, bouncing Ciara, her eldest daughter, on her lap and she looked entirely at home. Afterwards, the organizers asked the athletes to go and sit at individual tables and let the hacks approach them with more specific, feature-type questions.

There was a deathly crush at Sonia's table. Virtually no interest at the other half-dozen tables. I went and stood with Eamonn Coughlan, who was once the king of this city himself. He looked at the forest of bodies around Sonia.

'That's Sonia,' he said. 'When she goes, there's nothing like her coming through.'

He's right. She's a one off. An exception to all the rules.

Later this month, Sonia will be thirty-three. I've been interviewing her for ten years and it gets easier and more enjoyable. She used to hate the questions. Now she sees them as a competition, I think. She anticipates them, works out what I'm going to ask or why I would be asking it.

Running is no longer an adventure to be had while yomping around the European grand-prix circuit with a small knapsack on her back. That's how I saw her the first time I went to interview her. She arrived into the Omni Hotel in Oslo with Yvonne Murray, the two of them looking like schoolgirls, all giggles and chat and just their spikes, vests and tracksuits in the little bags they toted.

Running, though, is about a finite number of choices, a limited number of things that are left to be done. That was almost a decade ago. Now Sonia is in the second half of a career of waning velocity that has been filled with other things. The clutter of her grown-up life. Love. Death. And babies.

She talks here in the wind about coming to New York as a kid. Good stories. She had a scholarship interview in Villanova, but the girls who picked her up decided that a night in New York was in order. So many thousands of people have made the journey from Cobh to New York City, but not many in this style.

Back then, Sonia had a mulish streak in her that survives, but you can see she has mellowed. Something else too. She wants to devour this race. Big city. Same girl. Still ready for it.

Yesterday, she spent some time chatting with Greta Waitz, the great Norwegian runner. Waitz has won the New York marathon nine times. Sonia and Waitz have known each other for quite a while and Sonia was happy to sit and listen.

'I just wanted to speak to her. She said things I needed to know. She said get warm and stay warm. She said the second half is tougher, so don't get carried away. Central Park is hilly but not the worst yet, after twenty miles, it probably will look worse. Sometimes it's better facing the unknown, than fearing what you know.'

We complete the interview and the photos in a matter of hours and zoom back towards the city. Afterwards, Patrick and I speak. It's funny how infectious optimism is. We both solidly believe Sonia is going to win this sucker of a race. She shouldn't, but damn it, she will.

I don't know why we feel this. I read a wonderful piece by David Walsh recently about Paula Radcliffe and the scientific manner in which she prepares for a marathon. By comparison, Sonia's build up seems haphazard and full of daring-do. Apart from giving birth at the start of the year, running the marathon means that she will have competed at every distance from 800 metres to marathon this season. This is at a time when a lot of the advice coming to her is that she should concentrate on one event and get to Athens with that event as her speciality.

She says she's come here to win, however. She looks great. She's relaxed.

I'm a believer.

Sunday, 3rd November – Central Park

There's a knot of us standing and waiting. Waiting for Sonia. She hasn't won, she has lost. Badly.

Spiderman could have told her it would end where it did. During the summer, Sonia O'Sullivan was speaking to the Welsh runner Jon Brown about the experience of running in the New York marathon. Sonia suggested that the course seemed largely flat and manageable. Brown shook his head.

'Wait till you get to the slope up to the Queensboro Bridge and your legs are heavy,' he said.

That's where the *Spiderman* movie climaxes, we say to each other. It's a small nugget of trivia to nourish us as we wait.

We ask a marathon volunteer to go and tell Sonia we are here. Deadlines are beginning to worry us. Nothing happens.

We wait and wait. We interview Mark O'Carroll, who has come sixth in the men's race. We are genuinely pleased for Mark. Good guy. But he knows what the lead story is.

'What's the story with Sonia?' he asks.

We shake our heads.

'Aw shit,' he says.

Eventually, we give up and head, in resignation, back through Central Park to the press room in the New York Athletic Club. Hopefully somebody will bring Sonia to us.

These meetings with her after defeats are never easy and, if the paper wasn't clamouring for quotes, we'd just as soon avoid them. Sometimes Sonia is defensive and spiky. Other times she is just crushed, and asking her anything at all just seems cruel. It's been said before, but running isn't merely what she does, it is what she is. Losing leaves her desolate. No point in saying that she should get some perspective. Lack of perspective is what makes the great ones.

On the way, I get cut off in the crowds from the rest of the guys. I spend ten minutes trying to get past a cop at Columbus Circle. He makes me take the underpass. When I meet the boys again in the press room, they've already met Sonia. She's come here, spoken to a few people and was making her way back when she bumped into the lads.

My old friend Tom O'Riordan shares the quotes out with me. He says he hasn't seen Sonia so upset in a long time. Tommo, 'The Runner', as we affectionately call him, is like myself, a student of Sonia. When we go to races, we like to speculate on whether she looks well or not, capable of giving us a thriller or of it all ending in tears.

If Tommo says she's upset, then she's upset. Tommo has seen it all.

I write a quick, harsh piece, condemning Sonia's tactical naïveté. I'm a bit disappointed myself and I can't believe I bought in to so much optimism. Maybe I like Sonia and New York City too much.

Anyway poor old Sonia gets a good going over in the piece. When it is written and sent, I look over the words. I hope Sonia feels the same way about the New York marathon. I hope we share the perspective. It's one of those pieces where you have to lay aside your fondness for the person involved and remember that you are working for the readers and not the athletes.

I did that. Still I shudder when I imagine Sonia adding my words and those of most of us here to the pile of woes she has tomorrow.

Monday, 4th to Saturday, 30th November – Sweepings

It's a wicked month. A month when all the subplots tie together and the story ends. I am still in New York when Mick McCarthy decides to walk the plank. In fact, oddly, I am distractedly walking down Broadway talking to Mary, who has come over for a few days, when I notice a man passing us who looks a lot like Matt Dickinson, the soccer writer of the London *Times*. When he has gone a few yards past us, the man calls my name.

'Mick's gone,' he says, and he keeps walking.

I turn to Mary.

'Hmm. You know, I think that man was Matt Dickinson of the London *Times*.'

That moment on Broadway ends our evening in New York. I write a quick obit to throw into the mix back home in the office.

By the time I get back to Dublin, a couple of days later, the death of the King is history. We are looking for a successor.

Mick's departure leaves a small wash. To many, including Mick, we press guys are the villains of this long drama. I get many letters rebuking me for my part in the assassination of a good man.

I'm not so sure. Certainly, Mick McCarthy is a good man, and certainly his attitude towards the media got under my skin, and the skin of a few other people, as this year wore on. But the rap sheet was long.

The actual things that Roy Keane complained of in Saipan should have been provided. When Mick and Roy met in Roy's house before the World Cup qualifying campaign ever started, Roy Keane said to Mick that he was ready for the sort of consultative captaincy that Mick himself had enjoyed with Jack Charlton. He made the effort. Saipan was a letdown.

And losing our best player while we were there was bad. Not getting him back was bad. Using other players in the press conference as a human shield was bad, and sundered friendships for ever.

Not practising penalties. I'd argue that one for eternity.

Not speaking about Keane until the book came out? The *Daily Mail* column?

Continually making it obvious that he rated English journalists more highly than Irish ones? Poor judgement.

And then losing two games at the start of the campaign.

Too much in one summer. Too much baggage. And, after six years in which the Irish media largely supported Mick through thick and thin (and were branded 'liars' by him in an English paper) perhaps it was time to move on, for everyone.

There was little sympathy at the end, but the media don't make the decisions. Mick resigned from a high-profile job in which he was decently paid and part of the brief was to weather criticisms. The criticism was rough on occasion, but there was never a time when it didn't relate to football or football management.

I don't know why relations got so bad. Many of us felt let down in Izumo when, despite the pressures of editors and readers, we had given Mick the space for several days to get over the Keane affair, and then he popped up telling his side in a ghosted column for the *Daily Mail*. Things grew more adversarial after that and rightly so. There were hard questions to be asked. Mick refused to answer them except via the medium of his book.

For Mick's part, he never liked the Irish media. There were moments when we rubbed along fine, but he always listed us among those 'outside the tent pissing in' without appreciating that this was where we were supposed to be.

I don't know why he distinguished between the Irish media and our English colleagues, but I suspect it goes back to his playing days under Jack Charlton. By then, there had emerged a different and distinct pattern of Sunday paper criticism of Irish managers, first pioneered by Eamon Dunphy, when he was viciously putting an end to the era of what he termed 'decentskinsmanship' in Irish football. The target in the 1980s was Eoin Hand. Although the pieces were often hard to the point of being cruel, they established a style. Sunday paper reviews of Irish matches have always been tougher since then.

Mick, while he never had to endure what Eoin Hand endured, had a thin skin anyway. This was a man who responded to that challenge by an Irish journalist to run against him in a sprint, the point being to prove how slow Mick was. Any other pro would have walked away laughing, but Mick took the bait.

He wasn't helped either by the tendency of people around the team to get up early on Mondays and fax critical pieces to his home so that he could see what was being said about him. Naturally, the broad run of favourable comment never got faxed, so Mick sat there stewing in the criticisms that he pretended he never read. He couldn't bring himself to see it all as part of the job. It hurt too much.

Personally, I like Mick and enjoyed his company, especially in the earlier years when he seemed a little more loose. He endured two qualifying campaigns that ended in failure before he got us to the World Cup this year, and I was always among those who defended what he was trying to do. It's odd to think that his finest success would be wrapped around the seed of his greatest failure. He was at his best motivating the team this summer but Keane, Keane, Keane. The name will forever haunt him.

In the week after Mick resigned, we gathered in the same hotel that he'd said farewell from and received something called 'The Genesis Report', an independent investigation into the debacle of Ireland's World Cup preparation. We'd all spoken to the people who compiled the report. Generally, it was a validation of Roy Keane's complaints.

I think, though, that even Roy would agree there were more things going on in Saipan than were dealt with in those complaints about logistics. More personal aspects than can be dealt with in any report.

Niall's book came close to winning a prize as best sports book of the year. Sadly, there is no category for most speedily written sports book, or most enjoyable to write. We went to London for the awards ceremony and had a miserable night on the town the evening before. Chicken Chernobyl in some tourist-trap joint in Leicester Square and then a fruitless trudge around in the cold looking for a late drink. Easily, the least enjoyable part of the entire process.

In the week after 'The Genesis Report', we hacks journey to Greece for the most boring and pointless friendly in the history of the game of soccer.

The year effectively ends with Greece.

On the bus back to the airport, Chris Davis of the *Telegraph* does a sweet thing. Philip Quinn, the soccer correspondent of the *Irish Independent*, is quitting the road, he is heading for a sensible life back in the office. Philip and I aren't close, but I'll certainly miss him. He's the funniest guy on these trips, his impressions of various managers, players and journalists have shortened a thousand journeys for us.

Chris gets up and takes the microphone and, in the course of an epic poem that he has put together, he says all the things about Philip that we'd all like to say if we weren't such hard cases.

And, when it's done, we clamour for a speech from Quinner, but, for once, he has nothing to say. Just thanks.

We lapse into thoughtful silence as the bus moseys its way through the morning traffic of Athens. It's a weird and sometimes uncomfortable job this. It's on my mind that at the beginning of the year, I had good relationships with Mick McCarthy, Padraig Harrington and Sonia O'Sullivan, and now, in all likelihood, I don't have any relationship with any of them. And that's how it goes.

My favourite Philip Quinn moment is a recent one. A Kenny Cunningham press conference. Philip starts up. 'Kenny, a long, long career now, several hundred appearances with Wimbledon, now on to Birmingham, an established international with many caps and a career stretching back to the mid-1990s.' (pause) 'Can you talk us through your goal please?'

And Kenny took it on the chin. 'Well I don't like to brag . . .'

That's the way it should be. That's the template. We should be there to praise and to puncture. We should be sceptical about the raging idiocy of fame, the vacant lives of the heroes.

Instead, our relationships with sportspeople mirror the arc of their own careers. Progress. Apex. Decline. With us it's build-up, in close and then bam, the punch comes. The criticism from the source they least expect, at the time they least expect it, just when they begin to wane. We're the first off the bandwagon. That's our nature. The scorpion always stings.

Generally, it's not about friendships anyway. Fundamentally, it's lonely and competitive and it's not even about the sport that much. It's about getting it done. It's about deadlines, headlines and expense sheets. It's about getting there, getting organized, getting access, getting the words out. About feeding your curiosity so that it stays alive till next week.

We roll on through Athens. Probable home of the first sportswriters, of the original cliché makers.

Nobody likes us. We don't care. The only people who understand what we do are on this bus. Most of the time we don't even like each other.

There's not one of us who doesn't secretly wonder here and now what it must be like to be Quinner, to be stepping out of the hamster wheel next month, to be on the last trip, to have harvested the last quotes, honed the last intro.

The sun is coming up. We're shuddering.

Tuesday, 17th December

I did one of those radio shows today, a sort of look back at the sporting year affair. I hate being on radio or television but, once in a while, I go along just to push myself out of the comfort zone.

There we were, skimming away over various sporting subjects, when it struck me that somewhere, in the last ten years, I have acquired the ability to talk about anything. Anything. I notice it when I am interviewing people. I can keep the conversation going with questions and bland observations for hours, even when my brain is on autopilot. Today, on the radio, once I got over the fright of being there, I just found myself tossing out glib answers on any topic imaginable. Stuff I knew nothing about. How does this happen? When did I become this?

Afterwards, myself and Dermot Gilleece, who was on the show as well, stood in the car park outside the radio centre and chatted for a while. Dermot was with *The Irish Times* for many years, his painstaking and brilliant golf-writing illuminating our pages for the longest time. This year, he took the redundancy package and has moved his show to the *Sunday Independent*. Newspapers are like that. You're there. You're gone. No sentiment. You come in the front door and go out the back door.

I look at Dermot and wonder how he keeps going, how he keeps generating the ideas and making the trips and gathering the snippets. I'm convinced that sportswriting is a young man's game, that it gets harder and harder to keep your standards and to keep your mind open as you get older. It's a survivor's art being a decent sportswriter after a decade in the business.

Dermot knew the wonderful LA sportswriter, Jim Murray, and occasionally, when Murray would visit Ireland, Dermot would do him the kindness of fixing up rounds of golf on pleasant courses. This makes Dermot a direct link to the gods for me. I love those old guys, love the easy-swinging accounts of the lives they led, the smart savvy crackle of their prose. I like nothing better than dipping in and out of collections of their works and absorbing the gentle rhythm of pieces written about people I know nothing about. They knew sport in its heydey and they made the heydey of sportswriting.

Things have changed since then. We have the dimensions of the world wrong. One man went home from Saipan this summer and more was written about it – many, many times more was written about it – than was written about 40,000 people dying on that island a couple of generations ago.

But when I look closer at the sportswriters of that generation, the great heroes of sportswriting, there's another disturbing lesson. It seems that virtually all of them became cranky or irrelevant or comically self-aggrandizing in their old age.

The best of them, perhaps, and an old hero of mine, is Jimmy Cannon, a protégé of Damon Runyon's and a guy who, for years, had the ear of New York City. Jimmy ended his days as a press-box crank, boring the pants off younger guys, decrying the new styles, the new stories. No New York paper would have him any-more and he spent his time hustling, believing, correctly and with some pathos, that he hadn't changed, the business had.

There's a yarn I like that captures some of Cannon's wit and curmudgeonliness at the same time. A recent arrival in New York press boxes had been making quite an impact with his dry statistical analyses of big games. He arrived to work at the ball park one day carrying a large briefcase. Cannon leaned back and sneered, 'Whaddya got in the briefcase son? Decimal points?'

When I started as a freelancer in my late twenties, there were a whole bunch of us who arrived on the scene at roughly the same time. By and large, the older guys despised us and cut us down behind our backs. We chuckled at them and did imitations of the way they spoke and wrote.

Any day now I expect to wheel around in a press box and find the younger guys having a chuckle at my expense. I'm forty next birthday, and that's old in a young guy's game, but there are moments when you could see yourself doing this job for ever, when you realize that you've just nailed a good paragraph down, or watched the sweetest game of hurling or seen Jordan drain a three pointer. And you wonder how grey life might be away from the deadlines, the flashing cursor, the rush to be part of the nanny goat mambo.

When I was at the Winter Olympics this year, I noticed that Malachy had begun using one of the new guys, Keith Duggan, as a Saturday columnist. Keith is younger, better and funnier than me, qualities I despise in a journalist, and my only solace is that Keith is losing his hair a little. At least he doesn't look like a boy wonder. I find, though, when I read Keith's gentle and wise columns from Saturday mornings, and then look at my own Monday-morning efforts, that I have been sinking into some of the habits of meanness that marked the later Jimmy Cannon years, the time when his wit waned and his bile rose.

Don't know why: It just happens. You set up the targets and throw the knives. And next thing you know, you are pressing the button to file your 1,100 words of poison.

It's a problem, and it seems to me to be a problem that all sportswriting has. The games have got meaner. So has the coverage. A lot of the time the pleasure is gone. We are at war with sport.

The attention to detail is gone too. The sense that it is a business about people. I read recently that another hero of mine, Gary Smith of *Sports Illustrated*, likes to interview at least fifty people before he considers that he has researched a feature sufficiently. That's the sort of fine filigree work that doesn't ever get done anymore. What paper do you know that would trust its readers to stay with a 6,000 or 7,000 word piece, even if it had fifty interviews' worth of research propping it up?

We are too quick to look at the finish line, instead of studying or enjoying the race. We want winners, even if losers have better tales to tell. We want controversy instead of wisdom. We live in the era of breaking news. Too much, too quick, all the time.

Even our interview pieces have a certain tabloid inflection, the systematic redefining of ordinary mortals as either goats or lions. That's what Keane was about this year. A broad English sports-writing tendency to write him off as a fightin' 'n' drinkin' thicko up against an equally broad Irish tendency to beatify a complex man.

It was an extreme example of what we do all the time, we pick little fragments of people's lives, little threads of their DNA and reconstruct them hurriedly in the lab. For instance, if you score goals for a living and we, once, see you at the theatre, it will be many years before we stop referring to you as the theatre-going centre forward who took centre stage.

Keane was one of the biggest global sports stories of the year, and probably the biggest Irish sports story ever. I have worked on two major Irish sports stories in ten years. Michelle de Bruin and Roy Keane. The Keane story was bigger by far yet much less important. It told you nothing about modern sport and sports reporting that the de Bruin story hadn't highlighted already.

Newspapers reacted cautiously and dishonestly after the 1996 Olympics because they feared that criticism of de Bruin would hurt them. Sports stories aren't worth getting hurt over. With Keane, though, the heavy artillery was marched in. Whichever side of the argument you took as your own, the story would sell papers so we pumped it out, the good the bad and the indifferent. We kept pumping. Yet nobody died, nobody cheated, the basic premise of sport wasn't subverted.

In the Toy Department, we are all breadth and short-term impact. Special effects. We die to create the illusion of insider access when being outside could be our salvation. We'd rather have a bland column of nanny goats from ten bleating players who give the official version, than one of those considered pieces on a game, which Con Houlihan or Red Smith or Jim Murray used to pen so irresistibly.

No wonder people burn out more quickly. No wonder you see old guys with gin bottles inside brown paper bags stashed inside their desk drawers. Queuing outside dressing-room doors, being pushed around by stewards, extracting quotes from nineteen-year-olds. It's no job for serious people.

Nobody ever told me I was a serious person though. I try not to be. There are a few things that keep you going in this game. The mortgage. The knowledge that you failed at everything else in life. The odd good quote. The rare moment of genius from a D. J. Carey or a Sonia O'Sullivan.

And the anticipation. Just waiting to see how it all turns out, next weekend, next season, next year. Waiting. Watching. Wondering if you have the words left in you to fill the space that the occasion wants.